THE LIFE & TIMES OF REVD JOHN REDDAWAY LUXMOORE
(1829-1917)

WITH SPECIAL REFERENCE TO HIS RENOVATION OF
HOLY TRINITY CHURCH, ASHFORD-IN-THE-WATER

IAN PYKETT

INCLUDING AN APPENDIX ON
THE HISTORY OF THE DISSENTING CHAPELS IN ASHFORD

DAVID WINDLE

THE LIFE AND TIMES OF
REVD JOHN REDDAWAY LUXMOORE (1829-1917)

ISBN 978-1-910489-82-6

First published in 2022, by

Spiral Publishing Ltd   *in association with*   Country Books

38 Pulla Hill Drive
Storrington
West Sussex RH20 3LS
www.countrybooks.biz

British Library Cataloguing in Publication Data.
A catalogue record for this book is available from the British Library.

Front Cover:

Left: Revd John Reddaway Luxmoore, 1911.

Right: Proposed post-restoration south elevation of Holy Trinity Church, Ashford-in-the-Water, 1868.

Printed and bound in England by 4edge Ltd, Hockley, Essex.

'What a delightful treasure house we find
in the records of the past'

Thomas Brushfield
Ashford, 1864

TABLE OF CONTENTS

III RENOVATION OF HOLY TRINITY, ASHFORD-IN-THE-WATER

PREFACE

When bell-ringing one Sunday at Holy Trinity Church, Ashford-in-the-Water, I became intrigued with a parish priest named in a list hanging on the wall in the tower – a priest who had been the incumbent for the remarkably long period of 52 years.

He and his family would have lived in Ashford vicarage (formerly my home) for longer than any other resident. If any shade should linger there, it must surely be that of this man: John Reddaway Luxmoore.

Having googled his name, I gained the impression that he was a descendant of Bishop John Luxmoore of St Asaph, and that he therefore came from a highly privileged and very wealthy family background. If so, why would this clergyman, with so many opportunities available to him through well-developed and influential social and ecclesiastical networks, be content to spend half a century in a small village in rural Derbyshire?

My insatiable curiosity led me into the fields of genealogy and Victorian social history, where I searched for answers to my questions about this man and his family, and about the society in which they lived. I also became fascinated with the details of Revd Luxmoore's restoration of the Church of Holy Trinity, Ashford – his most visible legacy.

I am no historian. I have stumbled into the far corners of the World Wide Web without a guide. My journey has been at once fascinating, thrilling and frustrating. But I have discovered that I share my new-found amateur enthusiasm for such matters with many Victorians, and with some contemporaries considerably more experienced than myself.

Derbyshire, it transpires, has had more than its fair share of passionate chroniclers. Names that crop up repeatedly include Llewellynn Frederick William Jewitt (1816-1886), the 17th child of Arthur and Martha Jewitt of Sheffield. He founded and edited his own illustrated multivolume antiquarian journal, *The Reliquary*, which is both a factual treasure trove and, with its many illustrations, a work of art in its own right. Jewitt, who lived in Winster Hall in later life, was also founder and editor of the *Derby Telegraph*; secretary of the *Derby Town & County Museum and Natural History Society*; author of the two-volume history, the *Ceramic Art of Great Britain*; and editor of the even more lavishly illustrated volumes of the Anastatic Drawing Society.[1]

Then there is Revd John Charles Cox (1843-1919), a native of Parwich, who was first a partner in the Wingerworth Coal Company, but latterly an Anglican priest, and said to be 'perhaps one of the most influential English local historians of the 19th century.'[2] He published dozens of books – including a four-volume history of Derbyshire churches – and took over the editorship of *The Reliquary* on Jewitt's death.

The village of Ashford-in-the-Water can boast of having its own much-published antiquaries in the father-and-son duo, Thomas Brushfield (1798-1875) and Thomas Nadauld Brushfield (1828-1910) – but more of them later.

Two things become immediately obvious on flicking through Cox's vade-mecum *How to Write the History of a Parish:*[3] firstly, how fortunate we armchair antiquarians are in being able to obtain so much information, often from original sources, by merely logging on to the World Wide Web; and secondly, how shallow is the research I have undertaken myself so far on my chosen subject, compared to the depths that were plumbed by Cox and his contemporaries.

John Reddaway Luxmoore himself clearly had an interest in the history of his church. He hosted a British Archaeological Association lecture on that very subject on July 22nd 1899, given by Thomas Nadauld Brushfield in Holy Trinity, Ashford. He had taken the time beforehand (possibly at Brushfield's

---

[1] *Anastatic drawing was a process of printing from a zinc plate on which a transferred design was left in relief by etching out the rest of the surface. Invented ca.1840 by CF Baldamus in Germany, attempts were made to commercialise it by Sir Carl Wilhelm Siemens, founder of today's Siemens high-technology manufacturing company. Printing and Piracy – New Discovery. The Athenaeum, December 4th 1841.*

Use of the Anastatic Printing Process in Ireland. Edward J Law. J Roy Soc Antiquaries of Ireland, Vol 136, 2006, p 30.

The Anastatic Drawing Society was founded in 1854 by Revd JM Gresley, and a similar association, the Ilam Anastatic Drawing Society, was founded in 1859 by the then Vicar of Ilam, Revd GR Mackarness. In 1875 the two societies were merged and Jewitt assumed the editorship. The Anastatic Drawing Society. Llewellynn Jewitt (ed). Vol 20, SH Cowell, Ipswich, 1882, Introduction.

[2] *J Charles Cox. Nick Poyntz. Mercurius Politicus (blog), https://mercuriuspoliticus.wordpress. com/2011/05/02/j-charles-cox/*

[3] *How to Write the History of a Parish: an outline guide to topographical records, manuscripts, and books. J Charles Cox. George Allen & Sons, London, 1879, (fifth edition, 1909).*

request) to discuss with his erstwhile architect some points related to his restoration of the building 30 years earlier.[4]

But it is Revd Luxmoore's eldest son, John Stonhouse Luxmoore (1863-1940), who was so absorbed with the history of his father's church that he invested a great deal of time researching and writing his *Notes on the Church of Holy Trinity, Ashford-in-the-Water*.[5] He followed his father in taking Holy Orders, and before taking up his first curacy he returned to live for a few years in the vicarage, where the major part of his *Notes* were composed, around the turn of the century. They are in the form of a draft typewritten booklet of about 30 pages, with many insertions and handwritten annotations, figures and sketches, and additional relevant information cut and pasted (literally) from other publications. The *Notes* are informed and augmented by his handwritten booklet, *Mr S Birley's Remarks on the Church Copied Verbatim, Jan 1900*. Later in his life, when he was living in Sheffield, JS Luxmoore compiled further notes concerned principally with Ashford village matters and the genealogical details of some of its families.

Another reference work is the pamphlet *Ashford-in-the-Water and its Church* by John Norman, Vicar of Ashford with Sheldon from 1957 to 1964. He wrote the first version in 1960, commenting in the vicar's report for that year:

> *'Preparing a new history of the church cannot fail to bring home the relative insignificance of our day-to-day labours when seen against the great sweep of history which has passed since first a House of God was built in this village. Any 'results' which may follow what we attempt here must be viewed in the light of the passing years. If it can be seen, looking back, that in this age of materialism and lack of conviction, the Christian religion was faithfully proclaimed and a little practised, then indeed there can be no further commendation of our work than that.'*[6]

The first run of 500 copies, printed using a 'new duplicator with automatic feed', went on sale for 6d each in February 1961. With the support of advertisers, an extended version, with a run of 2,500 copies, was printed professionally in 1962; half the copies had already been sold in the first year 'to the surprise of the author.'[7]

---

[4]   *His architect, James Medland Taylor, writes, 'If you give me the exact date, I might be able to come over when Dr Brushfield reads his paper.' Derbyshire Record Office, D7672/Lx.C-29/15.*

[5]   *John Stonhouse Luxmoore. Derbyshire Record Office, D7672/Lx.C-30.*

[6]   *Vicar's annual report. Holy Trinity Church, Ashford-in-the-Water, 1960. Derbyshire Record Office, D747/A/PC/1/2.*

[7]   *Vicar's annual reports. Holy Trinity Church, Ashford-in-the-Water, 1961 and 1962. Derbyshire Record Office, D747/A/PC/1/2.*

Revisions and augmentations were written and printed in 1979 and 1996 by his successors. I have referenced these pamphlets frequently, but reading my text in conjunction with the most recent version will give a more comprehensive insight into the history of the parish church and the village, especially as I have concentrated on the period of Revd Luxmoore's incumbency.[8]

Many residents of Ashford and Sheldon found their spiritual homes not in their parish churches, but in one of the Nonconformist chapels. Despite the fragmented nature of the Nonconformist movement, the Established Church struggled against its advance, frequently finding itself on the back foot as it grappled at the same time with its own internal divisions between low and high church. The story of the Dissenting chapels in Ashford therefore parallels, and frequently bumps into, the story of Holy Trinity Church, creating a colourful, if sometimes unsettled, backdrop to Revd Luxmoore's ministry. Indeed, the Anglican Church's national campaign to counter Nonconformism is directly and powerfully reflected in the dramatic architectural changes that were made by Revd Luxmoore as he rebuilt Ashford Church. David Windle's history of Ashford's Dissenting chapels, to be found in the Appendix, is therefore wholly integral to Revd Luxmoore's life and times, and adds an essential further dimension to the Dissenting perspectives that I touch upon.

Notwithstanding the fact that there had been some tensions with Dissenters, it was said at Revd Luxmoore's Golden Jubilee that 'there could only be a very few residents in the village who had not, at some time or another, benefitted by their vicar's ministrations, and by both his and his wife's practical sympathy and kindly help in times of sickness and need.'[9] I have chosen here to focus on just a small number of his village acquaintants, some of whom were celebrated in their own right.

The diaries and letters of Maria Gyte and Fred Brocklehurst provide valuable firsthand accounts of the social and agricultural histories of Ashford and Sheldon in the early 20th century.[10] Revd Luxmoore lived to witness the initial consequences of the First World War that were delivered so cruelly on the small rural villages that he served, and that are portrayed so poignantly in these accounts.

---

[8] *The most recent version (1996), retitled 'Holy Trinity Church, Ashford-in-the-Water', is available directly from the church or from the Derbyshire Family History Society, Bridge Chapel House, Sowter Road, Derby DE1 3AT, https://www.dfhs.org.uk*

[9] *Vide infra, p 135.*

[10] *The Diaries of Maria Gyte of Sheldon, Derbyshire, 1913-1920. Gerald Phizackerley (ed). Scarthin Books, 1999.*

FW Goes to War: from the diaries and letters of FW Brocklehurst of Sheldon, Derbyshire. Brian Greasley. Country Books, Little Longstone, Derbyshire, 2016.

A revealing insight into Ashford village life at the close of Revd Luxmoore's ministry is contained in the heartfelt recollections of Alice Mary Dawson (née Thorpe).[11] Alice's father, Frank, was baptised by Revd Luxmoore in 1871, and Alice was born in 1912, three weeks before the vicar preached his farewell sermon. I would not presume to improve upon these reminiscences, and I am very pleased, therefore, to be able to quote from them directly.

In the earlier years of Revd Luxmoore's ministry, pressure for school reform was taking root with the passage of the 1870 and 1880 Education Acts. The resulting national debates regarding who should provide the funding, whether attendance should be compulsory, and what should be the function (if any) of religious bodies, were all played out on the miniature stage of the hamlet of Sheldon, and have been recorded for us by Brian Greasley in his book, *This Remote Little School.*[12] I have referred to a few vignettes that illustrate the central role that Revd Luxmoore played in this drama.

I mention only briefly some of the industries that were prevalent in the area in Revd Luxmoore's time, since these are described elsewhere.[13] Quite remarkable, of course, was the Ashford marble industry which flourished in the Victorian era and put the village on the national – indeed, international – stage, via displays of its finest work at the Great Exhibition of 1851 and other events as far afield as Paris and New York. Products made in Ashford and nearby communities were prized then, as now, for their decorative beauty. One such example is Abel Tomlinson's marble mosaic tabletop that stands in Ashford Church.[14] Samuel Birley (1824-1906) – the same Birley who provided his firsthand recollections for JS Luxmoore's *Notes on the Church of Holy Trinity* – was another of the marble trade's master craftsmen, whose work was purchased by the Victoria and Albert Museum. To learn more about the Ashford marble industry, the reader is encouraged to consult John Michael Tomlinson's definitive history.[15]

---

[11] *My Ashford: A Century Past. Alice Mary Dawson. Robert Dawson (ed). Peak Advertiser, Bakewell, 2017.*

[12] *This Remote Little School. Brian Greasley. Country Books, Little Longstone, Derbyshire, 2013.*

[13] *E.g., Bygone Industries of the Peak. Julie Bunting. Wildtrack Publishing, Sheffield, 2006.*

[14] *Derbyshire Black Marble. John Michael Tomlinson. Peak District Mines Historical Society Special Publication, No. 4, 1996, fig. 15, facing p 33.*

[15] *Derbyshire Black Marble. John Michael Tomlinson. Op. cit.*

Abel Tomlinson (1834-1909) was John Michael Tomlinson's granduncle and a churchwarden at the time the plans for Revd Luxmoore's renovation of Holy Trinity Church, Ashford, were submitted to the diocese. Abel's Ashford marble tabletop in the church was donated by Mrs Emily Marsden, his niece and adopted daughter. It was awarded the silver Industrial Prize Medal at the Derby Corporation Art Gallery in 1882.

As I began to discover the facts about John Reddaway Luxmoore's life, it became impossible for me to divorce them from the context of the social transformations of the Victorian and Edwardian eras; his wife and family; the people he met; and the projects that he undertook. His *times*, then, are comprehensively integral to his *life*, as is his renovated Church of Holy Trinity, Ashford-in-the-Water.

Ian Pykett
Ashford-in-the-Water
December 2021

Note added in proof

Plans were underway to celebrate, on Trinity Sunday 2020, the 150th anniversary of the reopening of Ashford Church following Revd Luxmoore's restoration of 1868-1870.

Then Covid-19 struck.

This has reminded us of the 1918 'Spanish Flu' pandemic, which reached its peak of devastation in the UK at the end of the First World War. It gained its moniker because the neutral Spanish press freely reported on the unfolding medical disaster, whereas many other western countries were subject to news censorship and media blackouts, in order that the pandemic would not lower morale. The virus killed an estimated 50 million people worldwide – three times more than died in the First World War.[16] Young adults between 20 and 30 years old were particularly affected, and when the disease struck it progressed very quickly.

The rapid deaths from influenza or pneumonia of several local people, recorded in Maria Gyte's diary during the final months of 1918,[17] seem certain to be the result of the 1918 pandemic, and must have darkened the joy and relief of the Armistice celebrations:

November 2nd 1918. 'There are many people all over the country in every village and town down with some sort of influenza.'

November 11th 1918. 'What dreadful things are happening besides the war ... News was telegraphed throughout that the Armistice had been signed by the Germans at 5 o'clock this morning. Bells were ringing all round the different towns and villages and flags were out.'

---

[16] *The Deadly Virus: The Influenza Epidemic of 1918. The US National Archives and Records Administration, https://www.archives.gov/exhibits/influenza-epidemic/*

[17] *The Diaries of Maria Gyte of Sheldon, Derbyshire, 1913-1920. Gerald Phizackerley (ed). Scarthin Books, 1999, pp 197, 199, 200, 208.*

November 18th 1918. 'Influenza and pneumonia is making terrible work with people all over the country. Two, three and more in some places lying dead in the house all at once.'

November 20th 1918. 'People keep dying of influenza and pneumonia.'

Then, finally, she writes,

February 2nd 1919. 'The influenza made terrible havoc in 1918. It seems abating, but we hear of one now and then dying of pneumonia.'

A little over a hundred years later, in December 2020, a 90-year-old grandmother became the first person in the UK to be given an injection as part of a mass vaccination programme to protect against Covid-19.

I

HISTORICAL PREAMBLE

The origins of Ashford-in-the-Water

The area around Ashford-in-the-Water has seen human habitation for thousands of years, as evidenced by the Neolithic stone circle at Arbor Low, about seven miles away, that was probably built between 3,000 and 2,500BC; and by the late Bronze Age or Iron Age settlement at the hill fort at Fin Cop, two miles away, dating from between 440 and 390BC.[18]

Situated close to the border between the early Middle Age kingdoms of Mercia and Northumbria, the region was of great strategic relevance to King Edward the Elder (ca. 874-924) and his efforts to capture control of the northern territories from the Danes. To help assure support of his interests, Edward encouraged the purchase of lands at Ashford and nearby Hope by Uhtred, the younger son of the English ealdorman of Northumbria.[19] Subsequent to Edward's establishment of a burh (an embanked fortification) at Bakewell in 920, the whole of the north submitted to his control and in 930 Uhtred himself became an ealdorman – essentially the founder of the town at Bakewell.

> *'to Uhtred, 60 manentes of land at Hope and Ashford, the estate he had bought from the Danes by order of King Edward for 20 pounds of gold and silver.'*
>
> *Land Charter, 906*

---

[18] *Evidence of a massacre linked to Iron Age warfare was discovered in a recent archaeological dig at Fin Cop: nine skeletons of women, babies, a toddler and a teenager were discovered, believed to have been massacred after the fort was attacked and captured. Massacre at Fin Cop. Clive Waddington. Current Archaeology, Vol 255, 2011, pp 20-27.*

[19] *Hope and Ashford were probably the main settlements in the area at that time since the principal trackway, the Portway, passed through them, bypassing Bakewell. Bakewell: The Ancient Capital of the Peak. Trevor Brighton. Halsgrove, 2005, p 10.*

> • In ASHFORD-IN-THE-WATER – with its BEREWICKS, Rowland,
> Longstone, Hassop, Calver, Baslow, Bubnell, Birchills, Sheldon,
> Taddington, Flagg, Priestcliffe, [and] Blackwell – King Edward
> had 22 caracutes of land to the geld and 1 caracute of land exempt
> from geld. There the king has now in demesne 4 ploughs; and 18
> villans have 5 ploughs. [There is] land for 22 ploughs. There is 1
> mill [rendering] 12d, and the site of 1 mill, and 1 lead mine, and
> 40 acres of meadow, [and] woodland, not for pasture, 2 leagues
> long and 2 broad.

The entry in the Domesday Book for Ashford.

Named *Aisseford* (a Saxon word meaning 'the ford of the ash') when the Domesday Book was compiled in 1086, Ashford was the nucleus of a manor which encompassed a dozen communities in a region of some 35 square miles.

One of those communities was nearby *Scelhadun* (deriving from 'scylf', a peak or crag; and 'heth-dun', a heather covered hill), now known as Sheldon.

It is said that Henry II (1133-1189), who built the keep of Peveril Castle at nearby Castleton, also built, and sometimes occupied, a hall in Ashford.[20] In 1199, King John (1166-1216), Henry's fifth son, was experiencing trouble from the turbulent Welsh. He persuaded the powerful Welsh chieftain Wenunwyn to switch sides in return for the grant of lands in England, including, for the sum of £30, the manor of Ashford.[21] But within two years Wenunwyn was

---

[20]   *The Village of Ashford-in-the-Water, Derbyshire. Howard Needham Walters & Moyra Burnett. 1999. Wishful Thinking, http://places.wishful-thinking.org.uk/DBY/Ashford/Village.html*

[21]   *Notes on the Churches of Derbyshire, Vol II, The Hundreds of the High Peak and Wirksworth. J Charles Cox. Bemrose & Sons, Derby & London, 1877, p 47.*

Hall Orchard, Ashford-in-the-Water, as it appeared ca.1920, showing the 'Ashford Castle ditches'. These were subsequently made level to provide a recreation field.

back fighting with the Welsh and the gift of the Manor of Ashford remained in abeyance for some years. When Wenunwyn died, his son, Griffin, resumed control over the manor that his father had forfeited.

On the Feast of the Purification (February 2nd) in 1257, Griffin founded a chantry (a chapel for the saying of masses for his soul) in Ashford Church. Ashford Manor later returned to Crown ownership, and was given by Edward II (1284-1327) to Edmund Plantagenet, Earl of Kent. In 1408 ownership transferred to the Nevilles, one of two major powers in the north of England that played a central role in the Wars of the Roses. This family built a residence or hunting lodge (sometimes called the 'castle') in Hall Orchard, now the village recreation ground.[22] Although this residence disappeared long ago, a building known as Neville Old Hall, which stood in front of the mediaeval tithe barn on Church Street, was demolished only in 1938.

In 1550, the manor was sold to Sir William Cavendish and was held by his

---

[22] *Monument No. 308447: 'A homestead moat, probably associated with the fortified house of the Nevilles (1408-1550). The site is traditionally that of Ashford Castle but there is no evidence to substantiate or refute this assertion.' Historic England. 'The site is too small to have been a castle, but as a manor house of the important Neville family likely to have been dressed up with martial symbols, such as battlements'. Philip Davis. Castlefacts, http://castlefacts.info/ castledetails/castledetails3?uin=10771#description*

Neville Old Hall, Ashford-in-the-Water, prior to its demolition in 1938. The 'Bottom Pump', a former source of water, is on the left, beneath a shelter erected in 1880 (see p 242).

successors, the Earls and Dukes of Devonshire, for the next four centuries. It was partly sold off in the 1950s to pay death duties, during which the estate's original 120,000 acres were reduced by almost a half, and Hardwick Hall and fine works of art by Rembrandt, Rubens, Holbein and Memling were sold.[23]

Many members of the Cavendish family have lived at various times in the village: at Ashford Hall, at Churchdale Hall, and at the Rookery. Several of them are commemorated by memorials in the parish church.

Early history of Ashford Church

There was a church in Ashford well before Griffin founded his chantry in 1257 – and probably as long ago as the Saxon era.

The tympanum, which is now above the inner entrance of the 1870 south porch, is the most compelling physical evidence that a church stood in Ashford in the Norman period. Tympana are frequently found in church doorways, occupying the area between the top of the door and the Norman arch that supports it, and they are often decorated with sculptured ornaments, figures or other imagery.[24] Regarding the carving on the face of the Ashford tympanum, JS Luxmoore comments:

---

[23] *Accidents of Fortune. Andrew Devonshire. Michael Russell Publishing, 2004, pp 44-51.*

[24] *On Norman Tympana, with especial reference to those of Derbyshire. TN Brushfield. Journal of the British Archaeological Association, Vol VI, Bedford Press, London, 1900, pp 241-270.*

'By some the tympanum has been taken to be a typical representation of Peak Forest, the borders of which came down close to Ashford.[25]

NORMAN TYMPANUM, CHURCH AT ASHFORD-IN-THE-WATER. [Geo. S. Banbury, del.]

Ashford Church's Norman tympanum, on which are carved 'the rude representations of a wild boar and a wolf, beneath a tree that occupies the centre of the stone'. See also p 164.

... The Peak District of Derbyshire is known to have been infested by wolves, which could not be killed under severe penalties, since they were reserved for sport. On the other hand, when their numbers became excessive, they were mercilessly slaughtered, lands being held by certain families for this particular service. In any case, such animals as the boar and the wolf would appeal to the feelings of Peakrels [men of the Peak of Derbyshire] ...

'Here it may be added that in a croft close to the 'castle' mound [on what is now Hall Orchard] some boar 'tusks' ('tusshes' as they were described) were found several years ago.'[26]

Lithograph by TN Brushfield of a Norman corbel in the chancel of Ashford Church.

Further evidence of the church's possible Norman origin are the corbels in the north chancel walls that support the main roof beams. One is decorated with a fleur-de-lis, a symbol of the Trinity; and another with a head supported by hands (John Norman wonders whether this illustrates 'a case of

[25] *John Stonhouse Luxmoore. Derbyshire Record Office, D7672/Lx.C-30.*

'The King's Forest of the High Peak, or De Campanâ, as it was invariably called in the old law papers, formerly comprised the whole of the parishes of Glossop, Castleton, and Chapel-en-le-Frith, and part of Hathersage, Hope, Tideswell, and Bakewell ... the wild boar sharpened his tusks against the rugged bark of the forest trees; whilst from their mountain fastnesses the hungry wolves came howling in search of their prey.' Henry Kirke. The Reliquary, Vol 8, Llewellynn Jewitt (ed). Bemrose & Sons, Derby & London, 1867-1868, pp 34-35.

[26] *These could be the 'stag's horns' noted by T Brushfield: Regarding 'the building once occupying the space ... in the field called the Hall Orchard, in Ashford' ... 'it may reasonably be concluded that it was a hunting seat in the then existing forest. ... I have seen stag's horns, which were found about 50 years ago, on digging a trench close by where the building once stood.' The Old Hall at Ashford. T Brushfield. The Reliquary, Vol 8. Llewellynn Jewitt (ed). Bemrose & Sons, Derby & London, 1867-1868, p 128.*

toothache'[27]). The latter was said by Thomas Nadauld Brushfield in 1900 to have previously 'served as a bracket, not many feet from the ground, at the end of the north aisle, on its north wall', although it is not clear what its function or ornamental use would have been at this level.[28]

Finally, a carved Norman lintel that had once appeared over a door in the south wall of the chancel is said to have dated from the Norman period:

'In the old church, there was a gritstone lintel over the chancel (south) door, containing in the centre a much-weathered carving. Lysons, in his drawing of the stone, represents it as a head,[29] but Dr [Thomas Nadauld] Brushfield thinks it was intended for a tree, surrounded by a garland. That it was Norman is fairly certain.'[30]

The old Norman lintel that once stood over the south chancel door of Ashford Church.

Beyond the Norman tympanum and the corbels in the sanctuary, the oldest major structural part of the current building is its tower. The battlements at its summit date from the 14th century, and the pinnacles at each corner are more recent. The lower levels (which possibly once adjoined a nave and short chancel) most likely date from the late 12th or early 13th century, while the tower arch is late 14th or early 15th century.

It is surmised[31] that there may have been a small north aisle added by Griffin to act as his chantry chapel. However, the north aisle as we see it now was probably added in the 14th century, the present late 16th-century arches and octagonal pillars following the line of the original north wall.[32]

The source of materials used for the construction of the old church is the subject of some discussion:

---

[27] *Ashford-in-the-Water and its Church. John Norman, 1961.*

[28] *In architecture, a bracket is a projection from a wall that typically supports a statue, a shelf, an arch, etc. Although its function is usually to bear weight, it is sometimes purely decorative. Architecture: Bracket. Editors of Encyclopædia Britannica. Encyclopædia Britannica, 2002.*

   Ashford Church. TN Brushfield. Journal of the British Archaeological Association, Vol VI, Bedford Press, London, 1900, p 278.

[29] *Sketch by Samuel Lysons. British Museum Additional MSS 9463.*

[30] *John Stonhouse Luxmoore. Derbyshire Record Office, D7672/Lx.C-30.*

[31] *Ibid.*

[32] *Ashford Church. TN Brushfield. Op. cit., p 278; Ashford-in-the-Water and its Church. John Norman, 1961.*

'There is a tradition that the first church, probably a small one, was enlarged by means of stones taken from the 'castle' in the Hall Orchard.'[33]

And Thomas Brushfield comments,

'I think there can be no doubt that the village church was partly, if not entirely, built of material from the old hall [the building once occupying the space ... in the field called the Hall Orchard, in Ashford].'[34]

On the other hand, John Norman states,

'Much more likely is the tradition that Greatbatch Hall in the village was built of the [old hall] stones in the early 17th century.'[35]

The 'first church' itself could not have used material from Neville's fortified house or hunting lodge on Hall Orchard (the latter having been built several hundred years later), but the building has undoubtedly undergone many repairs and (as JS Luxmoore suggests) enlargements in its history. Stone being difficult and expensive to transport, resourceful builders would have always used local materials whenever possible. So, depending on the time that the Neville residence fell into disrepair, its ruins would have represented a valuable resource of raw materials for any village construction project of the 16th or 17th century.

Dissenting chapels in Ashford and Sheldon

At various times since the early 18th century the small village of Ashford-in-the-Water has been served by not only the main parish church, but also by three 'Dissenting' or 'Nonconformist' chapels, as well as by a Dissenters' graveyard, the fascinating histories of which are described in detail by David Windle in the Appendix. Briefly:

A Presbyterian meeting house was built on Cliff End Lane[36] in 1701, for the influential 'Apostle of the Peak', William Bagshawe (1628-1702).[37] However,

---

[33]   *John Stonhouse Luxmoore. Derbyshire Record Office, D7672/Lx.C-30.*

[34]   *The Old Hall at Ashford. T Brushfield. The Reliquary, Vol 8, Llewellynn Jewitt (ed). Bemrose & Sons, Derby & London, 1867-1868, p 128.*

[35]   *Ashford-in-the-Water and its Church. John Norman, 1961.*

[36]   *Cliff End Lane, near the bottom of Vicarage Lane, is now called Buxton Road.*

[37]   *The extent of the influence of William Bagshawe is underlined in a recollection of the words of the Vicar of Bakewell, Revd Hubert Kestell Cornish, in 1851: 'Whatever religion existed a few years ago in the High Peak was due to Bagshawe'. Nonconformist Register Guide: Introduction. Derbyshire Record Office.*

The Derbyshire Returns to the 1851 Religious Census. Margery Tranter (ed). Derbyshire Record Society, 1995, p xliii.

William died a year after it was opened, and was succeeded by his nephew, Revd John Ashe (1671-1735).[38] From 1761, successive ministers of the chapel benefitted from a legacy of 40 shillings a year given by Thomas Roose, otherwise known as Thomas Goodwin. Although initially established as a Presbyterian chapel, in 1830 it became Unitarian and, in 1870, Congregational. By 1877 it was said that the chapel was 'disused, and in a dilapidated condition'[39] and it eventually collapsed in 1937 (see pp 120, 240).

A Baptist chapel, located approximately ¾ mile north of the village on Ashford Lane, was built in 1761, followed shortly thereafter by a house for the minister.

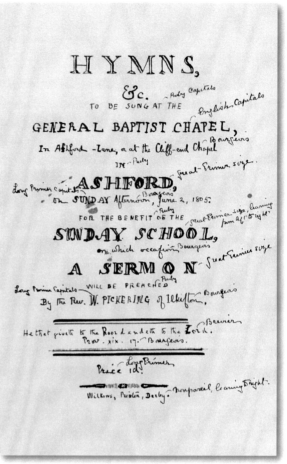

A mark-up of a flyer for an 1805 event at the Baptist Chapel, Ashford-in-the-Water.

By the time of the Religious Census in 1851, George Birley – 'one of the persuasion' – stated that the chapel was 'not used but standing void … has been closed about 4 years', i.e., since 1847,[40] the local Baptist Society having dissolved some years earlier.

Across the road from the site of the Baptist Chapel is the graveyard that was in use as late as 1904, and which has been called the 'infidels' cemetery'

[38] A transcript of the will of Revd John Ashe of Ashford-in-the-Water (and Tideswell) can be seen at: Original Documents. William Swift. The Reliquary, Vol 8, Llewellynn Jewitt (ed). Bemrose & Sons, Derby & London, 1867-1868, pp 59-60.

[39] Notes on the Churches of Derbyshire, Vol II, The Hundreds of the High Peak and Wirksworth. J Charles Cox. Bemrose & Sons, Derby & London, 1877, p 52.

[40] The Derbyshire Returns to the 1851 Religious Census. Margery Tranter (ed). Op. cit., p 172. This was possibly George Birley (1824-1892), brother of Samuel Birley (1824-1906). See p 94. His namesake, the Baptist minister, George Birley (1746-1824), latterly of St Ives, Huntingdonshire (see p 248), was probably from the Bradwell branch of the Birley family.

because none of the headstones is inscribed with a biblical text.[41]

The most recent of Ashford's Nonconformist chapels was the Wesleyan Methodist Chapel, built in 1830 on Court Lane, 50 yards north-east of Holy Trinity Church, on the site of a blacksmith's forge. A new building was constructed on the same site in 1899. Although well supported during its early decades, it closed in 1994. The building is now a private house, its exterior almost unchanged from the date it was built.

A Primitive Methodist chapel was established in Sheldon in 1848, at the bottom of the lane leading to the parish church. At the time of Revd Luxmoore's arrival two services were held each Sunday. It was active prior to the First World War, but by 1928 services had ceased and the building was subsequently demolished.[42]

---

[41] *Baptist Burial Ground, Ashford-in-the-Water. Derbyshire Places of Worship. Rosemary Lockie. Places of Worship Database, 2010-2019.*

[42] *The Diaries of Maria Gyte of Sheldon, Derbyshire, 1913-1920. Gerald Phizackerley (ed). Scarthin Books, 1999, p x.*

FW Goes to War: from the diaries and letters of FW Brocklehurst of Sheldon, Derbyshire. Brian Greasley. Country Books, Little Longstone, Derbyshire, 2016, p 25.

II

REVD JOHN REDDAWAY LUXMOORE

Roots in rural 19th-century Devon

John Reddaway Luxmoore – we'll call him 'our' John to differentiate him from many other John Luxmoores – was born in 1829 in Jacobstowe in west Devon to Samuel Luxmoore, a yeoman farmer, and Patience Luxmoore, née Reddaway. His paternal grandfather and great-grandfather were blacksmiths,[43] and his maternal grandfather and great-grandfather were yeoman farmers.

He was born at a time of extraordinary change: the 19th century witnessed unprecedented population growth; industrial and agricultural mechanisation; improved understanding of disease and its prevention; the birth of the steam locomotive and the railway, and the gradual decline of the canal system; the establishment of a national system of state education; and the revolution of the telegraph.

Whilst not immune to these transformations, change was slower in rural communities, especially those in the southernmost parts of the country where less industrial activity was taking place. This was particularly so in Devon, where the proportion of workers employed in agriculture was substantially above the national average. But, as time went on, even rural villages were forced to adapt to these new circumstances, including associated changes in the demand for food, the growth of competition from abroad in the supply of agricultural products, and a decline in rural trades and crafts.

Almost 90 per cent of farmers at this time were tenants of the great landowners, typically working around 100-300 acres.[44] Farmers of less than

---

[43] *John Reddaway Luxmoore's grandfather is identified as a blacksmith in CFC Luxmoore's family history, but as a retired farmer in the 1851 census, and he may therefore have worked in both capacities. The Family of Luxmoore. Charles Frederick Coryndon Luxmoore. William Pollard & Co Ltd, Exeter & London, 1909, p 27.*

[44] *The average farm size in Devon was 109 acres in 1851. Family Farms and Capitalist Farms in Mid 19th-Century England. Leigh Shaw-Taylor. Agricultural History Review, Vol 53, No. 2, 2005, p 180.*

50 acres were barely distinguishable from labourers, and would make only a tenuous living from their small plots. The most prosperous tenant farmers would have 500 acres or more at their disposal: they were at the threshold of upper middle-class living, doing no manual work themselves, mixing socially with the landowners, and seeking to live the more dignified life of their immediate social superiors.

Alongside the tenant farmers there were a smaller number of independent 'yeoman' farmers who, in the 19th century, were owner-occupiers of about one tenth of the land. Although some were wealthy, the appellation in a number of cases provided the illusion, rather than the reality, of an elevated social status. If they did not acquire their property through an inheritance, purchase of the farm and land would typically return only around 3 to 4 per cent by way of saved rent, whilst a tenant farmer's investment in extending the scale of his operations, or buying new capital equipment, could provide a return of 10 per cent or more.

Despite their extensive knowledge of many aspects of agricultural practice in the area in which they lived, most labourers who worked for mid 19th-century farmers earned no more than the subsistence level – certainly not exceeding 10 shillings a week, and often considerably less. This was well below the national average, not least because there were few opportunities at that time for rural labourers to find non-agricultural employment.

Before they were married (and sometimes afterwards, if their new wife could help with domestic or farming chores), some labourers managed to save a little from their meagre wages by living rent-free in the farmhouse.

Until the final quarter of the 19th century, the world of the farming community was largely restricted to the village and its nearest market town – not surprising when the fastest thing on earth was a galloping horse, covering 100 miles a day at best.[45] However, the railway reached Okehampton in 1871; Plymouth in 1876; and Holsworthy in north-west Devon in 1879. This accelerated dramatically a migration of labourers away from rural Devon that had started some years earlier, and the wages of those that remained began to rise rapidly. Early in the Devon exodus, one local complained that it was the 'very best and most industrious of our agricultural labourers and small tenant farmers' who were moving away, 'leaving us the old, the idle, and the reckless.'[46]

The business of farming supported a large and diverse number of tradesmen and craftsmen – at least 15 per cent of the workforce – whose skills as thatchers,

[45] *All Change in the Victorian Age. Bruce Robinson. British Broadcasting Corporation, 2011,*
    http://www.bbc.co.uk/history/british/victorians/speed_01.shtml

[46] *Exeter Flying Post, June 12th 1851.*

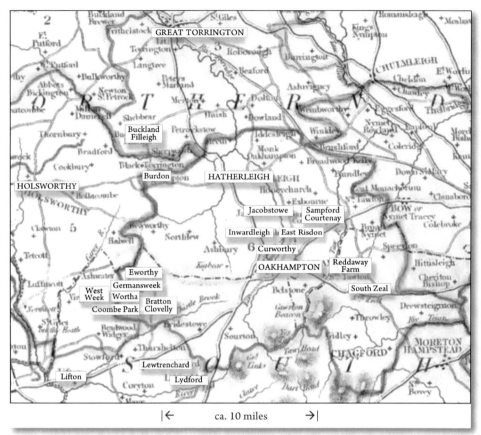

The west Devon area, with approximate locations of some of the places mentioned in the text and using original spellings. Map by Samuel Lewis, 1848.

blacksmiths, farriers, wheelwrights, stonemasons, millers, limeburners, coopers, hurdle-makers, carriers, foresters and gamekeepers kept farms in working order.

Blacksmiths, as highly skilled artisans with the essential ability to handle horses, had an economic and social position considerably higher than farm labourers. Whilst most blacksmiths were independent, large farms of around 500 acres or more may have established an 'in-house' smithy.

The horse was, of course, the mainstay of the blacksmith's work – it remained a vital source of power until the late 19th century, when steam engines finally eclipsed horse-driven farm machinery. Indeed, the total number of horses was still rising in the 1880s and 1890s, reaching a peak in the early years of the 20th century. However, the type of products that a blacksmith could make and repair extended well beyond horseshoes, to include ploughshares, gates and fences, and domestic utensils such as fire grates, shovels, pokers, hinges and lamp brackets.

This diversity of products and services certainly helped to maintain demand. But competition from factory-made substitutes that could be quickly transported over the new railway network, together with the arrival of tractors and motor cars, resulted in the closure of many village forges by the end of the first quarter of the 20th century.

Our John left his family home in about 1848, well before the railways had arrived, and we can therefore tell the story of his parents and their ancestry without straying far beyond the districts immediately surrounding the parish of Okehampton. Indeed, the Luxmoore and Reddaway names (and their variations) are still frequently encountered there today.

Luxmoore family ancestors

The family of our John's father, Samuel Luxmoore, can be traced back to Jordan de Lukesmore, who is recorded in the Manor Rolls of Lydford, Devon, in 1297. Lukesmore meant 'more of Luc', with 'more' meaning 'dwelling by a moor or marish ground' – a description of Lukesmore's sheltered home close to Lydford Castle on the western edge of what is now Dartmoor National Park. His descendants quickly populated Bratton Clovelly and Okehampton.

By the mid 1500s, a yeoman farmer Thomas (1550-1606) was recorded as living at and owning 'Moreston' (likely Morson Farmhouse in Bratton Clovelly), at which time his surname had become Luxmoore.

Some 200 years later, our John's father Samuel (1805-1832) is also found, like his ancestors, to be working in the farming tradition, reversing his father's and grandfather's diversions into blacksmithing.

Samuel had four brothers who survived infancy: William (1802-1847), Charles (1808-1880), James (1810-1860) and John (b.1816);

The body of a cholera victim is carried away in Exeter in 1832. The bedclothes are being washed in the stream, which is the local water supply for the other inhabitants.

and two sisters: Alice (1812-1891) and Elizabeth (1818-1912). Tragically, he was the first of these siblings to die, aged only 27.

Cholera arrived in Britain in 1831, having entered via seaports around the country when infected sailors came ashore. Devon was second only to London in its cholera casualty rate; it was not appreciated that water was the carrier of the disease, and it spread quickly as a result of the primitive level of sanitary arrangements throughout the county.

In 1832 – the year of Samuel's death – there were outbreaks in Exeter (402 deaths) and also in Plymouth, Stonehouse and Devonport (1,031 deaths in total).[47] It seems possible, therefore, that our John's father died of cholera.

The entwining of the Luxmoore and Yeo families

Our John's paternal grandfather, James (sometimes Thomas) Luxmoore – let's call him 'Grandpa Luxmoore' – was born in 1776 at Germansweek. Nine years earlier, one John Andrew Yeo – 'Grandpa Yeo' – had been born 10 miles distant, in Inwardleigh. They married their respective partners within one year of each other: Grandpa Luxmoore at the age of 24 in Lewtrenchard, and Grandpa Yeo at the age of 32 in Jacobstowe. Grandpa Luxmoore was to have seven surviving children; Grandpa Yeo six.

If the two grandpas did not know each other at the time they were each married, they certainly did by the time their children had grown up: Grandpa Luxmoore's

John Yeo and Alice Yeo (née Luxmoore) of Orchard Barton, Lewtrenchard, and (inset) a younger Alice.

---

[47] *History of the cholera in Exeter in 1832. Thomas Shapter. John Churchill, London, 1849.*

Local politics and public health in mid 19th-century Plymouth. M Brayshay & VFT Pointon. Medical History, 1983.

In 1854, physician John Snow used Shapter's analytical methods to pinpoint a particular water pump as a source of a cholera outbreak in London. From this work, it was discovered for the first time that water was the carrier of the disease, and it led to the great Victorian initiative of sewer construction across all the large cities of the country.

Samuel Luxmoore Yeo, son of John and Alice Yeo, and cousin of John Reddaway Luxmoore, at the age of about 23 years.

two daughters (our John's aunts), Alice and Elizabeth, married two of Grandpa Yeo's sons, John and Isaac, in Germansweek and Okehampton respectively. Their intertwined lives are memorialised through the names of John and Alice Yeo's sons: John Luxmoore Yeo (1841-1878) and ginger-haired Samuel 'Sandy' Luxmoore Yeo (1847-1918) – our John's cousins.

Around the time of his marriage in 1839 to Elizabeth Luxmoore, Grandpa Yeo's son Isaac (1816-1901) was a tenant farmer of some 260 acres at East Wortha in Germansweek, land that was owned by Thomas Bridgman Luxmoore, brother of Bishop Luxmoore of St Asaph, whom we shall meet shortly.[48] Isaac subsequently moved his family to the 208-acre Bitchcombe Farm in Lewtrenchard – owned by the then Conservative MP for South Devon – which he farmed well into his 60s.

Grandpa Yeo's other son, John Yeo (1803-1891), was living on the day of the census in 1851 with Alice and their six children at Orchard Barton[49] in Lewtrenchard. John held the tenancy to this 350-acre farm, owned at that time by the Lord of the Manor, Edward Baring-Gould, and Alice would no doubt be in charge of managing the household. They had the help of six farm labourers, two servants, and those children who were old enough to lend a hand (including the three characterised as 'scholars', who most likely did not escape their share of domestic duties).

The intertwining of the Luxmoore and Yeo families went beyond the naming of John and Alice Yeo's sons. By this time, John Yeo had invited Alice's father

---

[48] *The remains of East Wortha and West Wortha farms, as well as Combe Park, Thomas Bridgman Luxmoore's home at the time, were flooded in 1989 when the Roadford Lake reservoir was created (see p 78). Prior to the flooding, a large-scale excavation of West Wortha had been performed.*

[49] *Barton [Anglo Saxon: bere (yard) + tún (barley)] means 'that part of the farm premises which is specially enclosed for cattle ... because it is here that large quantities of straw are strewed about to be eaten and turned into manure .... The term 'Barton' is also applied to the entire farm and homestead, but in this case it is only to the more important farms; very often it is the principal farm in the parish, whether occupied by the owner or not – generally not.' West Somerset Word Book: A Glossary of Dialectical and Archaic Words and Phrases used in the West of Somerset and East Devon. Frederick Thomas Elworthy. English Dialect Society, 1888.*

and mother – Grandpa and Grandma Luxmoore (née Bickle) – to reside at Orchard Barton on a permanent live-in basis in their older age, and Grandma was still living there 10 years later.

Also at the Yeo farm in 1851 were Alice's brother Charles Luxmoore (our John's uncle) and two more Luxmoores: Samuel Rison Luxmoore, Alice's eight-year-old nephew, who had been orphaned aged four when both of his parents (William and Johanna Luxmoore) died;[50] and Alice's five-year-old niece Agness Luxmoore (daughter of James and Agness Luxmoore),[51] who was visiting from St Andrews, Plymouth. Another visitor was Elizabeth Davy, a family friend from Jacobstowe.

With 22 inhabitants on census day – eight Yeos, four Luxmoores, eight servants and labourers, and two visitors – this would have been a full, and possibly rather chaotic, farmhouse.

The 'other' Luxmoores

When he was 20 our John would have heard of the fate of his contemporary, John Nicholl Luxmoore, who had been killed in a riding accident whilst an undergraduate at St John's College, Cambridge. The story was widely reported because of the fame and, in the view of some, the notoriety of certain members of John Nicholl Luxmoore's family. The Luxmoores in this branch of the ancestral tree were local luminaries owning considerable property in Okehampton, and many were clergymen.

Networking has always been one of the best ways of finding employment opportunities. But 'networking' in its more disagreeable forms of cronyism and nepotism flourished in ecclesiastical circles in the 19th century, under the guise of patronage: the right to present a nominee for appointment to a vacant benefice.[52] This was no better illustrated than in the memoirs of the radical speaker and agitator Henry Hunt (1773-1835):

> 'My father then, on condition of my taking orders, and going into the Church, proposed to send me to Oxford ... 'If you should like to be a clergyman, I have now an opportunity of purchasing the next presentation to a good living,[53] and you will then have secured to you for life a

---

[50] *William (1802-1847) died as a result of 'phagedena, purpura, and great exhaustion' brought on by 'syphilis'; and Johanna (1803-1847) died of 'phrenitis and effusion on the brain'. The loss of both parents had thrown the family into 'a state of mass confusion, not to mention depression and remorse.' William Luxmoore: Biography. Charles Emerson Luxmoore, 2003.*

[51] *James Luxmoore (1810-1860), born in Germansweek, was a gardener living at this time in the St Andrew's parish of Plymouth.*

[52] *Patronage is also known as 'advowson'. The Local Historian's Glossary of Words and Terms. Joy Bristow. Countryside Books, Newbury, Berkshire, 2001.*

[53] *'Living' is the guaranteed income for the lifetime of a clergyman.*

thousand pounds or perhaps twelve hundred pounds a year; and you will have nothing else to do, for six days out of the seven, but hunt, shoot, and fish by day, and play cards and win the money of the farmers' wives and children by night. ... All that will be expected of you is to read prayers, and preach a sermon, which will cost you three pence once a week.'[54]

The importance of being connected to the 'right' people at that time cannot therefore be overemphasised, as the curate of Headington in Oxfordshire bemoaned in a note written to a friend at Balliol College Oxford in 1806:

'If I had been the nineteenth cousin of a lord, I might have attained hopes of a living, but I have not one drop of duke's blood in me that I know of, and have no one to patronise or assist me, so that probably I shall continue a curate all my life.'[55]

In an extreme form of patronage, 'pluralists' held multiple ecclesiastical livings at a time. Although challenged by the 1803 Residence Act, the practice continued long afterwards. John Nicholl Luxmoore's grandfather, another John Luxmoore, who was Bishop of St Asaph in North Wales from 1815 to 1830, was one of the most infamous pluralists, along with his sons Charles Scott Luxmoore (John Nicholl Luxmoore's father) and John Henry Montagu Luxmoore (his uncle).

Bishop Luxmoore gained a reputation less for his intellect than as an example of episcopal avarice; to Revd David Richard Thomas, author of an 1874 history of the St Asaph diocese, he was the worst offender in the matter of nepotism and plurality in its annals.

Bishop Luxmoore's eldest son, Charles, was Dean of St Asaph; Rector of Bromyard and Cradley; Vicar of Guilsfield; and simultaneously drew a stipend from Hereford. Charles' living as Rector of Cradley was one of

The present-day modest memorial to Bishop John Luxmoore is mounted in the north transept of St Asaph Cathedral.

---

54 *Memoirs of Henry Hunt, Esq. Vol 1. Henry Hunt. T Dolby, London, 1820, pp 94-95.*

55 *The Victorian Clergyman. Trevor May. Shire Publications, 2006, p 12.*

the most valuable in the Diocese, though he was rarely seen there. Being prodigiously wealthy, he determined to build a church and a rectory in Cradley in memory of his son John Nicholl Luxmoore. Completed after his death by his two sisters, the rectory was considered one of the finest in the region: in 1946, an internal plan showed there were 14 bedrooms, and when on sale in 2018 it was said to offer around 7,300 sq ft of living space.[56]

In the family tradition of pluralism, the bishop's other son, John Henry Montagu, was Vicar of Berriew, Registrar of Hereford, and also received an income from St Asaph.

It has been estimated that this particular 'other' Luxmoore family at one time absorbed as much as £27,000 per annum of church income in the two dioceses of St Asaph and Hereford,[57] a purchasing power of around £2.1 million per annum in today's money.

Such was their notoriety that St Asaph Cathedral dismantled 'a massive memorial to the avaricious Bishop John Luxmoore and his sons … and replaced [it] by a simple stone memorial to the bishop.'[58] The Latin inscription on this more recent memorial reads:

Below are buried the remains
of John Luxmoore, Professor of Sacred Theology,
first Bishop of Bristol, then Hereford,
[and] recently of this Diocese for fifteen years;
who, to the utmost of his ability,
carried out all his duties towards God [and] towards
all the good children of the vicinity.
He took care of the clergy entrusted to him
courteously [and] kind-heartedly, yet with an applied seriousness.
He was quick to support the poor.
He was active in education and taught with such delight and friendliness
that great crowds cheerfully listened to him.
Yet, the same man was not unskilled in passing on the Classical education
he had imbibed at Eton and Cambridge
to his country's Church and the Christian world.
Died: 21st day of January
In the year of our Salvation: 1830
In the year of his age: 74.

---

[56]   *The Old Rectory, Cradley. Andrew Grant Country Homes, https://www.youtube.com/watch?v=KjFviVMnEMw*

[57]   *John Luxmoore (1756-1830). Matthew Cragoe. Oxford Dictionary of National Biography, Oxford University Press, 2004.*

[58]   *St Asaph Cathedral. Ven TW Pritchard. 1997.*

Our John's branch of the Luxmoore family tree, and the 'other' Luxmoores' branch, meet eight generations earlier with their common ancestor, William Luxmoore, son of the yeoman farmer Thomas Luxmoore of 'Moreston', whom we encountered previously (see p29). William was born in 1581, midway through the reign of Elizabeth I. The future vicar of Ashford-in-the-Water was descended from William's younger son, John Luxmoore (1614-1680); whilst the branch of his con-

Robin Stonhouse Luxmoore, grandson of Revd John Reddaway Luxmoore, with the bronze bust of Henry Elford Noble Luxmoore (1841-1926), Housemaster of Eton College from 1871 to 1902. Luxmoore's Garden, Eton College, 1989. (Henry, of the 'other' Luxmoore branch, was the first cousin twice removed of Bishop John Luxmoore of St Asaph.)

temporary, John Nicholl Luxmoore, was descended from his elder son, Thomas Luxmoore (1610-1636) of Breazle and Combe Park.[59]

Although the two Luxmoore branches diverged in the 17th century, many of the respective descendants remained living in the west Devon area, and we will find them bumping into each other 200 years later.

Reddaway family ancestors

Early ancestors of our John's mother Patience Luxmoore (née Reddaway), dating back to 1238, likely came from the ancient Radeweie farm in Sampford Courtenay parish. Surviving now as 'Reddaway Farm', it left the family in 1760, but was acquired and owned again by a 20th-century Reddaway family until about 1999.

The name Reddaway probably derives from either 'red way', perhaps because of the colour of the soil (Old English reade weg); or 'ride way', a track fit for riding horses (Old English rad weg).

Patience's branch of her family tree has been traced back at least six generations to Oliver Reddaway, born in 1568.[60] Named after her mother Patience Reddaway (née Tucker), our John's mother was born in 1805 in the parish of Inwardleigh, five miles from the old Reddaway Farm in Sampford Courtenay, and three miles from Jacobstowe, where her future husband Samuel

---

[59] 'Combe' is the common spelling today. It is also variously spelt 'Coombe' (particularly in the 19th century) and 'Comb'.

[60] The Reddaways of Devon. Tony and Denise Poole, http://redway.com.au/reddaways.htm

was born in the same year. Her father and grandfather – both John Reddaways – were also born in Inwardleigh. She was the middle child, with two older siblings, John (1801-1868) and Mary (1803-1881); and two younger siblings, James (1808-1870) and Elizabeth (1806-1874).

Some of her close relatives were significant landowners, and some prospered greatly. Her father (1772-1863) and grandfather (1735-1806), and her uncle, Richard (1756-1810), were all landowning yeoman farmers, and her elder brother John was a tenant farmer of 213 acres at Higher Westacott and, subsequently, 350 acres at Curworthy, one of the Domesday manors of Inwardleigh.

When her younger brother James was 33 years old, he was farming at his father's 204-acre Bradley Farm in Buckland Filleigh, a property that he was to inherit in 1863. Shortly before this, in November 1862, James purchased the manor, farm and lands of Burdon and Down End (190 acres) for the sum of £3,400. Known as 'Buerdune' at the time of the Norman Conquest, it was thought to be one of the oldest manors in Devon and, until purchased by James, it had been held for some 13 generations of Burdons. James Reddaway thus became 'Squire James' Reddaway.[61]

Upon James' death in 1870, the Burdon Manor estate and Bradley Farm property passed to his nephew John Reddaway (1827-1908), our John's cousin, who was at that time 43 years old (two years older than our John), and now also the owner of Curworthy House and estate.[62]

Reddaway Farm in Sampford Courtenay, Devon.

---

[61] *The ancient feudal manor of Burdon, Devonshire. Highampton Local History Group, www.highampton-lhg.co.uk*

[62] *Shortly after inheriting the Burdon Manor estate, John Reddaway advertised the property 'To Let' for a 14-year term as a 'large and commodious dwelling house ... and about 231 acres of good arable, meadow, pasture and orchard land.' Western Morning News, June 16th 1870.*

OAKHAMPTON CASTLE, DEVONSHIRE.

An 1829 engraving of Okehampton Castle, Devon, made at the time that it was owned by Albany Savile (1783-1831), Mayor of Okehampton. For some time during the prior century it had been owned by John Luxmoore (1692-1750), and it was purchased by John Reddaway of Curworthy & Burdon in 1890.

This John Reddaway 'of Curworthy & Burdon' amassed further property when the citizens of Okehampton could not (or were not sufficiently motivated to) raise enough funds to purchase the ruins of the borough's castle.

Originally built in 1058, Okehampton Castle was dismantled in 1539 by Henry VIII, and subsequently descended by marriage to Baron Mohun of Okehampton. For a period during the first half of the 18th century, the castle was owned by John Luxmoore (1692-1750) of the 'other' Luxmoore family tree branch. A successful lawyer, this John was the grandfather of John Luxmoore, Bishop of St Asaph. Prior to its acquisition by John Reddaway of Curworthy & Burdon, it had been bought by the Earl of Devon with the intention of presenting it to the borough. But after the Earl's death this did not come to pass. The 'relic' was thus sold to our John's cousin at an auction in June 1890 for £1,010 [approximately £112,000 today]. The auctioneer congratulated the purchaser, 'expressing his pleasure that it had been acquired by someone in the district and the owner of property that adjoined the castle and its grounds.'[63]

---

[63] *Western Times, June 30th 1890; Magna Britannia, a concise topographical account of the several counties of Great Britain. Vol 6 (Devonshire). Daniel & Samuel Lysons. T Cadell, London, 1822, pp 371-372.*

Our John's mother died in 1886, and so did not live to see her nephew acquire this landmark building in Okehampton, which nowadays is part of the portfolio of English Heritage.

Family homes

In 1841, nine years after the tragic death of her husband, Patience Luxmoore is found living in South Street, Great Torrington – about 15 miles north of our John's birthplace in Jacobstowe – with John aged 12 and his sister, Patience Reddaway Luxmoore, aged 10. A second tragedy befell the family five years later in 1846, when our John's sister Patience died, aged only 16 years; it is possible that she could have been an early casualty of the 'Irish Fever' typhus epidemic.[64] Two years after our John's sister's death, his grandmother Patience died at the age of 74.

By 1851, at the time we were observing the Luxmoores and Yeos in their farmhouse in Lewtrenchard (see p31), our John, now aged 22, had left the family home. His mother, Patience (aged 46), his maternal grandfather John Reddaway (now retired and aged 79), and his maternal aunt Elizabeth (aged 44), had moved into two adjacent cottages in Bridge Street, Hatherleigh, and each was employing a servant girl.[65]

Our John's mother, her father and her sister were living modestly, although comfortably, and in that much they were fortunate: in Devon at this time, one person in 18 was officially classed as a pauper, and this number increased when the price of wheat doubled temporarily between 1851 and 1855. The workhouses, however, remained below capacity simply because they were so dreaded, and many would rather resort to the out-relief which was being provided by an increasing number of charities.[66] But, as Charles Dickens so vividly described, the stress and uncertainty of not knowing where the next meal was coming from was hard to bear, with many remaining destitute rather than entering the workhouse or accepting the demeaning hand of charity.

---

[64] *The so-called 'Irish Fever' typhus epidemic of 1847 claimed more than 30,000 lives that year. A History of Epidemics in Britain Volume 2. Charles Creighton. Cambridge University Press, 1891, (reissued 2013), pp 205-208.*

[65] *Domestic help was very affordable at that time. In 1891 it was estimated that, countrywide, one in three women between the ages of 15 and 20 was in domestic service. Kitchen maids and maids-of-all work (sometimes referred to as 'slaveys') were paid between £6 and £12 a year; 'tweenies' (maids who helped other domestics, moving between floors as and when they were needed) were paid even less. Women and domestic service in Victorian society. Kate Clarke. The History Press, 2020, https://www.thehistorypress.co.uk/articles/women-and-domestic-service-in-victorian-society/*

[66] *Outdoor relief ('out-relief') was assistance in the form of money, food, clothing or goods, given without the requirement that the recipient enter a workhouse.*

A view of Bridge Street, Hatherleigh, Devon, looking north, ca. 1890. JR Luxmoore lived in this street until he left home in approximately 1848. His mother remained here until her death 38 years later.

The trial of John Yeo

The apparently comfortable lives of Patience, Elizabeth and their father in Hatherleigh, and the unexceptional 1851 census return from Orchard Barton in Lewtrenchard, provide no clue that, within weeks of the census being taken, the Yeo-Luxmoore household was to become the epicentre of a dramatic and very public spectacle, when John Yeo was indicted for 'unlawfully assaulting Charles Luxmoore, knowing him to be a destitute person of unsound mind.'

The case, tried at Exeter Crown Court on July 29th 1851, 'excited great interest, and occupied the Court the greater part of the day' as 'few such cases have ever been brought before the public.' Indeed, the story competed successfully for column inches in both the local and national press,[67] against stories of the 75 per cent eclipse of the sun in England that had occurred the previous day, and the ongoing attractions of the Great Exhibition and Sir Joseph Paxton's Crystal Palace. It provided an opportunity for the sub-editors to compose some colourful headlines: 'Extraordinary Case'; 'Horrible Treatment of a Lunatic'. Indeed, the case is still cited today.[68]

The terms used at that time to characterise those with mental illnesses are

---

[67] *Exeter and Plymouth Gazette, August 2nd 1851; Exeter Flying Post, July 31st 1851; Sherborne Mercury, August 5th 1851; Taunton Courier & Western Advertiser, August 6th 1851; Bell's New Weekly Messenger, August 3rd 1851; Evening Mail, August 1st 1851; Reynolds' Newspaper, August 3rd 1851; The Atlas, August 2nd 1851; Morning Post, August 1st 1851; Wiltshire Independent, August 7th 1851; Devizes and Wiltshire Gazette, August 7th 1851; Cork Examiner, August 8th 1851; News of the World, August 3rd 1851.*

[68] *Inconvenient People: Lunacy, Liberty and the Mad-Doctors in Victorian England. Sarah Wise. Vintage Books, 2013, pp 187-191.*

now derogatory and offensive. A 'lunatic' was someone who was 'sometimes of good and sound memory and understanding and sometimes not'; an 'idiot' was a 'natural fool from birth'; and an 'imbecile' was anyone who had acquired a permanent cognitive impairment after birth, such as a traumatic brain injury, encephalitis, meningitis, or poisoning by toxins.

In the earlier part of the 19th century, pauper lunatics were dealt with locally under the Poor Law, vagrancy law or criminal law, and were therefore likely to end up in workhouses, houses of correction, or prisons. They were often manacled to outhouses, chained to the wall, and kept in appallingly squalid conditions, often with little food and water and no heat. Through no fault of their own, the mentally ill had become the most vulnerable class of British society: to their families, they could become a financial hardship; and socially they were hidden away from public view because of the stigma of their condition. But by the middle of the century more progressive attitudes and new legislation had started to usher in change: the 1845 Lunacy and County Asylum Acts mandated the provision of a network of county lunatic asylums, to be regulated by a new Lunacy Commission, and insanity was recognised as primarily a medical, rather than a moral, problem.[69]

Our John's uncle, Charles Luxmoore, was born three years after John's father, Samuel, and had been a blacksmith in his early youth, probably working alongside Grandpa Luxmoore. Although he had been of 'weak intellect since childhood', his mental capacity had become significantly impaired 18 years before the trial, when he was 25. There were several alleged instances of violent and unusual behaviour:[70]

> 'A young man helping me to take some iron out of a carriage, Luxmoore was taken all at once in a great rage, and said he would kill the young man';
>
> 'He would have killed me [a servant] many times if he could have got at me';
>
> 'I have seen him tear up a mouse and put it in his pipe and smoke it.'

He was even said to have been violent against his mother:

> 'He then used his mother very badly, and said he would kill her if he could get at her. He knocked her down, and she was almost senseless';
>
> 'He once took a billhook and threatened to kill his mother.'

It was also alleged that he had 'committed an outrage upon a girl.'

In order to contain his violent behaviour, his father, Grandpa Luxmoore,

---

[69] *Insanity. Marilyn J Kurta. In: Sally Mitchell (ed). Victorian Britain – An Encyclopædia. Routledge, Abingdon, Oxfordshire, 2011, pp 397-399.*

[70] *Except where otherwise stated, quotations are from contemporaneous press reports, op. cit.*

*'had a chain made and fastened round his leg by a rivet, and then through
the floor of his bedroom to a beam; but after he had been so confined for
some years, a sort of cell of wood was made on the ground floor.'*

When Charles was 39, and had been confined in this 'cell' for nine years,
'his father and mother became bedridden' (Grandpa Luxmoore was then 71
and Grandma Luxmoore was 73), and John Yeo,

*'determined to remove all the family to his own house at Orchard
[Barton], and he caused the cell to be taken down and carried to his
house [with the help of Charles' younger brother, our John's uncle, John
Luxmoore[71]], and there erected.'*

Charles remained in this rebuilt 'cell' at Orchard Barton for a further four
years when, in March 1851,

*'attention of the parish officers was called to the circumstance. He was
visited, and under an order of the magistrates he was removed to the
County Lunatic Asylum. The while of this being communicated to the
Commissioners of Lunacy, they ordered the present indictment.'*

Extensive testimony was given about the alleged conditions in which
Charles had been kept, and the care which had (or had not) been provided
to him. The prosecution described in great detail the state in which various
witnesses had observed him: often completely naked and soiled; in the very
small 'cell' without light; and without access to clean (or any) bedding.

The defence countered that John Yeo had been required to take Charles into
his farmhouse when Grandpa and Grandma Luxmoore had become bedridden,
the blood relatives having distanced themselves from the situation. He had
therefore done all he could to help, whilst simultaneously struggling to run his
farm.[72] Witnesses described the good food they had seen him eating, but also that
he quickly destroyed any new clothing and bedding, and the fact that a servant
charged with cleaning his cell was afraid for her life. The local clergyman,
Revd Charles Thomas Carpenter, Curate of Germansweek, testified:

*'I should say the manner in which he was kept was not improper. I do not
think he could have been kept in any other mode in his own house, from
the general terror there was of him in the neighbourhood ... I never saw
a more affectionate mother in my life, and I may say the same of all the*

---

[71] *This John Luxmoore, the youngest of our John's uncles (b.1816), was a saddler and harness
maker. In 1851 he was living in Tapton's Cottage in Lewtrenchard, close to Orchard Barton.*

[72] *Inconvenient People: Lunacy, Liberty and the Mad-Doctors in Victorian England. Sarah Wise.
Vintage Books, London, 2013, p 189.*

family, particularly as regarded the lunatic. The defendant is a humane, kind man.'

The defence attorney also noted by way of a mitigating context:

'the jury must be told, that no very long time ago, it was the constant practice in lunatic asylums to put the unfortunate in dark cells, to chain them, and even to flog them.'

It was mentioned that Grandma and Grandpa Luxmoore 'thought if the parish took care of him they would have to pay for it', and that they did not therefore avail themselves of this option because they 'were very poor, having only a moderate income … [of] … £30 a year [£3,200 today] – an annuity'; plus 'a cottage or two that brought in about £10 [£1,070] per annum'; and that 'they were so poor that they were already impoverished from the quantity of linen he destroyed'.

Summing up, the judge, Mr Justice Coleridge, stated:

'There did not appear to be any motive in what the defendant had done … although it might seem a little hard, still it was perfect justice, that if a man broke the law of the country to the injury of another it was no justification that he had done it through ignorance of the law, or that he had not done it from a bad motive … they had heard it said by the counsel for the prisoner, that by the law of this country magistrates had been authorised to chain lunatics, and that it had been the practice in lunatic asylums to chain lunatics there confined. Both these propositions were perfectly true, but it was never the law.'

The jury returned a guilty verdict, 'but very strongly recommended the defendant to mercy.'

In sentencing, Justice Coleridge declared:

'This has been to me really a difficulty … I am glad that they have so expressed their earnest desire that, now the verdict is pronounced and the law made clear, your case should be dealt with mercifully by the Court. I don't apprehend that the commissioners would desire anything else. [The Commissioners in Lunacy so assented.] … they agree with the jury that no severe punishment should be inflicted … I am about to pass a sentence of imprisonment, but not in the House of Correction. I don't mean to subject you, a respectable man, to the punishment of hard labour. The sentence therefore is, that you be imprisoned in the common gaol for six months.'

Some commentators (notably in the press from outside Devon) were critical of the judge's decision:

'A case was tried on Tuesday before Mr Justice Coleridge at Exeter which affords a very striking illustration of the danger which arises from leaving a lunatic to the treatment of his friends, unless that treatment be carried out under the vigilant superintendence of properly qualified persons.'[73]

On April 5th 1851 Charles was admitted to the Devon County Asylum. The medical superintendent, Dr Charles Bucknill, had used the opportunity of the trial,

'to advertise the wonders of the county asylum system, detailing the progress Luxmoore had made since his admission: 'The lunatic has been very quiet and tractable since I have had charge of him ... He is good tempered and perfectly harmless.' But this could also suggest that the 13 years in a darkened cell had not wrought half as much damage as the prosecution [had hoped] to demonstrate.'[74]

Charles died in the asylum 29 years later on April 13th 1880, at the age of 72.

The reality was that it was only in 1845 – six years before the trial – that the Lunacy Commission had been established, and the Devon County Asylum at Exminster for pauper lunatics had been opened. The welcome positive changes in attitude and treatment had had almost no time to become embedded; and the as yet undiminished social stigma would not have encouraged family members to inquire diligently about alternative care options for their mentally ill relatives. Indeed, it is only in recent times that John and Alice Yeo's descendants became aware of this episode.[75] In Charles Luxmoore's case, there was a real danger of harm to others if he was not kept under controlled surveillance at all times; and there was no money available to even consider private care provision.

As to the claim that 'none of the blood family had taken on the burden of care, once the lunatic's parents were no longer able to do so',[76] Charles' sister Alice was living in the same house. She could not possibly have avoided

---

[73]   *Cork Examiner, August 8th 1851.*

[74]   *Inconvenient People: Lunacy, Liberty and the Mad-Doctors in Victorian England. Sarah Wise. Vintage Books, London, 2013, pp 188-189.*

[75]   *'The little dark room [Charles Luxmoore's 'cell' at Orchard Barton] was destroyed in recent years during restorations, but is still remembered by the Yeo family of Orchard as 'the prison' without knowing the reason'. Never Completely Submerged: The story of the Squarson of Lewtrenchard as revealed by 'The Diary of Sabine Baring-Gould'. Ron Wawman. Grosvenor House Publishing, Ltd, 2009, end note 41, p 260.*

[76]   *Inconvenient People. Op. cit., p 191.*

'the burden of care', even if she had wanted to. But she was also caring for her own six children; her bedridden father and mother; her orphaned eight-year-old nephew, Samuel Rison Luxmoore; and – in the month that the parish officers visited Orchard Barton – her brother James' five-year-old daughter, Agness.

James himself lived 25 miles away in Plymouth, too distant to provide any meaningful level of regular assistance. Charles' brother John, who did live nearby in Lewtrenchard, had helped with the relocation of the 'cell' from Grandpa and Grandma Luxmoore's house to Orchard Barton, so had at least been willing to help out on that occasion. Charles' other sister, Elizabeth, lived about six miles away in Germansweek – perhaps close enough that she could have lent a hand from time to time if Alice or her husband John had asked her. Indeed, she would hardly have been able to refuse, as she was married to John Yeo's brother, Isaac. But she had four children of her own to look after. And, of course, Charles' only other sibling, Samuel, our John's father, had died 19 years earlier.

Should our John, Charles' nephew, have come to the assistance of his Aunt Alice and Uncle John Yeo? Although he was a fit 22-year-old, he was at that time a student living 15 miles distant, almost certainly without any means of personal transport. His Uncle Charles' other nephews and nieces either also lived too far away, or else were children in their teens or younger.

So John Yeo and Alice had little option but to struggle to cope with Charles by themselves. Both judge and jury appeared to understand these and the other practical issues when passing the relatively lenient sentence.

When recalling the sad story some 30 years later, Sabine Baring-Gould, inheritor of the Lewtrenchard estates, was of the opinion that 'Mr Yeo – who is still alive, a kind-hearted man – was not conscious that he was acting cruelly'.[77]

Grandpa Luxmoore had prepared a new will on July 24th 1851, five days before the date of John Yeo's trial at Exeter Crown Court. It was manifestly written with this event at the forefront of his mind, since it provided that:

> 'all the expenses of the trial at Exeter concerning son Charles Luxmoore shall be paid out of my property to John Yeo, my son-in-law, for ignorantly breaking the law.'

It also provided for John Yeo, Isaac Yeo and John Davy, his Executors-in-Trust, to:

---

[77] John Yeo was 79 years old at the time of Sabine Baring-Gould's recollection. Never Completely Submerged: The story of the Squarson of Lewtrenchard as revealed by 'The Diary of Sabine Baring-Gould'. Ron Wawman. Grosvenor House Publishing, Ltd, 2009, p 129.

'sell my property in the village of Eworthy, in the parish of Germansweek, also my freehold property consisting of three cottages on the south side of the road leading from Eworthy to Germansweek called Overlake Cottages, also orchards and gardens belonging.'

Overlake Cottage in Eworthy, Germansweek, Devon. This property was owned by JR Luxmoore's grandfather, James Luxmoore, but was sold upon his death in 1851.

Grandpa Luxmoore had purchased a 99-year lease to the Eworthy properties from Sir William Pratt Call for £50 in 1813;[78] the cottages, orchard and garden comprised a total area of about ½ acre.[79] This, and the amount of rent that the cottages were bringing in, confirm that their sale value would be very modest. He clearly had little other money: he bequeathed only nominal amounts of £5 to his invalided widow, £5 to his son John, and £1 to Charles. The residue of his estate was bequeathed to his other children – James Luxmoore, Alice Yeo and Elizabeth Yeo – with the share to his deceased son William Luxmoore to be given in trust to his five orphaned grandchildren, who included the young Samuel Rison Luxmoore.

Grandpa Luxmoore died a few weeks after he had made his will, in the same month that the newspapers carried the story of the trial across the country. On his deathbed, and with no little compassion, he had done the only thing he could to support his convicted son-in-law who had taken him into his home, and his mentally-ill son for whom, during most of his life, there had been no possibility of affordable independent care.

His will was proved on August 30th 1851 and before the year was out his property had been purchased by Revd Charles Thomas Coryndon Luxmoore, whose father was a cousin of Bishop Luxmoore of St Asaph. One of the great landowners of Devon, CTC Luxmoore's properties included Witherdon Manor; Northmore House (subsequently Okehampton Town Hall); and the

---

[78] *Notice and Grounds of Order for Maintaining, October 8th 1851. (A document from the parish of Lewtrenchard substantiating the grounds for charging the cost 'for the maintenance, medicine, clothing and care' of Charles Luxmoore in the Devon Asylum to the parish of Germansweek.)*

[79] *Tithe Apportionments, Germansweek, 1842.*

great tithes of Broadwoodwidger and Germansweek.[80] In addition, he was Lord of the Manors of Southweek and More Malherbe and of Germansweek.

Seventeen years after the trial – in the year our John embarked on the great restoration of his church in Ashford-in-the-Water – Mary Rosalie Carpenter (1836-1893), the eldest daughter of Revd Carpenter, who testified in John Yeo's defence, married Revd CTC Luxmoore's son – another Charles Luxmoore. As inheritor of his father's great estates, this Charles (1824-1890) would have found no difficulty in paying for the very best care available, should he have ever needed it.[81]

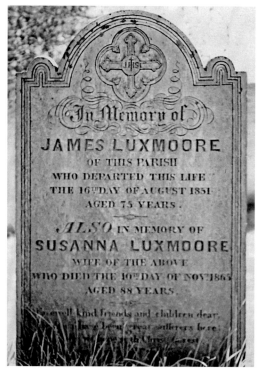

Headstone of James and Susanna Luxmoore, grandparents of JR Luxmoore, St Peter's Church, Lewtrenchard, Devon.

The money trail

Becoming a widow in the 19th century could mean destitution, especially for those of the working class. If they had small children they could be particularly vulnerable, as they had to support not only themselves but also their dependants. Some would survive by finding work in domestic service or in retail trades; others might turn for assistance to members of their own family or their late husband's family. If all else failed, then they would have to rely on charity.

As Samuel Luxmoore died intestate, his heir-at-law was our John, who at that time was only three years old. Samuel was a yeoman farmer, so would have owned at least some land. His widow, Patience, would have had an

---

[80] *Tithes were an obligation of parishioners to support their parish priest from the fruits of the earth in his parish. Great tithes were of corn, hay and wood; small tithes were of everything else (wool, and the annual increase of farm stock, eggs, fruit, etc.). The Tithe Commutation Act of 1836 replaced this ancient system of payment-in-kind with monetary payments. The Local Historian's Glossary of Words and Terms. Joy Bristow. Countryside Books, Newbury, Berkshire, 2001.*

[81] *Mary and Charles' son, Charles Frederick Coryndon Luxmoore, was to author in 1909 a Luxmoore family history (see Bibliography).*

opportunity to enjoy all of the income it could yield through the right of usufruct: a lifetime legal entitlement to manage and use land that would pass to her son on her death. Could this land have contributed a meaningful amount towards Patience's household expenses?

Could our John also have been named at this time as the direct beneficiary of an estate from some other family forebear? If so, until he had reached the age of majority, the testator would have named a guardian to manage the estate's finances, and potentially to make decisions regarding his education. In that event, could they possibly have provided to Patience a contribution to the cost of our John's upbringing?

Looking first at our John's parents' closest relatives, it is clear from the Yeo trial record that our John's grandfather, Grandpa Luxmoore, had no money to spare for his deceased son Samuel's family: most or all of what was received from the sale of Grandpa's cottages at Eworthy would have gone to pay John Yeo's legal bills. If any was left, it was to be shared between our John's aunts, uncles and orphaned cousins.

On our John's mother's side, Patience's grandfather had died a widower in 1806 when she was one year old. His estate was distributed to various of his children, the residue – valued at £660 5s [£52,000] – being left to Patience's father, John Reddaway. When her father died in 1863 (31 years after the death of Samuel), his most valuable asset, the 204-acre Bradley Farm, passed to Patience's younger brother, Squire James of Burdon.

However, as we have seen, after Samuel's death his wife could afford to live with her son and daughter in a house in Great Torrington town centre, rather than having to rely on her parents for accommodation at Bradley Farm, along with her other family members. And later, she is found living relatively comfortably on Bridge Street, Hatherleigh (see p 38).

In fact, for several decades following Samuel's death, and until she died herself aged 81, Patience enjoyed a continuous stream of unearned income.[82] So what was the source of this income?

The first clue lies in the 1840 Tithe Apportionments which show that, within a few years of Samuel's untimely death, our John, then aged 11 years, is the owner of record of two houses in the hamlet of Lifton, with 1 acre and ¼ acre respectively, plus 272¾ acres of land at West Week Barton in the same parish.

A second clue lies in John Yeo's comment at his trial that:

---

[82] *We find Patience in the 1841 census records, nine years after her husband Samuel's death and when John was approaching his teens, living with 'independent means'. In later censuses, she is identified as an 'annuitant'.*

'about 20 years ago an uncle left him [the mentally ill Charles Luxmoore]
£100 which he soon spent.'

In fact, we need to skip a generation to Charles' granduncle and namesake, Charles Luxmoore (1765-1833), a Regency gentleman who worked as a porter in the Customs House in London and who made a will on July 2nd 1832, one year before he died. It was proved on September 16th 1833, a time roughly consistent with John Yeo's recollection of 'about 20 years' before the date of the trial.

In this will, Charles bequeathed £100 each to Grandpa Luxmoore, Grandma Luxmoore, and to each of their two daughters and four sons (explicitly including Charles, even though his mental capacity had already become significantly impaired by that time); and an annuity of £15 per year each for Grandpa and Grandma Luxmoore.[83] This is also consistent with the trial testimony.

The will, made only four months after his grandnephew Samuel had died, also made provision for his great-grandnephew, our John, then 4½ years old; and his great-grandniece, our John's sister Patience Reddaway Luxmoore, then 2¾ years old. To John he bequeathed in trust his lands and property of West Week Barton, West Week Moor and Eastcotts (known as Longalands); and to Patience he bequeathed in trust an annuity of £1,200.

Clearly wishing his funeral and the associated mourning to proceed in a suitably elaborate manner, as might be expected for a Regency gentleman of high social standing, Charles specified his requirements for a 'good and substantial coffin which is to contain my body' with a 'good mattress and pillow on which my body is to rest', the coffin to be made 'of good and solid heart of oak of the best quality to be cover'd with good black cloth properly nail'd'.

Astutely recognising that a lack of funds on the part of some of his

West Week Barton, Lifton, Devon, which was inherited by JR Luxmoore from his great-granduncle Charles Luxmoore (1765-1833).

---

[83] *He also left £100 for Thomas Bridgman Luxmoore (1762-1844), an Okehampton lawyer who*
was then the owner of Combe Park (and Isaac Yeo's landlord), 'for the great pains and trouble
he has hitherto taken in and about the management of my affairs'.

family members could potentially lower the tone of the event, he provided to his executors and to 'Patience Luxmoore, widow of my late grandnephew Samuel Luxmoore, deceased', 'a full suit of mourning', and 'the like' also to Grandpa and Grandma Luxmoore and their sons and daughters. He further made provisions for the Luxmoore sons to wear black silk armbands and gloves, and for the daughters to wear black silk neckerchiefs and gloves.

After Charles died on July 28th 1833, his will was proved before the Surrogate of the Rt Hon Sir John Nicholl (1759-1838), King's Advocate, and father-in-law of Charles Scott Luxmoore, Dean of St Asaph. Sir John died in January 1838, six months before the birth of his grandson: our John's contemporary, John Nicholl Luxmoore (see p 32).

Up until her death in 1846, John's sister Patience's £1,200 annuity would yield £60 a year (around £5,500 today), assuming an interest rate of 5 per cent.[84] The trustees were instructed to use this income to support her upbringing and education, but it would not have supported the whole family.

Similarly, the trustees would have been able to generate approaching £300 a year net (around £26,000) from the West Week lands,[85] but they would have wished to invest as much of this as possible for the later benefit of our John.

A third clue is to be found in the Tithe Apportionments (of 1838), where John's mother Patience is recorded as owning 185½ acres of land at East Risdon in Jacobstowe, six years after the death of her husband, Samuel. At the same time, she was leasing a further 1½ acres in the adjacent Little Risdon. The East Risdon land had, in fact, been inherited by Samuel from his grandfather, Benjamin Bickle – Grandma Luxmoore's father.[86] It is this land that conferred upon Samuel a legitimate designation of 'yeoman' farmer.

The Jacobstowe tax rolls show Samuel as the owner of 'East Rison' starting in 1829,[87] and he probably inherited the estate in about 1828. Our John and his

---

[84] *In order to end the practice of usury, maximum interest rates were successively reduced during the 16th to the 18th centuries, ending at 5 per cent with the Statute of St Anne in 1713. However, usury laws were repealed in 1854, it being argued that interest rates should be determined by the market forces of supply and demand.*

[85] *Assuming a rental value in Devon and the South West of £1.30 per acre; tithes of 13.4 per cent; Poor Rates of 10.1 per cent; and taxes of 3 per cent. Land rental values and the agrarian economy – England & Wales, 1500-1912. Gregory Clark. University of California at Davis, 2001.*

[86] *East Risdon had been sold in 1826 to Benjamin Bickle by Jonathan Luxmoore (1797-1873), solicitor, first cousin once removed of Bishop Luxmoore of St Asaph. The Family of Luxmoore. Charles Frederick Coryndon Luxmoore. William Pollard & Co Ltd, Exeter & London, 1909, pp 9, 27.*

[87] *William Luxmoore: Biography. Charles Emerson Luxmoore, 2003. (Charles Emerson Luxmoore indicates that the name 'Risdon' was also variously spelt 'Reson', 'Ryson' and 'Rison'.)*

Farm building at East Risdon, Jacobstowe, Devon. This farm was the likely birthplace of JR Luxmoore.

sister were therefore born and lived here, before they moved with their mother to Great Torrington.

For approximately one or two years around 1828, Samuel's elder brother, William (a cordwainer), and sister-in-law, Johanna (née Weeks), were also living at East Risdon; their second child, Thomas Weeks Luxmoore (1828-1849), was born there in the month following Samuel's marriage to Patience.[88] Some years later, by which time they had moved to Plymouth, William and Johanna named their third son Samuel Rison Luxmoore, to commemorate his late Uncle Samuel and the East Risdon estate.[89]

Assuming that Patience had secured the right of usufruct over the East Risdon estate, she would have received during her lifetime an income of around £180 per year [£16,000]. This, together with the funds the trustees would have provided to support the children's upbringing, would have been enough to sustain a relatively comfortable lifestyle.

The trustees named on Charles Luxmoore's will of 1832 included various members of the Reddaway and Bickle families, the latter being the family of Grandma Luxmoore. This suggests that strong bonds between the Luxmoores and Reddaways extended historically well beyond our John's immediate family.

Finally, when our John's maternal grandfather John Reddaway (1772-

---

[88]   *Ibid. Cordwainer = shoemaker.*

[89]   *We met Samuel Rison Luxmoore (1843-1902) when he was living with his Aunt Alice and Uncle John Yeo as an orphan at Orchard Barton in 1851 (see p 32).*

1863) died, he bequeathed to our John's mother, Patience, who was then aged 58, £100 plus the house and orchard on Bridge Street, Hatherleigh; and to her sister Elizabeth, then aged 57, the adjoining house and orchard. Upon their respective deaths, he stated that the properties should pass to his son John Reddaway (1801-1868) and his heirs. Since this John Reddaway predeceased Patience and Elizabeth, the two houses passed to his son, John Reddaway of Curworthy & Burdon. Grandfather John Reddaway also bequeathed to Elizabeth various lands in Hatherleigh: Week Marsh near Passaford Ford; Higher, Middle and Lower Rimmon Parks; Little Comfort field; and Mile Gutter fields.[90] Elizabeth

Headstones of the parents of JR Luxmoore: Samuel Luxmoore (foreground right) and Patience Luxmoore (left), St James' Church, Jacobstowe, Devon.

named our John as her executor and, upon her death in 1874, she passed to him these lands in Hatherleigh, and also the lease to the Grenville estate in Bratton Clovelly. By then, he had been living in Ashford for 13 years.

In her will, made ten years before she died, Patience Luxmoore bequeathed everything to her son, John Reddaway Luxmoore, who was the sole executor.

---

[90] *The 'three fields or closes of land called Runnen Parks' in the will of John Reddaway are identified as 'fields or closes of land called Higher, Middle and Lower Rimmon Parks' in the will of Elizabeth Reddaway. Also, in Elizabeth's will, Little Comfort field is said to be known also as the 'Hannaborough Lane plot'. Hannaborough Lane is a single-track road that runs south from the A 3072, on the south-western edge of Hatherleigh. Passaford Lane runs about ½ mile to its east. Passaford Ford would have been where the lane crossed the River Lew; a footbridge was constructed in the early 20th century, and another was built in the mid 20th century.*

Household effects from her house at Hatherleigh, which included a Brinsmead pianoforte with a mahogany stool, were sold by auction on March 30th 1886.[91]

Divergence from agriculture for a life in the church

Rather than follow in the footsteps of so many generations of both his mother's and father's ancestors (by continuing the tradition of farming or an allied trade), our John's guaranteed future ownership of the properties at West Week and Risdon provided him with the opportunity to choose a different path.

As a 19-year-old 'gent', we find him leaving the family home in 1848 and assuming a mortgage on Peards Acre – a house and land in South Zeal. His mother, or his maternal grandfather, may have introduced him to this property: it stands just three miles south of Reddaway Farm, in a village where the name is still found locally today.

Three years later, he transferred his mortgage on Peards Acre to its next occupier (the Town Clerk of Okehampton) and became a pupil at a private college in the handsome vicarage of St John the Baptist Hatherleigh, where the incumbent was Revd Samuel Feild, 'a prominent second-generation Evangelical Anglican.'[92] This was the start of our John's training for his future ecclesiastical life.[93]

He would not know this until later, but his timing was fortuitous. Had he continued to follow in the farming tradition of his forebears he would have been thrust, twenty years later and at the peak of his working life, into the hardship and misery of a major depression in the British agricultural market.[94] The catalysts for this economic disaster – that lasted for almost the entirety of the last quarter of the 19th century – were the perfect storm of the advent of free trade following the repeal of the Corn Laws; the opening up of the American prairies to cultivation following the US Homestead Acts; and dramatic improvements in US and British domestic and transatlantic transportation (railways and steamships). Against an increase of 43 per cent in the population of England and Wales between 1871 and 1901, the proportion of male agricultural labourers decreased by over one-third, and by 1895 wheat prices were at their

[91]   *Western Times, March 26th 1886.*

[92]   *The significance of JG Deck 1807-1884. Peter J Lineham. Christian Brethren Research Fellowship Journal, 1986, pp 4-5.*

[93]   *In parallel with his studies with Revd Feild, he was also becoming educated in some of the less exciting aspects of being a landowner: At the age of 25, we find that 'JR Luxmoore of Hatherleigh' applied for a government loan of £750 'for drainage of the lands' at West Week. Notice of the Inclosure Commissioners for England and Wales, 1854.*

[94]   *Where was the 'Great Agricultural Depression'? A geography of agricultural bankruptcy in late Victorian England and Wales. PJ Perry. Agricultural History Review, Vol 20, 1972, pp 30-45.*

lowest levels in 150 years. Sheep farmers in Devon were particularly hard hit as their animals were severely affected by disease early on in this period.[95]

Agricultural prosperity started to return as the new century approached: the fortunes of the next generation of Edwardian farmers revived as prices stopped falling, farming costs were reducing, and investments in new and more efficient technologies – such as steam cultivation equipment – were increasing. Indeed, by 1912 it was concluded that farming 'is at present sound and prosperous'.[96]

Although our John avoided the agricultural depression, he would find that life in the church did not guarantee an entirely peaceful existence. The year he started his education under Revd Feild was the year the government conducted a Religious Census, which determined that across England and Wales fewer than 11 million worshippers of all faiths – 61 per cent of the population – attended services on Census Sunday. The number was significantly higher in Devon, at 70.5 per cent; however, this was split between Anglicans at 40.1 per cent, and mostly Nonconformists at a startling 30.4 per cent.[97] In other parts of England the population attending Anglican church services was much lower: the textile town of Bradford, for instance, recorded only 12 per cent.

These were alarming figures for the Victorian Established Church, which had already become a target for a great deal of hostility, with growing demands for disestablishment. The middle and working classes saw no reason to support a body that seemed to provide them with little in return, and this census refuted any claims that it represented the greater part of England's population. Rather, the Anglican Church was now a minority interest, especially in the rapidly expanding northern towns.

The shock of the census gave greater urgency to reforms, already underway, to reinstate the authority and primacy of the Established Anglican Church over Nonconformism.

The general turmoil was felt in Devon, not least in the growing appeal of the Plymouth Brethren, a low church movement that traces its roots to Dublin in the late 1820s. As the name implies, some of its most prominent adherents were to be found in Plymouth.

One such supporter was James George Deck (1807-1884). Previously an officer in the Madras Native Infantry, Deck enrolled in Revd Samuel Feild's

---

[95] *WC Little, assistant commissioner for the southern counties, noted that around Holsworthy the loss of sheep through disease on a group of more than one hundred farms equalled half the annual rental, or more than the average profit. Where was the 'Great Agricultural Depression'? PJ Perry. Op. cit., p 42.*

[96] *A pilgrimage of English farming 1910-1912. Daniel Hall, 1914, p 431.*

[97] *Early Victorian Devon 1830-1860. David Parker. Halsgrove, 2017, p 112.*

private college following a 'conversion experience' in 1826, some 25 years before our John commenced his studies there. Preaching in Devon and subsequently in New Zealand, Deck ultimately became one of the Brethren's most notable figures.[98]

Our John would have been aware of some of Devon's more influential clergymen at this time. And he would surely have perceived pluralist echoes of his namesake, Bishop John Luxmoore of St Asaph, in the Right Revd Henry Phillpotts, bishop of his own diocese. Bishop Phillpotts of Exeter evidently felt that the £3,000 p.a. stipend of the bishopric might not support both his aristocratic lifestyle and his 18 children, so he asked to retain in addition, on a non-resident basis, the £4,000 living of his former parish of Stanhope in Durham – the second or third most lucrative living in the country. As a 'compromise' he was offered instead an equally lucrative canonry at Durham, a post which he continued to hold until his death. This enabled him to build and live in a mansion in fashionable Torquay, rather than reside at the Bishop's Palace in Exeter.[99]

He was violently controversial – 'a genuinely religious man with his religion concealed behind porcupine quills.'[100] Broadly representing the conservative

---

[98] *ASIDE: James found his time at Hatherleigh vicarage to his liking – at least initially – for he took the time to marry Revd Feild's daughter Alicia in 1829 before returning with her to India. James and Alicia were visiting Hatherleigh again in 1835 when their third child, John Feild Deck, was born and baptised there. At the time, Revd Feild was engaged in theological disagreements with Baptists in the village regarding an Anglican doctrine that supported 'infant baptism' rather than the Baptists' doctrine of 'believer's (adult) baptism'. Not being able to find support for 'infant baptism' in the Bible, James came to the conclusion that he could not become ordained in the Established Church as he had planned: 'Approaching his loved wife he said, 'I have left the Army to become a clergyman, but now see that the Church of England is contrary to the Word of God; what shall we do?' Her noble reply was, 'Whatever you believe to be the will of God, do it at any cost.' James and Alicia found fellow feelings among a significant number of people across the West Country, who similarly rejected any teaching not found in the New Testament. Through these new associations with the 'Brethren', James abandoned hopes of ordination and decided rather to concentrate on lay Evangelism in villages around the coast of Devon. However, splits began to appear over scriptural interpretations, and around the time our John became a pupil of Revd Feild, the Plymouth Brethren divided into two irreconcilable sects: the 'Exclusive' and the 'Open' Brethren. James was saddened by the bitter attacks between the groups: ultimately exhausted, he became ill and emigrated in 1852 to New Zealand, partly for its climate and partly for its distance from England. He soon took up his preaching again, creating a 'considerable sensation', but sectarianism reared its ugly head there also. Until he died in 1884, at the age of 76, James Deck continued to waver in his desire for broader fellowship with other Christians, even though he was officially associated with the 'Exclusives'. The significance of JG Deck 1807-1884. Peter J Lineham. Christian Brethren Research Fellowship Journal, 1986.*

[99] *Henry Phillpotts (1778-1869). John Andrew Hamilton, 1895. In: A Web of English History. Majorie Bloy, http://www.historyhome.co.uk/people/phillpott.htm*

[100] *The Victorian Church – Part One: 1829-1859. Owen Chadwick. Wipf & Stock, 2010, p 217.*

high church wing of the Oxford Movement,[101] he fought against what he thought were the pernicious extremes of both Nonconformity and Roman Catholicism. Indeed, the biographer of the Plymouth Brethren's James Deck believes that Deck 'was a victim of the vindictiveness of Henry Phillpotts, who, after his consecration as Bishop of Exeter in 1830, made the lives of Evangelicals and low churchmen in the diocese extremely uncomfortable.'

At the same time, however, Phillpotts was a 'champion of lost causes', seeking to increase the rights of the poor and ease the plight of children employed in coalmines and as chimney-sweeps. He was generous in his gifts to the church, spending large sums on the restoration of the Bishop's Palace in a 'most creditable manner'. Hypocritically, on the face of it, he sought to reduce the number of absentee incumbents, and he earmarked funds to support the poorest paid clergy.

If Bishop Phillpotts was strong-willed, he might have met his match in Samuel Sebastian Wesley (1810-1876) – grandson of the celebrated hymnwriter Charles Wesley, and a grandnephew of John Wesley, the founder of Methodism – who was organist at Exeter Cathedral from 1835 to 1842. But with his salary of a mere £175 per year, Wesley certainly did not compete with Phillpotts in terms of income![102]

Wesley was notoriously belligerent, always having arguments with his employers. The standard of church music in England was poor and Wesley had taken it upon himself to improve matters, but without recourse to any kind of diplomacy. For example, in his 1849 pamphlet 'A Few Words on Cathedral Music and the Musical System of the Church, with a Plan of Reform' he wrote:

'The prospect of bringing the clergy to a just sense of the claims of music in the cathedral service of this country seems all but hopelessly remote. They still, in the main, view their own labours as all-important, and disparage the art in its most important bearings; as did the Puritans of Elizabeth's reign. The arts, in their connection with religion, are systematically decried, and preaching but too often viewed as the one thing needful in the public services. Surely the claims of music and architecture are too

---

[101] *A movement initiated by high church members of the Church of England at the University of Oxford, which sought to renew historic catholic doctrines and practice in opposition to Nonconformism. It became the 'Anglo-Catholic' wing of the Anglican church, which emphasises its Catholic, versus Protestant, heritage.*

[102] *Wesley's income at Exeter was almost three times what he had been paid previously at Hereford Cathedral. However, against a prevailing view that composers of sacred music should never expect to receive the full value – in monetary terms – of their work, he continually argued for better remuneration for church musicians. Samuel Sebastian Wesley: A Life. Peter Horton. Oxford University Press, 2004, pp 76, 83, 235.*

serious to be thus trampled underfoot. To be successfully developed, the arts demand as high, perhaps a higher, order of intellect than do any duties essentially appertaining to the clerical office.'

Fortunately perhaps – at least initially – Wesley's interactions were principally with the deans of the cathedral rather than with the bishop. At the time of his appointment, he had found a champion in Dean Whittington Landon, who said, 'everything I can learn confirms me in the opinion of Mr Wesley's personal respectability.' But this happy state of affairs did not last long and Landon's successor, Dean Thomas Hill Lowe, 'certainly contributed to the souring of relations between organist and chapter ..... with each passing year the prospect of a harmonious working life had receded further. This, unfortunately, had only served to bring out some of the worst aspects of [Wesley's] character.' Matters were not helped by Wesley's frequent absences, a pupil recording that he 'often left me for two or three days ..... to exercise his favourite pastime of fly-fishing.'[103]

Nevertheless, Wesley did succeed in improving the choir at Exeter, and even managed to persuade the authorities to renovate the organ, following which *The Musical World* proclaimed that the instrument 'from being the worst, may now be reckoned one of the best in the kingdom.' And his mission to enhance the quality of Anglican choral music nationally was indeed ultimately highly successful, although predominantly posthumously.[104]

When he looked back on his time at Exeter, Wesley wrote, 'I ever regret leaving Devon.' In 1870, he was asked to open the rebuilt organ at St Peter's and St Paul's Church in the north Devon market town of Holsworthy. This rekindled thoughts of settling in that part of the world – 'so charming in most respects.' Although he was not to retire there, his memory is perpetuated by a piece he composed on the occasion of the installation of a carillon in Holsworthy Church's 15th-century tower in 1874: *An Air composed for Holsworthy Church Bells and varied for the Organ*. This, one of his most appealing works, is still heard today, along with many of his anthems and hymn tunes.[105]

---

[103] *Ibid., pp 111, 127.*

[104] *'There can be little doubt that the vigorous protest Wesley uttered started a movement for reform which was to bear abundant fruit later. One has only to compare the singing that is heard today in our cathedrals, with what was all too prevalent in Wesley's time, to realise the vast improvements that have taken place. Obviously he did not take up his pen in vain, slow as the progress was at first.' Revd W Francis Westbrook. In: Reprint of SS Wesley's 'A Few Words on Cathedral Music and the Musical System of the Church, with a Plan of Reform'. Hinrichsen, London, No. 1961b, 1961, p i.*

[105] *Samuel Sebastian Wesley: A Life. Peter Horton. Oxford University Press, 2004, p 82, 287-289.*

Theological college

Our John had neither the social standing nor the influential ecclesiastical connections and family relationships enjoyed by the 'other' Luxmoores. And, although the income streams from the properties he had inherited allowed him to pursue a career in the church, he did not enjoy anything approaching their levels of wealth.

Should we need any further evidence of this, after a few years of study with Revd Feild he was admitted in 1855 to St Bees Theological College on the Cumbrian coast, a few miles south of Whitehaven. St Bees had been established specifically to train clergy for whom the cost of a traditional university degree course would have been prohibitive. Because most entrants would not have acquired any knowledge of the classics at school, the vast majority would, like our John, have been tutored privately by clergymen before arriving at the college.[106]

Founded in 1816 by George Henry Law, Bishop of Chester, St Bees was the first independent non-graduate theological college outside Oxford and Cambridge to be established for the training of Church of England ordinands. Prior to this time, the Church had faced considerable difficulties in supplying remote or poorly paid parishes with ministers, and the establishment of theological colleges such as St Bees created a 'two-tier system' of clerical provision: those benefices with an income that could support a gentlemanly, graduate clergy (such as the 'other' Luxmoores) were in demand and rarely without applicants, while the poorer parishes were supplied with curates from the non-graduate colleges, who did not have the social, intellectual or economic status of their wealthier colleagues.

John Luxmoore's cohort at St Bees therefore comprised mainly socially mobile, lower middle-class individuals who had managed to improve upon their largely working-class roots prior to entering theological college.[107]

St Bees became increasingly attractive because of its high standards and a good reputation for turning out reliable clergy. One commentator stated in 1872, 'A St Bees man has little chance of becoming Archbishop of Canterbury, but for more than half a century the quaint Cumberland College has turned out a very useful supply of hard-working clergy for the North of England and the Colonies'.[108] Some 2,600 clergy are believed to have trained at the college during the course of its 79-year history.

---

[106] *The Education of the Anglican Clergy. Kelsey Sterling. University of Leicester, 1982, p 85.*

[107] *Ibid., p 89.*

[108] *St Bees: The College Opens. Ian McAndrew and Doug Sim. St Bees Parish Council, 2020, https://www.stbees.org.uk/home/village/village-history/theological-college/college-opens/*

First curacy

Our John was ordained deacon in 1857, and priest in 1858. His first clerical appointment, at the age of 28, was as curate of St John the Baptist, Smalley, Derbyshire. He remained there for a little over two years, during which time he would have made some connections to clergy in other local Derbyshire parishes. Indeed, Smalley lies only 30 miles south-east of what was to become his long-term home, Ashford-in-the-Water.

Upon his departure in the autumn of 1859, the *Derby Mercury* reported that he was 'very much affected' by a rather gushing address given in his honour by one WT Barber, Esq, and at which he was presented with a pocket-sized communion service 'of very beautiful design and workmanship.'

An extract from the *Derby Mercury* article appeared soon afterwards in the *Exeter and Plymouth Gazette*, referring to 'a gentleman well known in Hatherleigh … and how his work as a clergyman of the Church of England has been appreciated', along with a quotation from the *Derby Telegraph* that,

'Mr Luxmoore has, since his residence at Smalley, so endeared himself to the inhabitants, and has so completely won not only their esteem but their affection, that the occasion of his leaving has been one of deep regret to all.'[109]

PRESENTATION TO THE LATE CURATE OF SMALLEY.

On Tuesday evening, the 18th inst., a large number of the inhabitants of Smalley met in the Girls' National School-room, to present a testimonial to their late curate, the Rev. J. R. Luxmoore, on the eve of his leaving Smalley. As soon as it became known in Smalley that Mr. Luxmoore was about to leave, a number of ladies formed themselves into a committee, for the purpose of obtaining subscriptions to a testimonial of respect. The money thus obtained was employed in the purchase of a pocket communion service. This, which was of very beautiful design and workmanship, was contained in an appropriate case, and on a plate affixed to the latter was engraved the name of Mr. Luxmoore, the date of the presentation, and by whom presented. We believe these were supplied by Messrs. Weatherhead and Walters, of the Irongate. At the request of the committee and the parishioners, W. T. Barber, Esq., kindly undertook to present the testimonial.

Report of a presentation to Revd JR Luxmoore on the occasion of his departure from Smalley Church, Derbyshire.

His next appointment was a brief curacy at St Mary the Virgin in Ross-on-Wye. Here he was to fulfill an important non-clerical assignment before taking up his position in Ashford: to meet and marry Rosalie – the woman who would support him throughout his new life as a rural priest.

Rosalie

Rosalie Stonhouse-Vigor was born in Clifton, near Bristol in Gloucestershire. Seven years younger than our John, she was christened there on August 31st 1836.

---

[109] *Woolmer's Exeter and Plymouth Gazette, November 5th 1859.*

Her great-grandfather was the physician and cleric, Revd Sir James Stonhouse (1716-1795), 11th Baronet of Radley. He studied medicine in France, but after returning to England he underwent a religious conversion. He became the rector of Little Cheverell, near Devizes, and subsequently Great Cheverell also.[110]

Sir James' son, Rosalie's grandfather Timothy (1765-1831), who assumed the additional surname of Vigor by royal licence on July 11th 1795, was successively Vicar of Sunningwell, Berkshire; Archdeacon of Gloucester; and Chaplain to the Bishop of Hereford. His half-brother was Sir Thomas Stonhouse (1744-1810), 12th Baronet.

No fewer than four of Revd Timothy's five sons were also clergymen, including Rosalie's father, Revd Arthur Stonhouse-Vigor (1810-1883), who was cousin to two further successors to the Radley baronetcy: Sir John Brooke Stonhouse (1797-1848) and Sir Timothy Vansittart Stonhouse (1799-1866).

Revd Arthur Stonhouse-Vigor's sister, Clara Rosalie Heathcote (1818-1896), after whom his daughter Rosalie was named, was the wife of Revd Gilbert Wall Heathcote. Revd Heathcote was Rector of St Peter's Church, Ash, Surrey, for 46 years, and was the grandson of Sir Thomas Heathcote (1721-1787), 2nd Baronet of Hursley.

Rosalie was therefore surrounded by numerous family members who were priests. Although there was undoubtedly ecclesiastical 'networking' – and maybe some nepotism – the Stonhouse family did not attract the opprobrium that fell upon the family of Bishop Luxmoore of St Asaph.

When her father died in 1883, Rosalie's younger brother, William, inherited his estate. Rosalie also did not benefit from her Aunt Clara Rosalie's substantial effects of £27,877 9s 4d: Clara's beneficiaries were, again, Rosalie's brother, William, and the son of her elder brother, James. Therefore, despite the affluence of some family members, neither Rosalie nor her father could be called 'wealthy'.

Marriage and honeymoon

John Reddaway Luxmoore met Rosalie at the time her father was Vicar of St Leonard's, Walford, in Herefordshire,[111] and John was curate at Ross-on-Wye.

---

[110] *A History of the County of Wiltshire, Vol 10. Victoria County History, London, 1975, pp 53-60. or: British History Online, https://www.british-history.ac.uk/vch/wilts/vol10/pp53-60*

[111] *Revd Arthur Stonhouse-Vigor was instituted at St Leonard's in 1842. Walford St Michael and All Angels, Herefordshire. Burgum Family History Society, https://www.burgumfamily.co.uk/pl_walford_2.php*

Walford. Littlebury's Directory and Gazetteer of Herefordshire 1876-1877 (transcribed by Rosemary Lockie), 2003.

Walford Church is now dedicated to St Michael and All Angels, having been St Leonard's until a major refurbishment in 1887. Walford Parish Newsletter, Walford, 2011.

The clergymen's respective churches were no more than two miles apart, and it came to pass that Rosalie and John were married in St Leonard's Church, on January 17th 1861, by her granduncle, Revd Canon Henry Huntingford. By marrying John, Rosalie perpetuated a long family association with the Church, whilst he immediately expanded his network of influential clerics.

In a pleasing symmetry, John and Rosalie were married in Walford – the village named after 'Wales Ford', where the old turnpike road to Wales crossed the River Wye that runs through Herefordshire; and they were to reside for most of their married life thereafter in Ashford – the village named after the 'Ford of the Ash', where the vicarage is just 300 yards uphill from the 'other River Wye' that runs through Derbyshire.

In the April following their marriage, with some time to spare before John was to take up his new appointment at Ashford, Rosalie had an opportunity to show John the area around Bristol where both she and her mother Sophia were born. They stayed in an elegant terraced Georgian house at York Place in Clifton Village, the home of Rosalie's mother's sister, Isabella Bennett. Isabella and Sophia had in fact both been married in Bristol within three years of each other.

About 70 years earlier, Rosalie's great-grandfather, Sir James Stonhouse, had spent many of his later years in Bristol 'for the sake of the waters'. In 1788, he had taken up residence permanently in Hotwells, 300 feet below Clifton – a district that takes its name from its hot springs:[112]

'This salutary spring, which 'pale-eyed suppliants drink, and soon flies pain' ... rises near the bottom of the cliffs ... forcibly gushing from an aperture in the solid rock ... possessing the rare quality of being warm. ... In consequence of these impregnations ... (1st, an uncommon quantity of carbonic acid gas; 2nd, a certain quantity of magnesia, soda, and lime, in

---

[112] *ASIDE: Sir James could evidently be rather petulant: 'In October, 1773, the Secretary [of Bristol Royal Infirmary] wrote, on behalf of the Board, to the Revd Sir James Stonhouse, Bart, MD, requesting him to give the anniversary address. This gentleman was formerly rector of Great and Little Cheverell, Wiltshire, but was at this time living in Bristol. As he had a 'triple handle' to his name, being a baronet, a doctor of medicine, and a clergyman, he thought rather highly of his own importance. He consented to give the sermon, but wrote in answer, 'I must own that I have thought it rather extraordinary that I should never have been apply'd to on this occasion by the governors during my ten years residence here and could consider it in no other point of view than as a personal disrespect." Also, 'There is a letter of his, dated January 3rd 1780, refusing a request to preach at the Mayor's Chapel. He complains that he has not been asked 'in his turn,' and concludes, 'but as the present mayor has thought proper to act differently from his predecessors, the doctor chooses to decline preaching at the chappell (sic) during Mr Miller's mayoralty." A History of the Bristol Royal Infirmary. G Munro Smith. JW Arrowsmith, Ltd, Bristol, 1917, p 25; p 25 footnote 3.*

*various combinations with the muriatic, vitriolic, and carbonic acids) ...
the water appears well-calculated to attemper a hot, acrimonious blood,
and to cure or palliate consumptions, weakness of the lungs, hectic heats,
and fevers. It is also successfully prescribed in uterine and other internal
hæmorrhages and inflammations; in spitting of blood, dysentery, chlorosis,
and purulent ulcers of the viscera. It is likewise beneficial in diarrhœa,
gleets, diabetes, stone, gravel, strangury, nervous atrophy, colliquative
sweats, loss of appetite, and indigestion. In all these complaints, it may
be used with success, particularly if resorted to in time.'[113]*

John and Rosalie would surely have visited Hotwells' Dowry Chapel,
a chapel-of-ease to Clifton Church. Founded in 1746, it was 'built for the
accommodation of fashionable visitors'. Monuments in the chapel were
dedicated to the memories of Sir James; his wife Sarah, née Ekins (1733-
1788); and son John (1762-1803). Each had a lengthy inscription written by
Hannah More (1745-1833),[114] an Evangelical moralist for whom Sir James had
been a supportive critic and mentor. More was a prolific religious writer: she
devised the prodigiously successful *Cheap Repository Tracts* – around 200
moral, religious and occasionally political pamphlets that were distributed to
the literate poor – and wrote many of them herself. More said that she owed the
first glimmerings of her spiritual awakening to Sir James, who also had
Evangelical leanings. He was the model for the 'good clergyman' in her story
The Shepherd of Salisbury Plain, which was translated into French, German
and Russian, and remained in print for nearly 100 years.[115]

The Dowry Chapel was pulled down about 10 years after John and Rosalie's
visit, and the Church of St Andrew-the-Less was built in the same location in
1873. However, that church was also demolished in 1962, and blocks of flats
now occupy the site.[116]

John and Rosalie were lucky to see Isabella's husband, Charles James Fox
Bennett, during their stay at York Place: he came to England only twice a
year, in winter and spring, to visit Isabella, who, as a member of Bristol's high
society, seems to have preferred to remain at home.

---

[113] *The Picture of Bristol; or A Guide to Objects of Curiosity and Interest in Bristol, Clifton, the
Hotwells, and their Vicinity. Second edition. Revd John Evans. W Sheppard, Bristol, 1818, pp
141-143.*

[114] *Ibid., pp 145-147.*

[115] *Hannah More: the First Victorian. Anne Stott. Oxford University Press, 2003.*

[116] *Dowry Chapel (Demolished), Hotwells, Bristol; St Andrew-the-Less Church (Demolished),
Hotwells, Bristol. Gloucestershire Places of Worship. Rosemary Lockie. Places of Worship
Database, 2010-2020.*

Born in Shaftesbury, Charles Bennett, when only 15, had followed in the footsteps of the 15th-century Italian explorer and merchant John Cabot, who travelled from Bristol to discover Newfoundland; and also (less glamorously) those of his elder brother Thomas, who had emigrated there a few years earlier.

One of Thomas' children who had been born in Newfoundland – Elizabeth ('Lizzy') Bennett – was sent at the age 13 to a private school in Brighton under the tutelage of a certain Arabella Theodosia Gauntlett. A fellow pupil was the 14-year-old Rosalie Stonhouse-Vigor; there were thus two generations of ties between the Stonhouse and Bennett families.

Charles established CF Bennett & Company in Newfoundland's capital city, St John's, to import European merchandise and export fish. His business interests soon spread to shipbuilding and distilling, and he became one of Newfoundland's wealthiest citizens. In 1842 he entered politics, ultimately becoming Premier of Newfoundland from 1870 until 1874.

During this time, Charles would have mixed both socially and professionally with Rt Revd Edward Feild, who was Bishop of Newfoundland from 1844 to 1876. Their friendship would have become cemented further because they were British expats, and also because they shared the same conservative high church views.

Charles Bennett and Bishop Feild were both outspoken, uncompromising and controversial. The bishop had as much disdain for Nonconformism as did Bishop Phillpotts. It was said of Edward Feild: 'the one flaw in his character was the want of Christian charity which he displayed towards the ministers of other denominations.'[117] But notwithstanding their confrontational personalities and immoderate views, Bishop Feild and Charles Bennett did much to shape Newfoundland's future, not least Bishop Feild's establishment of a new gothic revival cathedral at St John's.

The Anglo-Catholic bishop was the cousin of our John's first tutor, the Evangelical Revd Samuel Feild. Although there was an ocean that separated them – metaphorically (with respect to their churchmanship) as well as literally – their family ties may have helped oil what otherwise could have been an abrasive professional relationship. One of the bishop's deacons, Oliver Rouse, who originally hailed from Devon, may also have helped to keep lines of communication open. When he travelled in 1846 from Newfoundland to England to raise funds for St John's new cathedral, he met with Revd Samuel Feild, noting that the latter was suitably gracious in voicing his respect for his cousin.

---

[117] *Edward Feild Obituary. Dictionary of National Biography. Leslie Stephen and Sidney Lee (eds). Smith, Elder & Co, London, Vol 6, 1908, pp 1150-1151.*

No doubt always on the lookout for career opportunities for his past pupils, Revd Feild had asked of Oliver 'what salary [Bishop Feild] would guaranty to any clergyman who might feel disposed to come to Newfoundland.'[118]

It seems quite plausible that Revd Samuel Feild communicated a few years later to his cousin that one of his pupils, who had gone on to study at St Bees, would be looking for a suitable long-term living, not to mention a suitable spouse. The bishop would then have mentioned this to his friend Charles Bennett, who knew of course that his sister-in-law's daughter was not only of marriageable age, but also the daughter of a clergyman. In fact, Revd Samuel Feild may have come to know the Bennett or the Stonhouse families directly because, before he became Vicar of Hatherleigh, he had been Headmaster of Westbury College in Westbury-on-Trym,[119] two miles north of Clifton, and several of his children were born and christened there. Moreover, Bishop Feild may have known Revd Arthur Stonhouse-Vigor by virtue of the fact that they both matriculated at Wadham College Oxford.

One way or another, probably as a result of judicious networking between the Feild cousins, the bishop's friend Charles Bennett, and Charles' brother-in-law (Rosalie's father), our John had gained not only an appointment at Ross-on-Wye, but also his wife Rosalie.

In the 18th century Bristol was one of the country's leading slaving ports, contributing 40 per cent to British trade between 1730 and 1746. However, by the last quarter of the century, the tide of public opinion had turned against slavery.

---

[118] *ASIDE: Oliver Rouse (b. 1820 at Northlew), great-great-grandson of Revd John Rouse, a previous incumbent at Hatherleigh, was an Anglican missionary in Newfoundland. He arrived there a year before the appointment of Bishop Feild, and was ordained a deacon in the old decaying wooden cathedral at St John's, just two days before it was destroyed by fire in June 1846. Oliver documented in detail a visit he made to England in 1846 to help raise funds for the construction of a new cathedral. During that trip he visited Revd Samuel Feild at Hatherleigh, who 'spoke highly of Bishop Feild's humility', believing it was his 'earnest wish to do that which would most benefit his people.' Although Samuel Feild did not think the bishop's ideas were always the most judicious, 'he didn't doubt but that he would learn wisdom from experience.' Revd Samuel Feild thought that the bishop's motives for accepting the bishopric could not have been anything 'worldly' since he had had every comfort he could wish for in England: his parishioners loved and respected him, whereas now 'he was, by many, loaded with contumely and reproach.' In September 1850, Bishop Feild's dream of a new stone cathedral became a reality, and Oliver was one of three men ordained priest the day after its consecration. The Journal of Oliver Rouse, Anglican Missionary in Newfoundland. John C Street (ed). Madison, Wisconsin, 1983.*

[119] *John Thomas Graves (1806-1870). Adrian Rice. Oxford Dictionary of National Biography. Oxford University Press, 2004.*

Revd Samuel Feild's name appears in various records both as 'Field' and 'Feild', and he therefore seems not to have been fussy about which spelling should be used. The bishop, however, was displeased when his name was incorrectly spelled 'Field'. The Journal of Oliver Rouse, Anglican Missionary in Newfoundland. Op. cit., p 224.

Nonconformist Christians contributed significantly to the establishment of the Abolitionist movement. For example, in 1787 Quakers comprised nine of the 12 original members of the Society for the Abolition of the Slave Trade; and anti-slavery was one of the principal political themes embodied in the writings of Sir James Stonhouse's protegé, Hannah More.[120] Anti-slavery voices prevailed when the Slave Trade Act of 1807 abolished slavery in Britain; the subsequent Slavery Abolition Act of 1833 expanded the jurisdiction to the whole of the British Empire.[121]

During the 19th century Bristol was transformed: its population increased fivefold as a result of a growth in commerce that would help to push the engineering technologies of the Industrial Revolution to their limits. Like all the city's inhabitants, Rosalie would have heard of the engineer most associated with this transformation – Isambard Kingdom Brunel – whose great steamships, SS *Great Western* and SS *Great Britain*, were built in Bristol to ply the Bristol to New York route.[122] She and her new husband would have visited his railway station at Temple Meads and, just 15 minutes' walk from their lodgings, one of his – indeed, one of the Victorian era's – most challenging civil engineering projects: the Clifton Suspension Bridge. An inscription on the tower on the west shore of the Avon Gorge reads '*Suspensa vix via fit*' – a pun on the name of the original benefactor, William Vick (d. 1753), which loosely translates as '*A suspended way built with difficulty.*'

The challenges, however, were less to do with engineering and more to do with initially naïve business planning, inadequate funding, and difficulties in reacting to the parallel relentless changes in society, commerce and transport infrastructure.[123] By 1853 only the two towers on each side of the gorge had been built when the 1830 Act of Parliament[124] authorising its construction expired, and it was generally accepted that any ambitions to complete the bridge had been abandoned.

---

[120] *Hannah More wrote several anti-slavery poems, including 'The Sorrows of Yamba'. A Comparative Study of Three Anti-Slavery Poems Written by William Blake, Hannah More and Marcus Garvey: Black Stereotyping. Jérémie Kroubo. GRAAT On-Line Occasional Papers, 2010, http://www.graat.fr/krouboread3%5B1%5D.pdf*

[121] *Bristol and the Transatlantic Slave Trade. Bristol City Council, 2020, https://www.bristolmuseums.org.uk/stories/bristol-transatlantic-slave-trade/*

[122] *This lower-cost mode of transportation would inadvertently contribute to the onset of the depression of British agriculture, by opening up more efficient trade with the American continent.*

[123] *The Clifton Suspension Bridge: A Business Enterprise. Derek Portman. Derek Portman History Research Archive, 2000.*

[124] *Clifton Suspension Bridge Act, 1830: An Act for building a Bridge over the River Avon from Clifton in the County of Gloucester to the opposite Side of the River in the County of Somerset and for making convenient Roads and Approaches to communicate therewith. May 29th 1830.*

The Avon Gorge, showing New Hotwells House (right) and the 'monuments of failure':
the piers of the Clifton Suspension Bridge, ca. 1861.

The newlyweds would therefore have witnessed a very sorry scene: despite a last-ditch attempt to resurrect the project, by 1859 the cranes had been dismantled, the abutments railed off, the site office torn down, and there were calls for the two towers – characterised as 'monuments of failure' – to be demolished.

A wrought iron bar, placed across the gap to transport materials from one side to the other, remained in place even after work on the structure had been halted. Brave Victorians would pay to be pulled across in a basket – indeed, it was a tradition to propose to your loved one on the way over.[125] We have no record, however, whether John and Rosalie engaged in this exciting diversion. Ironically, Brunel's death in the year before John and Rosalie's wedding led to a revival of fortune for the project. The Institution of Civil Engineers wished to complete it 'as a fitting monument to their late friend and colleague'. Meanwhile, two fellow engineers, John Hawkshaw and William Barlow, suggested that ironwork from Brunel's Hungerford suspension footbridge in London, which was to be replaced by Charing Cross Railway Bridge, could be used at Clifton.

So it was that in the year Rosalie and John were married, stayed in Clifton, and contemplated their future life in Ashford-in-the-Water, a new Act of Parliament was granted[126] that reinvigorated Vick's dream, and led to the

[125] *Personal communication. Ross Floyd. 2020.*

[126] *Clifton Suspension Bridge Act, 1861: An Act for erecting a Suspension Bridge from Clifton in the City and County of Bristol to the Parish of Long Ashton in the County of Somerset, June 28th 1861.*

realisation three years later of 'the ornament of Bristol and the wonder of the age'. The completed structure featured prominently in advertisements for excursions that were being offered on the Avon Gorge and Bristol Channel in 1887, on Messrs P&A Campbell's paddle steamer *Waverley* – the first of what was to become a 13-vessel fleet.[127] But it has been argued that the great business success of this bridge today – built as it was during the era of the horse and steam-powered transportation – can be credited to the emergence of the motor car.[128]

THE BRISTOL CHANNEL DISTRICT GUIDE

9D NET

OFFICIAL HANDBOOK OF P.&A.CAMPBELL L⯑⯑ (WHITE FUNNEL FLEET)

Guide to P&A Campbell's Paddle Steamer Cruises on the Bristol Channel.

The Luxmoores relocated to Ashford-in-the-Water in 1861, with John commencing his appointment at Holy Trinity Church on May 19th, Whit Sunday. Given the length of his stay in the village, he must have found Ashford to his liking.

The livings of Ashford and Sheldon

Today, the majority of clergy receive a stipend which is paid for by the giving of congregations into diocesan 'common funds', that are distributed according to local needs and opportunities. Clergy are also usually provided with rent-free accommodation (which can, however, present a problem in retirement with regard to affordable housing). Whilst a minority do find their financial situation difficult, most report living relatively comfortably.[129]

---

[127] *Bristol Channel District Guide. A Levy Langfield & Frederick G Warne. 1936 Edition, pp 22-32.*

Bristol Channel. P&A Campbell. The Internet's leading database of Paddle Steamers Past and Present, http://paddlesteamers.info/PACampbell.htm

[128] *The Clifton Suspension Bridge: A Business Enterprise. Derek Portman. Op. cit., p 189.*

[129] *The Clergy Remuneration Package and recent work undertaken to evaluate its benefit to clergy. Archbishop's Council, June 15th 2018.*

By comparison, there were vast and anomalous differences in clergy income until well into the 20th century, depending on the historic endowments of each parish. An incumbent and his family in one parish might find themselves living in penury, within striking distance of a clerical 'colleague' in an adjoining parish living a life of luxury under the patronage of one of the Crown or Oxbridge colleges, and perhaps even ministering to a much smaller population. In the stereotype of Victorian literature, curates would frequently have endeavoured to maintain the social standing of beneficed clergyman without the income to match.

Some junior clergymen would have been lucky enough to obtain a grant from the Additional Curates Society (ACS). This organisation was founded in 1837 with a subscription of £500 from King William IV, for the purpose of augmenting the income of assistant curates in the increasingly populous larger towns. In the later 19th century, additional funds for the ACS were raised on an ongoing basis by the Ladies' Home Mission Association.

At the time Revd Luxmoore arrived in Ashford, the living at Holy Trinity Church was a perpetual curacy in the diocese of Lichfield.[130] It comprised £102 a year from the patron, the vicar of Bakewell, plus income from land and investments that had been generated using funds provided from the Queen Anne's Bounty – a 1714 Act of Parliament that provided money 'for the augmentation of the maintenance of the poor clergy'.[131]

The Bounty Board would have expected a return of 10 per cent on the £800 Bounty. This, together with the yield from a £200 private benefaction, would, in theory, have provided Revd Luxmoore with an additional income of up to £100 a year. In practice, however, there were frequent controversies, disputes and practical challenges regarding the management and administration of the Queen Anne's Bounty: whether or not there was land available to purchase, from which income could be generated; difficulty in collecting rents from the occupiers of the purchased lands; whether the land could reasonably provide

---

[130] *The archdeaconry of Derby was originally part of the Diocese of Lichfield, but was moved to form part of the Diocese of Southwell when that diocese was created in 1884. In 1927 the archdeaconries of Derby and Chesterfield became the new Diocese of Derby.*

[131] *History, Gazetteer and Directory of the County of Derby. Francis White & Co, 1857, p 490.*

Queen Anne's Bounty grants had been made to Ashford in 1737 (£200); 1745 (£200) – at which time a Mrs S Archer made a matching Private Benefaction of £200; 1786 (£200); and 1798 (£200). The £200 Parliamentary Grant to Ashford had been made in 1815. Derbyshire Record Office, D7672/Lx.C-29/2.

In the same year that Mrs Archer augmented the Queen Anne's Bounty in Ashford, she did the same at Sheldon, providing a Private Curacy there. St Michael and All Angels' Church, Sheldon. Derbyshire Places of Worship. Rosemary Lockie. Places of Worship Database, 2010-2019.

the required returns; whether the patron of the mother church should receive some or all of the income that was intended to augment the living of a chapelry; and even failures on the part of the patron or bishop to approve and return the necessary information to the Bounty administrators.[132]

Assuming Revd Luxmoore did in fact receive a full 10 per cent of the income expected from the Queen Anne's Bounty investments, his total stipend would have been about £200 a year [£13,000], which seems modest. However, relative to the very low average wage of the time, this income conferred upon him a prestige economic status as one of the high earners in the village. And, in addition to his personal income, there were funds available for maintaining and renovating the church properties, including the vicarage, via income from a £200 Parliamentary grant under the Church Building Acts of 1818 and 1824. Nevertheless, he may not himself have felt this income to be especially generous when compared to that of the 'other' Luxmoore clergy he had come to know, or to Bishop Phillpotts of Exeter, whose stipend amounted to a wage today of around £750,000 a year.

When they lived in the parish vicarage, incumbents were commonly called 'vicars', but it was only in 1868 that perpetual curates obtained the legal right to this title. At the time the Ashford vicarage was built (1853), the parish was a chapel-of-ease to the mother church at Bakewell. In 1872 it was created a separate parish in union with Sheldon, and Revd Luxmoore was formally appointed vicar of both parishes. He would then have been entitled to receive some or all of the living that had previously accrued to the assistant curate of Sheldon,[133] plus additional income from wedding and funeral fees from both parishes ('surplice fees').

Finally, he would be receiving income from his properties in Devon – if only sporadically during the agricultural depression of the last quarter of the 19th century[134] – including, from 1874 when he was 45 years old, the Hatherleigh

---

[132] *Queen Anne's Bounty and the poor livings of Derbyshire: 1772-1832. MR Austin. Derbyshire Archaeological Journal, Vol 92, 1972, pp 78-89.*

[133] *In 1891, the living of Sheldon 'is a vicarage, annexed to that of Ashford, joint gross yearly value £250.' Kelly's Directory of the Counties of Derby, Notts, Leicester and Rutland. London, 1891, p 298.*

[134] *Where was the 'Great Agricultural Depression'? A geography of agricultural bankruptcy in late Victorian England and Wales. PJ Perry. Agricultural History Review, Vol 20, 1972, pp 32-34.*

Managing his properties from 270 miles away and ensuring that they continued to produce income required time, effort and diligence, and incurred the overhead costs of local assistance and professional advice. On at least two occasions Revd Luxmoore's advisers placed advertisements for tenants for his East Risdon farm. Western Times, December 1st 1860; Exeter & Plymouth Gazette, January 14th 1887. In 1863 a tenant with whom he had contracted a lease on West Week farm was declared bankrupt. Exeter & Plymouth Gazette, March 6th 1863.

lands that were bequeathed to him by his aunt, Elizabeth Reddaway. In sum, his lifestyle in Ashford would have been reasonably comfortable, but insufficient to allow extravagance.

In view of his modest family upbringing, Revd Luxmoore would have remained keenly aware of the ongoing challenges faced by many young clergymen who lacked appropriate ecclesiastical connections or independent means. It is therefore not a surprise to find that one of his daughters had been Honorary Secretary for several years to the Bakewell Deanery's branch of the Ladies' Home Mission Association. The bishop of the diocese gave explicit credit to the work of 'the Ladies' Home Mission Association in Aid of the ACS, which in 1888 was scarcely known in Notts., [but] has branches now in all the deaneries of the Diocese, and has more than trebled its contributions.'[135]

Victorian engineering: a triumph and a disaster

The development of Victorian railway and waterworks projects at scales never before seen was felt even in the rural countryside and, within three years of settling in the Peak District, the Luxmoores would witness both a triumph and a disaster of 19th-century civil engineering.

Hailed as 'ambitious' and 'unprecedented', a new railway line travelling northwards from Rowsley to Hassop was opened on August 1st 1862 – a decade before trains were starting to reach the districts of Revd Luxmoore's childhood in west Devon. The project required blasting through some of the most unforgiving terrain in the country, and the construction of two viaducts and eight tunnels.[136]

The railway had reached Rowsley by 1849, where the 6th Duke of Devonshire's Head Gardener, Joseph Paxton – who had shares in the railway company – had designed and built a station.[137] The route further north, however, had been the source of some considerable dispute. The 6th Duke was in favour of a route that would follow the Derwent valley through Baslow (therefore supporting his travel needs), but the townsfolk of Bakewell argued against this as it would bypass them. The other proposed route would follow the River Wye though Bakewell. However, the Duke of Rutland objected because he did not want to see smoke and steam rising

---

[135] *Derbyshire Times & Chesterfield Herald, June 13th 1894; The Second Visitation Charge of George Ridding, DD, Bishop of Southwell, 1893, p 17.*

[136] *Ashford's closest station was Great Longstone, adjacent to Thornbridge Hall. The owner of this property at the time, barrister George Jobson Marples, had acquired and enlarged the hall in 1896, and in 1903 built himself a private station called Woodlands. When he wished to travel, the train had to make a second stop there, just a few hundred yards from Great Longstone station.*

[137] *John Robertson of Baslow: Architect. Ann Hall. Baslow, Derbyshire, 2015.*

above the gardens of Haddon Hall. But after the 6th Duke of Devonshire died in 1858, his successor was opposed to the line running through Chatsworth Park, and the Wye valley route was therefore the only alternative left. The Duke of Rutland's objections were assuaged by an agreement to construct a tunnel behind Haddon Hall, even though a simple cutting would have otherwise sufficed. In fact, at 1,058 yards, it was to become the longest tunnel on the line between Matlock and Buxton.[138]

After this long delay, construction of the railway continued apace along the Wye valley through Bakewell to Hassop and over a new viaduct at Monsal Head, eventually meeting another line being built southwards from Whaley Bridge. On May 30th 1863, a great celebration in Buxton attended the completion of Midland Railway's London to Manchester main line.

Nine years earlier, Charles Dickens had described the 1½-mile walk along the road north from Ashford to Monsal Head, at which point the dramatic surprise view into Monsal Dale suddenly unfolds:

'It is into the heart of this region that we propose now to carry the reader. Let him suppose himself with us now on the road from Ashford-in-the-Water to Tideswell. We are at the Bull's Head, a little inn on that road. There is nothing to create wonder, or a suspicion of a hidden Arcadia in anything you see, but another step forward, and – there! There sinks a world of valleys at your feet. To your left lies the delicious Monsal Dale. Old Fin Hill lifts his grey head grandly over it .... the sweet Wye goes winding and sounding at his feet, amid its narrow green meadows, green as the emerald, and its dark glossy alders.'[139]

Rosalie and John would have taken the same walk, now witnessing steam trains travelling across the new Headstone Viaduct.

There was widespread criticism at the time of the construction of the viaduct, with John Ruskin famously saying,

'The valley is gone, and the gods with it; and now, every fool in Buxton can be in Bakewell in half an hour and every fool in Bakewell at

---

[138] *Bakewell: The Ancient Capital of the Peak. Trevor Brighton. Halsgrove, 2005, p 72.*

A History of the Midland Railway Route through the Peak. Matlock Station, Matlock, Derbyshire DE4 3NA. Peak Rail plc, https://www.peakrail.co.uk/our-railway/historyofline/

[139] *The Miner's Daughter – A Tale of the Peak. Charles Dickens. In: Household Words First Series, No. VIII, Alden, Beardsley & Co, 1854. For the avoidance of doubt, the Bull's Head referred to by Dickens was located at Monsal Head (the location of the present-day Monsal Head Hotel), not the Bull's Head in present-day Ashford-in-the-Water. Derbyshire Map XXVIII.NW, Ordnance Survey, Survey of 1878-1879, National Library of Scotland.*

Headstone Viaduct in Monsal Dale, Derbyshire, showing Fin Cop peak in the distance (left-hand side), ca. 1914.

Buxton; which you think a lucrative process of exchange – you Fools everywhere.'[140]

A year after the triumphal opening of the London to Manchester railway, a civil engineering disaster was unfolding 20 miles to the north of Ashford, in the moorland parish of Bradfield. The Dale Dyke Dam, covering an area of some 76 acres, was built to meet the demand for water in the rapidly growing city of Sheffield. It was being filled for the first time when, at five o'clock on the very stormy afternoon of March 11th 1864, a crack was noticed in the embankment. By 7.00pm the crack was the width of a finger, and by 9.00pm it had opened still further to the width of a man's hand.

The resident engineer still felt that there was no danger, walking across the embankment as if to dare the waters to break. But suddenly, exclaiming 'it's all up, the embankment is going', the engineer had to be dragged from the path of the water by a companion, as an immense torrent of 690 million gallons of water swept down the Loxley Valley and on to Hillsborough, where the River Loxley joins the River Don. The flood continued along the Wicker to Attercliffe, past what is now the Meadowhall shopping centre, and on to

---

[140] *Fors Clavigera: Letter V. John Ruskin. George Allen, Kent, 1871. Ruskin was, with no little hyperbole, comparing Monsal Dale to the Vale of Tempe, celebrated by Greek poets as a favourite haunt of Apollo and the Muses: 'There was a rocky valley between Buxton and Bakewell, once upon a time, divine as the Vale of Tempe; you might have seen the gods there morning and evening – Apollo and all the sweet Muses of the light – walking in fair procession on the lawns of it, and to and fro among the pinnacles of its crags.'*

Rotherham. More than 600 houses were destroyed by the torrent of water.

Apart from maritime disasters, the Great Sheffield Flood was Victorian England's worst disaster, claiming 240 lives, and resulting in one of the largest insurance claims of the era. The collapse led to reforms in engineering practice and the introduction of new standards for the construction of such large-scale structures. The Dale Dyke Dam was rebuilt, although on a smaller scale, and recommissioned in 1875.[141]

The sound of music

An event of far less immediate drama, but nevertheless of lasting consequence in ecclesiastical circles, and also coincident with the arrival of the Luxmoores at Ashford, was the phenomenally successful publication in 1861 of *Hymns Ancient & Modern*.

In the first half of the 19th century, the singing of hymns by writers such as Charles Wesley and Isaac Watts was widely accepted and enjoyed in Nonconformist chapels. At the same time, although hymn singing was then not officially sanctioned in the Church of England, the Oxford Movement was working to re-establish the services of the ancient Greek and Latin churches, and translations of hymns from these traditions gradually entered worship services.

The growing popularity of hymns resulted in the publication of more than 100 hymnals from 1810 to 1850, but this fragmented effort prevented any of them from becoming successful. Several groups of clergymen had suggested the amalgamation of certain hymn books, when hymnwriter and vicar Sir Henry Williams Baker recommended that the compilation of a single book would be the best way forward. Together with about 20 other clergymen and editors of existing hymn books, he placed a newspaper advertisement inviting co-operation. Under the editorship of musician and church organist William Henry Monk,[142] *Hymns Ancient & Modern* was thus born.

It became one of the best-selling hymn books ever produced: by the end of the 19th century it was used in 90 per cent of rural Anglican churches and had deeply influenced Nonconformist hymnody as well.[143] Within a few years

---

[141] *The Great Sheffield Flood, 1864. Edward Goodricke Draper. Hillsborough Community Development Trust, 1995.*

[142] *'If one hymn must be chosen to represent the style, ethos, and sentiment of Victorian hymnody, it should probably be 'Abide with me' by Henry Francis Lyte (1793-1847), with its tune 'Eventide' by William Henry Monk (1823-1889).' Hymns. Nicholas Temperley. In: Sally Mitchell (ed). Victorian Britain – An Encyclopædia. Routledge, Abingdon, Oxfordshire. 2011, p 386.*

'Abide with me' was voted no. 5 on the list of the UK's Top 10 hymns in 2019. BBC News, September 29th 2019.

[143] *Hymns. Nicholas Temperley. Op. cit.*

of Revd Luxmoore's arrival in Ashford, we see him inviting his parishioners to the weekly choir practice 'so that our singing in church may become more general and hearty'[144] (see p 85).

Several of Samuel Sebastian Wesley's hymn tunes were to be found in the early editions of *Hymns Ancient & Modern*, including *Aurelia* ('The Church's one foundation') and *Harewood* ('Christ is our cornerstone'), and an increasing number have since been published in more modern editions, including the *New Standard Edition* of 1975.

Music in general, and singing in particular, were very popular Victorian and Edwardian entertainments and pastimes, enjoyed by all classes of society, both inside and outside the church, with very little excuse needed for villagers to burst into song or to enlist the local brass band for summer street parades.

We are therefore not surprised to see the schoolroom 'densely crowded' for the entertainment given on the occasion of the annual parochial parish tea in 1893, when Mary Luxmoore, then aged 31 years, 'who was in good voice, rendered her song with care and precision.'[145] In the same year, the church organ had been overhauled and 'new pedals, new [key]board and pipes added'. In order to defray the expense of this work, a 'very successful entertainment' was given in the school on a stage that had been specially erected for the purpose, 'Mr J Luxmoore undertaking this portion of the work.'[146]

The Luxmoore family also supported various charities and other worthy projects in surrounding parishes, by attending meetings and contributing to concerts, plays and tableaux vivants, particularly by lending their voices in solo songs and duets.[147]

In the early 20th century singing became embedded in the school curriculum, primarily as a result of the work of Cecil James Sharp (1859-1924). Sharp's research into, and promotion of, English folksong invigorated a national folk revival movement, of which the Anglican priest, Revd Sabine Baring-Gould (whom we have already met – see p 44), had been an influential early figure. The movement was later embraced by composers such as Ralph Vaughan Williams, George Butterworth and Frederick Delius. Sharp also collected and

---

[144] *Parish notice, 1867. Derbyshire Record Office, D7672/LxC/Lx.C-62.*

[145] *Derbyshire Times & Chesterfield Herald, February 11th 1893.*

[146] *Derbyshire Times & Chesterfield Herald, September 30th 1893.*

[147] *Tableaux Vivants at Darley Dale. Derbyshire Times & Chesterfield Herald, January 9th 1897; Entertainments at Great Longstone. Derbyshire Times & Chesterfield Herald, May 8th 1897; Concert and Tableaux Vivants at Chatsworth. Derbyshire Times & Chesterfield Herald, May 8th 1897; New Year Concert at Great Longstone. Derbyshire Times & Chesterfield Herald, January 7th 1888; Lady Manners Grammar School Speech Day. Derbyshire Times & Chesterfield Herald, July 31st 1897.*

published works on English country dancing and morris dancing: in 1911, he founded the English Folk Dance Society, which, in 1932, amalgamated with the Folk Song Society that had been established in 1898.[148]

During the 1920s the Thorpe family of Ashford would not have been alone in helping to perpetuate the singing tradition in the village. Alice Mary Thorpe recalled that, in her teens:

'Elsie [Alice's younger sister] and I loved music and we went together to Miss Barlow's for singing lessons when we could afford. Miss Barlow and Miss Coe lived in a cottage in Greaves Lane and organised the village choral society that met in a room alongside the cottage.'[149]

Revd Luxmoore was personally acknowledged for helping to provide information for the biography of Sir William Sterndale Bennett (1816-1875).[150] A composer, pianist, conductor and music educator, hailed as the 'most distinguished musician of the early Victorian period', Sterndale Bennett was rated by Sir John Betjeman as 'Queen Victoria's Senior Musical Knight', and it was Prime Minister William Gladstone who recommended his knighthood.[151]

He came from a musical family for whom Ashford had been home: 'the neighbourhood reverberated with music.' His grandfather, John Bennett – christened at Ashford Church on October 13th 1754 – had been a chorister at King's College Cambridge, as had John's sons, Robert (William's father) and Thomas (his uncle). Robert had become the organist at Sheffield Parish Church, and a piano teacher in both Sheffield and Bakewell ('whither he rode on horseback across the moors from Sheffield'). On one particular occasion, Robert had conducted a festival performance of George Frideric Handel's *Messiah* in Bakewell Church, at which his father, John Bennett, had featured as bass soloist.[152]

---

[148] *Cecil Sharp. British Musician. Editors of Encyclopædia Britannica. Encyclopædia Britannica, 2019.*

English Folk Dance and Song Society, Cecil Sharp House, 2 Regent's Park Road, London.

[149] *My Ashford: A Century Past. Alice Mary Dawson. Robert Dawson (ed). Peak Advertiser, Bakewell, 2017, p 32.*

[150] *The Life of William Sterndale Bennett. James Robert Sterndale Bennett. Cambridge University Press, 1907, p viii.*

[151] *William Sterndale Bennett (1816-1875). Nicholas Temperley. In: Sally Mitchell (ed). Victorian Britain – An Encyclopædia. Routledge, Abingdon, Oxfordshire, 2011, p 72.*

Sir John Betjeman quote in: Sterndale Bennett's 200th Anniversary Concert. Friends of the Bodleian, April 13th 2016.

Yorkshire Post, April 13th 2016.

[152] *The Life of William Sterndale Bennett. James Robert Sterndale Bennett. Op. cit., pp 2-6.*

Memorial to Sir William Sterndale Bennett and his father in Sheffield Cathedral. It quotes the opening bars of Sir William's anthem 'God is a Spirit'.

William was born in Howard Street, Sheffield, in 1816 during the time his father Robert was working there. He was orphaned at the age of three, however, and was raised by his grandfather, John, in Cambridge, so never lived in Ashford himself. But in 1853, on 'a pilgrimage to scenes and spots about which he had, in his youth, heard much talk at his grandparents' fireside', William 'passed through, for the first time, the village of Ashford-in-the-Water, the home of his forefathers. He played the little organ in the church where they had worshipped, and was more than satisfied with his visit.'[153]

The author of William Sterndale Bennett's autobiography was his son, James Robert Sterndale Bennett (1847-1928). James and Revd Luxmoore corresponded regarding the cottage in which the Bennetts had lived, which James stated was 'the middle one of three situated between the village school and a small building which is or was some kind of chapel':

'Though presenting plain features it is set amidst picturesque surround-ings, at the base of a steep crag and within a few yards of the entrance to the lovely dale, through which winds the high road from Ashford to Buxton – a fit birthplace for a poet or musician, and John [Bennett] became both, though in only a humble way.'[154]

Sir William Sterndale Bennett is buried in the north choir aisle of Westminster Abbey, not far from the graves of Henry Purcell and Sir Charles Villiers Stanford.

Red Spider country
Revd Luxmoore and his congregations would have become familiar with 'Onward Christian Soldiers' that appeared in the 1909 edition of *Hymns Ancient & Modern*, to a tune composed in 1871 by Arthur Sullivan of Gilbert & Sullivan fame. He would also have learned of the connection of the hymn's writer, Revd Sabine Baring-Gould, to Orchard Barton, in which his Grandpa Luxmoore and the Yeo family lived: in 1872 Sabine inherited from his father, Edward, the 3,000-acre estate that included Lewtrenchard Manor and Orchard Barton. The inheritance further bestowed upon him the gift of the living at Lewtrenchard Parish Church, to which he appointed himself, thereby becoming both squire and parson, or squarson. He was buried in the churchyard of his own church in 1924, as had been Revd Luxmoore's grandparents, James and Susanna, before him (see p 46).

---

[153] *Ibid., p 227.*

[154] *Letter from James Robert Sterndale Bennett to Revd John Reddaway Luxmoore, December 13th 1900. Derbyshire Record Office, D7672/Lx.C-47/6. 'Some kind of chapel' clearly refers to the now demolished Cliff End Chapel.*

As well as being a leader in the revival of English folksong, Sabine Baring-Gould wrote 30 novels; a series of books on folklore; *The Lives of Saints* in 15 volumes; and a number of other hymns. His poem, *The Building of St Sophia*, was one of the recitations selected for the children of Sheldon School to learn in the 1894-1895 school year.[155]

There is a strong literary connection between the Luxmoore family name and Sabine Baring-Gould: his 1887 two-volume novel, *The Red Spider*,[156] is set in and around Bratton Clovelly and the ancestral seat – Combe Park[157] – of Thomas Luxmoore (1610-1636), who sits atop the 'other' Luxmoores' branch of the family tree (see p 35). The plot centres around one Honor Luxmore (the eldest of a large family), who has been entrusted by her mother with the care of her young brothers and sisters, and who performs her duty to them irrespective of everything else, even sacrificing her own love affairs for the sake of this sacred charge.

Baring-Gould also wrote a libretto of the plot that was set to music by the Scottish composer Learmont Drysdale. First staged in 1898, it received more than 100 performances over the next few years.[158]

Regarded by the author as his finest work, the real purpose for his writing *The Red Spider* was,

> '*to recall on paper many and many a recollection of village life in the south-west of England in one of its most still and forgotten corners. ... Old customs, modes of thought, of speech, quaint sayings, weird superstitions are all disappearing out of the country, utterly and for ever.*
>
> *The labourer is now enfranchised, education is universal, railways have made life circulate freer; and we stand now before a great social dissolving view, from which old things are passing away, and what is coming on we can only partly guess, not wholly distinguish'.*[159]

Even Baring-Gould would have been astonished to see how eerily prophetic these last words now seem: exactly 100 years after the publication of *The*

---

[155] *This Remote Little School. Brian Greasley. Country Books, Little Longstone, Derbyshire, 2013, p 40.*

[156] *The Red Spider. Sabine Baring-Gould. Shatto & Windus, Piccadilly, London, 1887.*

[157] *'At the extreme limits of the parish, in a pretty situation, lay a good house of Queen Anne's reign, with some fine trees, and traces of gardens, and a fishpond, called Coombe Park, which had belonged to the Luxmoores or Luxmores.' The Red Spider. Sabine Baring-Gould. Op. cit., Vol 1, p xvii.*

[158] *Selected choral works of Learmont Drysdale, Scotland's forgotten composer. Kenny M Sheppard. Texas Tech University, 1987, p 78.*

Learmont Drysdale (1866-1909) in Opera in the British Isles, 1875-1918. Paul Rodmell. Routledge, London & New York, 2013, p 252.

[159] *The Red Spider. Sabine Baring-Gould. Op. cit., Vol 1, pp iii-iv.*

Red Spider, that very same 'still and forgotten corner' of Devon was to be the construction site for the west country's largest reservoir scheme. The Roadford Reservoir's massive dam across the River Wolf valley is actually sited on Combe Park Farm, which played a central part in both the fictional novel, and the real-world lives of many generations of Luxmoores. It is now lost forever under 30 metres of water.[160]

Quite coincidentally, Revd Luxmoore's grandson, Robin Stonhouse Luxmoore, had chosen to visit his family's roots in Devon in the year that the reservoir was about to be filled:

> 'A water resources engineer from Canada, Robin Luxmoore, came here last May to trace his roots, only to discover that his ancestral pastures were about to be lost forever in South West Water's largest reservoir project to date. However, he too was shown the site of Coombe Park by Mr Timms [County Archaeologist] and met two newly-discovered relations.'[161]

> 'The souvenir he most wanted to fly home with proved elusive, though. Nowhere could he buy a second-hand copy of Red Spider to remind him what traditional country life was really like.'[162]

The Roadford scheme cost in the region of £75 million. When inaugurated in 1989, it was anticipated that the reservoir would solve the drought problem that had plagued Devon for years.[163] Today's 730-acre Roadford Lake venue, managed since 2000 by the South West Lakes Trust, is now a 'must-see' visitor attraction in the area.

Buildings and restorations

A large number of new churches were built, and many more underwent renovations or complete rebuilding, during the Victorian restoration movement. It is therefore not surprising that Revd Luxmoore was invited to the various associated local dedications and celebrations. He no doubt obtained some helpful information and advice relevant to his own proposed restoration that was to occur from 1868 to 1870, or else dispensed the same after he had completed that project.

---

[160] *A large waterwheel from Combe Park Farm was re-erected in working order in 1989 at Okehampton Museum. Combe Park Farm waterwheel at Okehampton Museum, item MBRN-DPH-140, the Mills Archive Trust.*

[161] *Red Spider Country Disappears. Anne Dunbar-Graham. Sabine Baring-Gould Appreciation Society. Newsletter 1989-1990 No. 2, p 3.*

[162] *Racing against time before land flooded. Simon Timms. Western Morning News, August 2nd 1989.*

[163] *The Making of Roadford Reservoir. Simon Timms. Report and Transactions of the Devonshire Association for the Advancement of Science, Literature and Art, Vol 222, 1990, p 171.*

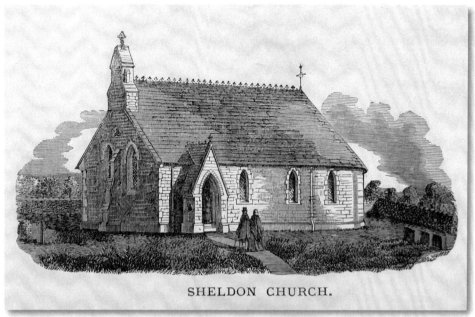

SHELDON CHURCH.

Engraving of St Michael and All Angels' Church, Sheldon, Derbyshire, ca. 1870.

Of all these events, the one that was to become the most personal to him (apart from his own restoration at Ashford) was the construction of the new St Michael and All Angels' Church in Sheldon, to a design by the architect Samuel Rollinson of Chesterfield. Revd Hubert Kestell Cornish, Vicar of Bakewell, laid the foundation stone on May 31st 1864. Built on land given by the Duke of Devonshire, this church replaced a smaller building which had stood in the village street since the 15th century.

The builder was the master carpenter Anthony Gyte (1816-1883) of Church Street, Ashford-in-the-Water. Anthony was the father of Elizabeth Gyte (1851-1929), who was at that time 14 years old and would become Revd Luxmoore's longest-serving domestic servant.

St Michael and All Angels' Church was consecrated on October 7th 1864[164] by John Lonsdale, Bishop of Lichfield. Eight years later, Revd Luxmoore was installed as Vicar of Sheldon, jointly with Ashford.

Bishop Lonsdale (1788-1867), who would oversee the diocese of Lichfield for only the first six years of Revd Luxmoore's incumbency, was a bishop utterly unlike the highly controversial Bishop Luxmoore of St Asaph and Bishop Phillpotts of Exeter:

---

[164] *Church of St Michael and All Angels, Sheldon, Derbyshire, a Grade II Listed Building. Historic England, list entry number 1334884.*

*'There was but one opinion of Lonsdale's episcopate during his time –
that he was the best bishop the diocese had ever had, and, if equalled by
any successor, was not likely to be surpassed. He was a perfect model
of justice, kindness, humility, and shrewd sense, and his undeviating
attention to diocesan duty he almost carried too far.'*[165]

'An outstanding man' of great modesty (initially declining the bishopric
until he was persuaded because he had been recommended by both
the Archbishop of Canterbury and the Bishop of London), he generally took the
liberal side in any controversy, even though his own sympathies were broadly
in line with the conservatism of the high church. He condemned and distrusted
adherents to the extremes of both the high church Oxford Movement and the
low church Evangelical Anglicanism.[166] He was highly successful in diffusing
the 'exciting ecclesiastical crises' which he faced during his episcopate and, as
a result, the Lonsdale era is mainly remembered for its unparalleled scale of
church building and restoration.

John Lonsdale died unexpectedly and was succeeded in 1868 by George
Augustus Selwyn (1809-1878), who had previously been the first Bishop of
New Zealand. Selwyn College Cambridge was founded in his name to honour
his life and contribution to scholarship and religion.

To assist in his transition from New Zealand to Lichfield, Bishop Selwyn
selected Edmund Hobhouse – whom he had previously appointed Bishop
of Nelson, New Zealand – to be his assistant bishop.[167] He also enlisted the
support of Charles John Abraham, whom he had appointed as the first Anglican
Bishop of Wellington, New Zealand.

It was during Bishop Selwyn's episcopacy that Revd Luxmoore was keen for
a proposed new school in Sheldon to become a church school. He was heavily
involved in the planning and acted as the chief liaison between the Education
Department, the Local Authority and – Sheldon being a 'Chatsworth Village' –
the 7th Duke of Devonshire. He was engaged in drawn-out discussions
(sometimes intense) regarding sources of funds and the potential financial
impact on ratepayers, and the size and type of the school. His view was that

---

[165] *John Lonsdale. Dictionary of National Biography. Sidney Lee (ed). Vol 34, 1893, p 129.*

[166] *The Derbyshire Returns to the 1851 Religious Census. Margery Tranter (ed). Derbyshire Record
Society, 1995, p xv.*

[167] *The dedication page of J Charles Cox's 'Notes on the Churches of Derbyshire Vol II, The
Hundreds of the High Peak and Wirksworth, 1877' reads: 'To the Rt Revd Bishop Hobhouse
these pages are, by permission, dedicated, in acknowledgement of the kind and generous help
received at his hands in furtherance of the author's attempt to elucidate the ecclesiastical history
of Derbyshire.'*

an infant school would be sufficient, since the older pupils could go to the existing school in Ashford.[168]

These discussions lasted several years, to the extent that the authorities in the Department of Education wrote to Revd Luxmoore expressing concern at an apparent lack of urgency. Rosalie sent a lengthy explanatory letter on his behalf to Chatsworth on February 7th 1877 stating, 'I write for my husband as he is not well enough to do so himself'. She explained that, moreover, he had been in Devonshire 'for about a month' and had had to 'go to Richmond in a hurry.' Finally, on July 12th that year, Anthony Gyte, who had completed St Michael and All Angels' Church 13 years earlier, contracted to build the new school. Revd Luxmoore then made it ready by ordering equipment, desks and benches, at a total cost of £263 11s 3d, including the building work and interior furnishings.[169]

This 'remote little school' (as Revd Luxmoore later referred to it)[170] was opened one year later on July 29th 1878 with a celebratory party in the village – 'a kind of gala day' – at which he and Rosalie were present. He visited the school regularly, signing himself in the school logbooks as 'Correspondent'.

Maria Brassington (1857-1934) was appointed as the first mistress and had the challenging task of teaching 36 children aged from 4 or 5 to 10+ in one room. Those challenges included circumstances clearly beyond her control, such as sicknesses (the school was closed for more than four months during the course of 1882 'in consequence of an outbreak of fever') and absences 'owing to working on farms'. Although the various inspectors' reports were not uniformly favourable, she received an excellent appraisal on more than one occasion: 'Discipline and order good. Elementary subjects nicely done'; 'The state of this small school reflects credit upon Miss Brassington for her industry and perseverance'.[171]

At the time of her appointment, Maria was 20 years old. Eight years later she married Anthony Gyte (1863-1945), son of the Anthony Gyte who built the village's church and its school. Their first child, Mary Louisa Gyte, was born on June 26th 1887, at which time Maria left the school. She was subsequently the author of *The Diaries of Maria Gyte* (see Bibliography).

The school closed in 1935, and in 1948 the building was gifted to the village by Andrew Cavendish – who was to become 11th Duke of Devonshire in 1950 – in memory of his elder brother William John Robert Cavendish, Marquess

---

[168] *This Remote Little School. Brian Greasley. Country Books, Little Longstone, Derbyshire, 2013, pp 11-12.*

[169] *Ibid., pp 14-20.*

[170] *Ibid., p 51.*

[171] *Ibid., pp 32-35.*

of Hartington, killed in action during the Second World War. It has since been known as the Hartington Memorial Hall.[172]

Another church building project with which Revd Luxmoore would have become very familiar was the restoration of St Giles' Church, Great Longstone. An appeal for subscriptions was issued in 1871, the year following the completion of the restoration of Revd Luxmoore's own church in Ashford. Revd John Paley, the Vicar of Longstone, officiated at the last service in the unrestored building on July 7th 1872, having only eight days earlier taken steps to resign his living there.

The new vicar, Revd Nathaniel A Wells, arrived in March 1873. In the meantime, and whilst the church restorations were in progress, the schoolroom was licensed 'for all offices of divine service, including the holy sacraments' and services were held there on Sunday afternoons, 'generally by the Revd JR Luxmoore, Vicar of Ashford'.[173] Revd Luxmoore also 'kindly assisted at both morning and afternoon services' on March 16th 1873, whilst the new vicar was instituted by Bishop Hobhouse.

The restoration work took 15 months and the church was reopened on September 22nd 1873 by Bishop Charles J Abraham, with Edmund T Chipp, Organist of Ely Cathedral, presiding at a new organ, and with hymns selected from *Hymns Ancient & Modern*.

Revd Luxmoore's assistance was further acknowledged in respect of Mr George Thomas Wright's excellent 1906 compilation of the *Longstone Records* pertaining to St Giles' Church, which, among much else, detail the restoration with 'before-and-after' photographs and floor plans.[174]

Bishop Selwyn, who had died three months before the opening of Sheldon School, was succeeded as Bishop of Lichfield by William Dalrymple Maclagan.[175] On July 26th 1880, Revd Luxmoore was in attendance when Bishop Maclagan consecrated the new church of St Anne's in Over Haddon – 'one of the most romantic villages in the county of Derby':[176]

'A large number were present, including most of the neighbourhood aristocracy.'

---

[172] *Ibid., pp 126-128. William John Robert Cavendish is one of the men from Ashford who died in the Second World War, and who are memorialised on a tablet inset into the exterior south wall of the tower of Ashford Church. The others are Sampson Lynes Gratton and Robert Harris.*

[173] *Longstone Records, Derbyshire. GT Wright. Benjamin Gratton, Bakewell, 1906, pp 134-135.*

[174] *Longstone Records, Derbyshire. GT Wright. Op. cit., pp 6-7.*

[175] *In 1891 Maclagan became Archbishop of York, a position he held for 17 years.*

[176] *This, and other quotations regarding the consecration, are from contemporaneous press reports: Sheffield Daily Telegraph, July 28th 1880; Derby Mercury, July 28th 1880; Derbyshire Times & Chesterfield Herald, July 31st 1880.*

Indeed, it is reported that,

'Owing to the large number present, it would be impossible to find
accommodation for them in the church for the dedication ceremony, and that,
in consequence of this, a service would be simultaneously held in [a] tent'.

The large marquee, holding around 400 people, had been erected in an adjoining field, lent for the occasion by a local farmer, Jonathan Heathcote. In a second tent were 'many useful and fancy articles', exhibited 'in order to empty the pockets in aid of the funds of the new church'. It is to be hoped that the tents were thoroughly waterproof, given 'the general downpour during the whole of 12 hours, and the drizzle and fog which hung around'.

St Anne's, designed in the gothic style by Henry Cockbain of Manchester,[177] was built by Messrs James, Rowland & Alfred Hill of Tideswell and Litton.[178] For 'the cost of the building … something over £2,000 … Over Haddon possesses one of the prettiest churches in the country'.

Revd Luxmoore served under yet another bishop, George Ridding, when the diocese of Lichfield was moved administratively to become part of the new diocese of Southwell in 1884. Along with many other local clergy, he attended the formal consecration by Bishop Ridding of the new All Saints' Church, Matlock Bank, on September 17th 1884. It was built to serve the Victorian spas of Matlock, but to what appears to have been an over-optimistic plan. On the day of the consecration the building was 'rather unfinished in its present state, and presents very far from an ornamental feature in the landscape, but it is intended to add a tower and other structural adornments when funds permit.' Ven Archdeacon Balston, Vicar of All Saints' Church Bakewell,[179] admitted that 'none could go into the church without noticing that the building was not complete … there had been a great amount of trouble in getting the church erected.'[180] The budgeted cost was £4,000, of which £1,200 had yet to be raised. (Unfortunately, sufficient funds to complete the church to its original design were never raised, and a more modest west end was built in 1958.)

In 1899, Revd Luxmoore was among the clergy present for the reopening and dedication of the restored west door at Bakewell parish church. This 'fine

---

[177] *A Biographical Dictionary of the Architects of Greater Manchester, 1800-1940. Manchester Group of the Victorian Society, https://manchestervictorianarchitects.org.uk/architects/henry-cockbain*

[178] *Likely to be from the same family as Messrs Alfred & Hedley Hill of Tideswell, who built the enlarged Wesleyan Methodist chapel in Ashford-in-the-Water in 1899. See p 243. Kelly's Directory of the Counties of Derby, Notts, Leicester and Rutland. London, 1891, pp 317-320.*

[179] *Edward Balston, Vicar of Bakewell from 1869 to 1891, was also Archdeacon of Derby from 1873.*

[180] *Derby Telegraph, September 20th 1884.*

old Norman doorway' had been 'restored at the expense of Mr [John Edward] Barker, QC, of Brooklands, Bakewell'[181] in honour of his deceased mother, Hannah Barker. Sadly, Mr Barker had been too unwell to attend, but 'had expressed his entire approval of the work, which he was able to inspect when in progress, and on completion.'[182]

Village events

The village churches of Ashford and Sheldon would, of course, be the centre of Revd Luxmoore's life, with their year-round Sunday services, and annual cycles of festivals in which his congregations would become busily involved.

In 1884, for example, the rural dean and vicar of Tideswell preached at Ashford in the morning and Revd Luxmoore in the evening on the occasion of the Harvest Festival. 'The church was very tastefully decorated with flowers, corn and fruit from the gardens of Lady [Louisa] Cavendish, Ashford Hall,[183] and others. The work was executed by the ladies of the parish, among whom were Mrs Luxmoore, and the Misses Fenton and Churchdale'.[184]

In return for their support, it was a custom of Revd Luxmoore and Rosalie each year to entertain the members of the Ashford Church choir, sidesmen, Sunday School teachers, and other church workers. In January 1912, this annual event took place in the schoolhouse 'where supper was partaken of' by about 50 people:

> 'Captain Fitch of the Church Army delighted the company with a lantern lecture depicting 'A Trip Down The River Wye' together with views of the Isle of Wight. Illustrated songs were thrown on the screen, and the choristers heartily joined in singing them. Games and dancing were also indulged in.'[185]

Captain Fitch likely provided the same entertainment when he visited Sheldon School a few days later.[186]

---

[181] *John Edward Barker, QC, baptised at Bakewell on September 11th 1833, was a member of the Inner Temple at the Inns of Court in London and was called to the bar in 1862. He inherited Brooklands House, Bakewell, and achieved prominence in the area of legal claims after the Great Sheffield Flood of 1864 (see p 71), https://www.wikitree.com/wiki/Barker-11574*

[182] *Derbyshire Times & Chesterfield Herald, July 15th 1899.*

[183] *Louisa Cavendish and her husband, George Henry Cavendish, MP, came to live at Ashford Hall on July 12th 1838. George's elder brother was William Cavendish, an accomplished scholar and founder of the famous Cavendish Laboratory at Cambridge University, who would in 1858 become the 7th Duke of Devonshire.*

[184] *Derby Telegraph, October 1st 1884.*

[185] *Derbyshire Times & Chesterfield Herald, January 20th 1912.*

[186] *This Remote Little School. Brian Greasley. Country Books, Little Longstone, Derbyshire, 2013, p 119.*

In addition to his ecclesiastical duties, Revd Luxmoore would frequently be called upon as vicar to support (with his wife whenever possible) all manner of local community events. We therefore see him in 1874 donating 10 shillings for the second prize for the 'neatest and best stocked cottage garden',[187] and in 1878 presenting the first prize for 'the best collection of vegetables',[188] at the annual Floral and Horticultural Society's exhibitions.

We have a lasting legacy of an occasion that took place shortly after his arrival in the village, in honour of the marriage on March 10th 1863 of the Prince of Wales, the eldest son of Queen Victoria and the future King Edward VII, to Princess Alexandra of Denmark. There were celebrations throughout the land, and at Ashford-in-the-Water Lady Louisa Cavendish planted two lime trees in the Hall Orchard, which have grown into very large and splendid specimens.

Revd Luxmoore was clearly keen to provide opportunities for his flock to enjoy themselves, whilst at the same time improving their education. In 1867, as an adjunct to a lending library, he opened a reading room, with coffee and biscuits on hand, as well as games of chess and draughts. He had also instituted a night school which, within two years, had an average attendance of about 40. Following the examinations in 1867, 'more than 30 young men sat down to partake of roast

PARISH OF ASHFORD.

The Choir Practice

Is held on Wednesday, in each week, at 8 p.m., in the Boys' School Room. The Parishioners are invited to attend, so that our singing in Church may become more general and hearty.

The Night School

Is held in the same Room, on Monday and Thursday, in each week, from 7 to 9. 2d. per week is paid in advance.

The Reading Room.

It is decided to open a Reading Room on February 11th, 1867, to be continued open on Monday, Wednesday, and Thursday, from 9 to 10 p.m., and on Tuesday, Friday, and Saturday, in each week, from 7 to 10. Newspapers and Periodicals will be supplied. Chess and Draughts will also be furnished. It is hoped that this may become a source of pleasure and profit to the parishioners.

The Subscription will be 2d. per week, payable in advance, or 1s. 6d. per quarter. Members of the Night School will be required to pay only an additional 1d.

Drawing will be taught gratis, on Tuesday evenings, from 7 to 8, to any who attend the Day or Night School, being also members of the Reading Room.

It is intended to provide, for such as desire it, Coffee and Biscuits at cost price.

The Incumbent relies upon the co-operation of his parishioners in maintaining that order which is essential to the comfort and success of any Reading Room.

The Lending Library

Is about to be renovated, and, it is hoped, enlarged. Members of the Reading Room will be entitled to the use of the Library, without any further Contribution. The subscription for others will be 1d. per week. Gifts of Books suitable for the Library will be thankfully received by the Incumbent.

Ashford-in-the-Water Parish Notice, 1867.

---

[187] *Derbyshire Times, August 4th 1874.*

[188] *Derby Mercury, August 14th 1878.*

beef and plum pudding … prizes were given away, songs were sung, chess and draughts and other games played, and a very pleasant evening spent.'[189]

Sunday June 20th 1897 marked the 60th anniversary of Queen Victoria's accession to the throne. The British Empire was at a high-water mark: Victoria sat at the head of a realm of 450 million subjects stretched across every continent, and her Diamond Jubilee Day was celebrated around the world.

The following Tuesday was declared a public holiday in Britain, and John Stonhouse Luxmoore had been made Honorary Secre-

ASHFORD DIAMOND JUBILEE CELEBRATION, JUNE 22ND, 1897.

Programme of Sports.

2-30 P.M.   BOYS AND GIRLS UNDER 15.

Girls'—50 yards Races	Boys'—Half-mile Race
Boys'—100 yards Races	Girls'—Skipping Race
Girls'—Hopping Race	Boys'—Sack Race.
Boys'—Three legged Race	Girls'—Potato Race
Girls'—Egg and Spoon Race	Boys'—Obstacle Race

6-30 P.M.   ADULTS.

Men's—100 yards Race	Men's—Wheelbarrow Race
Ladies'—Egg and Spoon Race	Old Folks (over 50)—Egg and Spoon Race.
Men's—Half-mile Race	Men's—Bicycle (Tortoise) Race
Ladies'—Potato Race	Men's—Obstacle Race
Men's—Sack Race	
Ladies'—50 yards Race	

All Competitors must be Residents in the Parish.
First and Second Prizes will be given for each event.
No Competitor allowed more than one First or two Second Prizes.
Starter, Judges, and a Referee (whose decision will be final) will be appointed by the Committee.
Names of Competitors to be given in to the Secretary as soon as possible.

A GREASY POLE (Prize, Leg of Mutton).   TUG OF WAR.

COMMITTEE:

Mr J. T. Dickinson.	Mr E. Marsden.	Mr. G. Thorpe.
Mr J. W. Daybell.	Mr Smalley.	Mr F. J. Wilson.
Mr Fisher.	Mr Stubbs.	

J. S. LUXMOORE,
Hon. Secretary.

Flyer publicising the Ashford Diamond Jubilee celebrations.

tary for the Ashford celebrations. The village was 'tastefully decorated, flags and arches being plentiful.' At Sheldon School, two Union Jacks, a Royal Standard and jubilee medals were purchased for the children, having been paid for from the proceeds of a concert.[190] An 'excellent sermon was preached at Ashford by the vicar (the Revd JR Luxmoore) from the text 'Ye shall hallow the fiftieth year. It shall be a Jubilee unto Thee' … [and] the organist played George Frideric Handel's [coronation anthem] *Zadok the Priest* at the conclusion of the Service.'[191]

[189] *Derby Mercury, May 8th 1867.*

[190] *This Remote Little School. Brian Greasley. Country Books, Little Longstone, Derbyshire, 2013, p 45.*

[191] *Derbyshire Times & Chesterfield Herald, June 25th 1887.*

1897 Diamond Jubilee celebrations in front of the school, adjacent to the Top Pump, looking east. From the far right: [unknown]; Revd JR Luxmoore (with wife Rosalie, in black, behind); daughter Mary Luxmoore (white dress with black trim); son William Cyril Luxmoore (moustached, with white suit and boater); daughter Edith Rosalie Luxmoore (white dress); son John Stonhouse Luxmoore (moustached, with darker suit and boater); William Daybell (homburg hat, bearded); John Wallwin of the Corn Mill (top hat, white sideburns); George J Marples of Thornbridge Hall (bowler hat, moustached, white buttonhole on his right lapel); [unknown in pale flat cap]. The flag-bearer is Sam Kitson.

Congregations at Ashford and at Sheldon – and, indeed, throughout the empire[192] – would have sung the hymn that had been chosen by Victoria herself for the celebrations: Revd John Ellerton's 'The day thou gavest, Lord, is ended', to the tune *St Clement* by Revd Clement Cotterill Scholefield. Although the hymn has an unmistakable imperial rhetoric ('each continent and island'), the overarching sentiment is that even the British Empire is transitory; only God's empire will last for ever ('So be it, Lord; thy throne shall never like earth's proud empires, pass away'). The international inclusivity of its words has been affirmed by its adoption in 1944 as the World Day of Prayer hymn,[193] as well as its use in the ceremony at which Hong Kong was handed back to China in 1997.[194] More than a century later, it remains one of the country's most popular hymns.[195]

---

[192] *A program of a thanksgiving service centered around prayers and hymns for Queen Victoria's Diamond Jubilee in a Canadian Protestant Episcopal Church. Library of Congress Control Number 91898204. Church of England in Canada, June 20, 1897.*

[193] *A History of the World Day of Prayer, http://www.wdpscotland.org.uk/dload/WDPHistory.pdf*

[194] *The story behind the hymn: The day thou gavest, Lord, is ended. Rupert Christiansen. The Telegraph, September 22nd 2007.*

[195] *'The day thou gavest' gained third place in a BBC 'Songs of Praise' poll in 2005. Press Office, BBC, October 27th 2005.*

In her journal, Queen Victoria called it 'a never-to-be-forgotten day.' 'No one ever, I believe, has met with such an ovation as was given to me, passing through those six miles of streets,' she wrote. 'The crowds were quite indescribable and their enthusiasm truly marvellous and deeply touching. The cheering was quite deafening, and every face seemed to be filled with real joy. I was much moved and gratified.'[196]

Temperance

Two years after Queen Victoria's Jubilee celebrations, Revd Luxmoore preached 'an appropriate sermon' to open the village Wakes Week on Sunday May 28th 1899. Afterwards, the Men's Friendly Society paraded behind the Darley Dale and Wensley Brass Bands 'to the Devonshire Arms hostelry, where a substantial dinner was awaiting them.'[197] If he accompanied them into that drinking establishment, Revd Luxmoore would not have partaken of any alcohol.

Revd Luxmoore (centre, behind tuba player) at a village parade, Greaves Lane, ca. 1900.

Despite deep and sometimes bitter theological differences with Dissenting Christians, Victorian Anglicans did attempt in selected circumstances to co-operate with Nonconformists, and sometimes with Roman Catholics, to confront common social problems. So it was that in 1894 the Luxmoore family (if not Revd Luxmoore himself) supported a children's entertainment held

---

[196] *Queen Victoria's Diamond Jubilee. Christopher Klein. History: A+E Networks UK, https://www. history.com/news/queen-victorias-diamond-jubilee*

[197] *Derby Daily Telegraph, June 1st 1899.*

in the Wesleyan Chapel in Ashford, to aid the Band of Hope, a temperance organisation that had been established in 1847. The adults had provided some entertainment, including songs performed on this occasion by Revd Luxmoore's son John and daughter Mary (then in their 30s); and there was 'an amazing dialogue, entitled *I wouldn't be a publican.*' Altogether, 'the programme was greatly enjoyed by those present.'[198]

Twenty-five years after the formation of the Band of Hope, the Church of England belatedly established its own Temperance Society (CETS), but even then it was following – rather than leading – efforts by individual clergymen to address the drinking problem. By extending the reach of the Established Church into social and cultural, as well as religious, realms, and by directing its practical activities towards those in the poorer classes who had no religious affiliation, it was hoped that CETS might also become a vehicle for countering the rise of Nonconformism. Anglican clergymen were told that if they did not soon join the fight against intemperance,

> *'There is no doubt whatever but that their indifference to the misery and vice and crime committed to their charge will be used as ... a most powerful argument for the entire destruction of our Church as the Established Church.'*[199]

But CETS came into conflict with some other factions within the temperance movement. For example, it was criticised for continuing to use alcoholic wine in the Holy Communion service, and for failing to advocate total abstinence. Methodists in the New World took umbrage at Bishop Feild's failure to support the Canadian temperance movement, and were shocked by his view that moderate drinking of alcohol could be morally right, 'the Church itself being the only temperance society to which anyone need belong'.[200]

The Ashford branch of CETS was formed in 1884, and on May 6th that year Sheldon School was the venue for the entertainment of its new members. Forty were present, among them Revd and Mrs Luxmoore and two of their daughters.[201] By the time of its annual meeting four years later, it had more

---

[198] *Derbyshire Advertiser & Journal, February 2nd 1894.*

[199] *The Church of England Temperance Magazine, new ser. V, September, 1868, p 284. Quoted in: Anglican Temperance Movements in England, 1859-1873. An Example of Practical Ecumenism. Gerald Wayne Olsen. Canadian Catholic Historical Association Study Sessions, Vol 40, 1973, pp 41-51.*

[200] *Edward Feild, Bishop of Newfoundland 1844-1876. Frederick Jones. Newfoundland Historical Society Pamphlet No. 4, 1976, p 16.*

[201] *This Remote Little School. Brian Greasley. Country Books, Little Longstone, Derbyshire, 2013, p 120.*

than eighty members. Although Revd Luxmoore would certainly have continued to use wine in the Eucharist, at this Ashford CETS public meeting he proposed a vote of thanks to an invited speaker who was a firm advocate of total abstinence – Dr Edward Mason Wrench of Baslow[202] – who had spoken on the subject 'from a medical man's point of view':

Mrs Brayshaw of the Elms was a long-term supporter of the Band of Hope, as evidenced by this plaque under the village's Top Pump shelter.

'Alcohol, he said, is clearly a poison, and cannot be taken, even in small quantities, without injury to the system. Eminent medical men, many of whom had formerly held out against total abstinence, after long experience admit that alcohol, taken as a beverage, is worse than useless, and that total abstainers live longer and have healthier bodies than moderate drinkers.'[203]

If there was a lack of a coherence within the Church of England Temperance Society, the temperance movement in general flourished among the British Nonconformist constituency: by 1897, the Band of Hope numbered 3.5 million children and adults, and it had become part of the fabric of Victorian society. Indeed, Ashford resident Alice Mary Dawson recalls that the village's branch was still going strong 30 years after the Luxmoores had provided their encouragement at the Wesleyan Chapel:

---

[202] *Dr Wrench (1833-1912), of Park Lodge, Baslow, a veteran of the Crimean War, attended to three Dukes of Devonshire and other members of the Cavendish family; various members of the Duke of Rutland's family; and King Edward VII on his visits to Chatsworth. He received the decoration of the Victorian Order in 1907 in recognition of his services, and he is memorialised in a stained-glass window in the north aisle of St Anne's Church, Baslow.*

Papers of Edward M Wrench of Baslow, Derbyshire, surgeon. University of Nottingham Manuscripts and Special Collections, ref. GB 159 Wr; Wre; Wr Ki; Wr/BT.

An Old Campaigner: Memories of a Derbyshire Doctor. Magazine of the Derbyshire Family History Society, issue 174, September 2020, pp 6-9.

[203] *Derbyshire Times & Chesterfield Herald, January 21st 1888.*

*'I signed the Band of Hope pledge ... declaring that I would never drink
alcohol. The Ashford Band of Hope was run by Mrs Brayshaw, who lived
in the Elms near the school. To interest the children in the Band of Hope,
she used to put up a notice advertising slideshows about once a month.*

*'First we'd go into the house and sing 'My drink is water bright' whilst
Mrs Brayshaw played her harmonium, after which prayers were said.
Then out to the stables for a magic lantern show, which of course was
the big attraction to us children in those days. The slides were mainly to
warn us about the evil effects of drink, showing men beating their wives
and poverty caused by drinking.'*[204]

Ultimately, however, and despite innumerable bills and legislative debate
between the turn of the century and the interwar years, the temperance
movement failed to make a significant mark on policy. This was not least
because, as we have seen, the movement was fragmented, its constituent
organisations pushing different moral and political agendas, ranging from
moderation to complete prohibition. At the same time, Victorian values were
dissipating; opportunities for other leisure activities were increasing; and some
public houses were being requisitioned and breweries converted into munition
stores or factories during the war.[205]

An ironic, but unambiguous, indication of the temperance movement's
diminishing influence was
to occur coincident with
the revelries celebrating
the 60th anniversary of
Queen Victoria's reign:
1897 also marked the
50th anniversary of the
founding of the Band of
Hope. The Queen had
agreed to become its
Jubilee Patron, and a com-
memorative medallion
was struck to be worn
with a ribbon.

A medallion was struck to commemorate the 50th
anniversary of the Band of Hope. The inscriptions on
the obverse and reverse sides read, respectively: 'HM
Queen Victoria. Patron of the Band of Hope Jubilee.
Unprecedented reign of sixty years, 1837-1897'; and
'Jubilee of the Band of Hope movement. 1897. Founded
in Leeds 1847 by Mrs Ann Jane Carlile and Rev
J Tunnicliff'.

---

[204] *My Ashford: A Century Past. Alice Mary Dawson. Robert Dawson (ed). Peak Advertiser,
Bakewell, 2017, p 30.*

[205] *A Force to be Reckoned With? The Temperance Movement and the 'Drink Question', 1895-1933.
James Clifford Dunn. University of Central Lancashire, October 1999.*

But in apparent defiance of Victoria's unmistakable support for the temperance movement, by order of the government pubs were to remain open on her Diamond Jubilee Day until 2:30am.[206]

High society

As Vicar of Ashford-in-the-Water and Sheldon, Revd Luxmoore would have been invited automatically to key events in the social calendars of the local aristocracy. So in 1880 he attended, as a 'distinguished patron', a Grand Morning Concert given in aid of the Over Haddon Building Fund by the Bakewell Choral Society, and hosted by the Duke of Rutland at Haddon Hall – described in the press as 'the most attractive and interesting of all the ancient baronial mansions in the kingdom'.[207]

In 1904, three years after Queen Victoria's death, her eldest son – now King Edward VII – and Queen Alexandra visited Chatsworth. A 'great programme of festivities' was organised, the principal events being 'shooting … over the Bakewell, Ashford and Beeley coverts[208] … and amateur theatricals'. Revd Luxmoore was invited by the Duke and Duchess of Devonshire, along with Rosalie, to attend the theatrical performance: 'a little pantomime on the subject of *Cinderella*'.[209]

Another memorable event for 'Revd JR and Mrs Luxmoore and party' was the 'brilliant gathering' of the 1899 County Ball at Chatsworth. An extensive report, which describes its every detail, is redolent of today's most glamorous and extravagant costume dramas.[210] Some extracts provide a taste of the affair:

'The arrangements, perfect as they were in every particular, must have entailed a tremendous amount of forethought and labour.'

The weather, however, did not co-operate:

'During the time the guests were arriving, a violent hurricane prevailed, and two trees were uprooted in the park, a large number of men having to be called out to remove one of the trees which had fallen across the carriage road.'

---

[206] *Queen Victoria and Britain's first Diamond Jubilee. Andy Sully. BBC News, May 22nd 2012, https://www.bbc.co.uk/news/uk-17368499*

[207] *The editor of this story took the opportunity to contrast 'the concert room of Haddon Hall to our cramped and musty-smelling Town Hall of Bakewell! How superior the former, how disgracefully shabby the latter, totally inadequate as it is for the purposes of a public gathering and for musical purposes in particular!' Derbyshire Times & Chesterfield Herald, May 15th 1880.*

[208] *Coverts are thickets in which game can hide.*

[209] *Derbyshire Advertiser & Journal, January 8th 1904.*

[210] *Derbyshire Times & Chesterfield Herald, January 14th 1899.*

For guests living further afield a special train had been chartered, taking passengers from Derby to Rowsley, where,

'every preparation had been made to ensure a comfortable journey to the mansion of their noble entertainers ... the platform was covered with crimson cloth, and there were other decorations, denoting that an important affair was in progress at the ducal residence.'

MENU.

Consommé aux Quenelles
Côtelettes de mouton aux Pois
Poulet a la Diable
Cailles roties

———

Petites Timbales d'Homard
Filets oe Soles a la Desabris
Mignons de Poulardes Belle Vue
Mauviettes a l'Ecarlate
Ballotines a l'Aspie
Noisettes a la Rachel
Faisans   Perdreaux   Grouse
Petits Pains et Sandwiches

———

Gelees   Patisserie
Macedoine de Fruits au Champagne

The talents of the head chef and his staff are evident from the menu for the 1899 Chatsworth Ball.

A welcome buffet was provided in the Painted Hall, after which the guests, having been received by the Duke and Duchess, proceeded up the Grand Staircase to the Ballroom, where,

'250 extra lights [were] arranged to obtain the greatest effect ... a marvellous effect was produced, and just sufficient clearness and natural light obtained to convey the impression of something between a bright moonlight and the breaking dawn ...

'All the rooms, staircases, and flats had been utilised – with the exception of the State Apartments – for floral and foliage adornment, the wealth of the greenhouses and the hothouses being skilfully requisitioned in all directions.'

Quadrille	...	Ziguener Baron	...	Strauss
Waltz	...	Gartenlaube	...	Ziehrier
Waltz	...	Donau Wiebchen	...	Strauss
Waltz	...	... Schatz ...	...	Strauss
Polka ...		... Puppen Fee		...Millocker
Waltz	...	Faschingskinder	...	Ziehrier
Lancers	...	Belle of New York	...	Kerker
Waltz	...	Wein Weib und Gesang	...	Strauss
Waltz	...	Serezelem	...	Waldteufel
Waltz	...	... Morena ...	...	Fetras
Barn Dance	...	... Ohio ...	...	Elkin
Waltz		... Bruder Lustig ...		Vollstedt
Waltz	...	... Weiner Blut ..		...Strauss
Polka	...	Dame de Cœur		...Farhbach
Waltz	...	... Verborgene ...		Ziehrier
Lancers	...	... Geisha ...		S Jones
Polka	...	Obersteiger	...	Zeiler
Waltz	...	Verlobung	...	Ziehrier
Waltz	...	... Donau Bleu ...		... Strauss
Gslop	...	... Jager ...		...

The Blue Hungarian Band provided the dance music for the 1899 Chatsworth Ball.

Seating for 150 diners had been provided in the Supper Room:

'The daintiest pastry, most tempting sweetmeats, and other appetising delicacies were served in sugar baskets as transparent as Venetian glass, and decorated in most seductive a fashion. Stands of cornflower were raised for the purposes of holding filets de soles and mauviettes à l'écarlate – in other words, larks hidden in 'something', both of which afforded proof of the skill and taste of the chef and those under his direction.'

'The very large number of horses and carriages for which accommodation had to be found taxed even the very extensive stabling at Chatsworth ... it is gratifying to record that there were no accidents, especially considering the boisterous weather.'

'The company dispersed about three o'clock, the special train to Derby leaving Rowsley at 3.30am.'

Samuel Birley (1824-1906)

Revd Luxmoore's poignant introduction to the Birley family was to occur just one month after he was installed as the new incumbent at Ashford Church: his first funeral was for Samuel Birley's infant nephew, Benjamin Birley. The vicar's predecessor, Revd James Burrow, had christened baby Benjamin and his twin brother Samuel – named after his uncle – only eight months earlier, on September 20th 1860. Samuel's own son, Richard, had also tragically died in 1853, aged only 4 years and 8 months.

This proved to be the beginning of a rather traumatic initiation for Revd Luxmoore, because Benjamin's was just the first of nine consecutive funerals of infants and children under the age of 14 at which he had to officiate between June and November 1861.

Happier times were to come for the Birley family in the following year, when Samuel Birley won prizes in both the furniture and the mining classes at the 1862 London International Exhibition, for one of the most elaborate examples of Ashford marble known to collectors. Made in his village workshop and showroom on Court Lane to a design by James Randall – an English draughtsman who worked in London and exhibited at the Royal Academy – this inlaid marble table was purchased after the Exhibition by the Victoria & Albert Museum for £240. Thomas Brushfield relates,

'an inlaid black marble table sent from this village to the great industrial exhibition of 1862 was universally admired, obtained a very high prize,

Samuel Birley's spectacular Ashford marble table. High-resolution colour photographs are available to view online (see p 260).

and caused the name of its inventor, Samuel Birley, to be placed as an artist among the celebrities of the day. [211]

Active in the marble trade for most of the second half of the 19th century, Samuel had enough work to employ four or five men, including his younger brothers John (baby Benjamin's father) and Charles.

Samuel was also active in community affairs. A churchwarden at Holy Trinity for many years, he was at various times secretary or treasurer of both the Women's and Men's Friendly Societies in Ashford.

---

[211] *Derbyshire Black Marble. John Michael Tomlinson. Peak District Mines Historical Society, Special Publication No. 4, 1996, pp 42,45,67.*

Victoria & Albert Museum. Museum Number 157&A-1864, http://collections.vam.ac.uk/item/O18958/table-randall-j/

Ashford-in-the-Water: The changes which have taken place there in sixty years. Thomas Brushfield. The Reliquary, Vol 6. Llewellynn Jewitt (ed). Bemrose & Sons, Derby & London, 1865-1866, p 91.

Friendly societies are mutual-aid organisations whose origins lie in ancient Greek and Roman cultures, that wished to satisfy the basic human instinct to bury the dead with appropriately sensitive rites and formality, even when this would often have been beyond the means of the surviving relatives.

In the absence of effective welfare systems, their missions expanded to insure against loss of income as a result of sickness or infirmity. Their rapid growth in the 19th century has been credited in large part to the Protestant refugees of Spitalfields, one of whose societies was founded in 1703.[212] They acted as supplements to the basic out-reliefs that might be available from charities, and as a means to avoid the perceived horrors of the workhouse. However, wages – especially of women – were low, and many were unable to afford the membership fees. Applications would not be invited from those thought unable to keep up the payments, or from those engaged in dangerous trades.[213]

On May 30th 1893 the Men's Friendly Society (also known as Ashford Men's Club), which at that time had a membership of 100, held its 'annual feast' at the Devonshire Arms Hotel, 'where a capital spread had been provided by the hostess, Mrs Frost.' In the presence of Revd Luxmoore and other members, the chairman of the meeting, William Hollis Bramwell (who had travelled

The Devonshire Arms, Church Street, Ashford, ca.1910.

up from London for the occasion), said he had a pleasing but somewhat difficult task before him, namely,

'to give expression to the feelings of the members of the club as well as his own towards their worthy treasurer, Mr S Birley. It would be hard to estimate the value of the services Mr Birley had rendered to the club during the last 51 or 52 years. His whole interest had been thrown into

---

[212] *Friendly Societies. Edward William Brabrook & Carroll Davidson Wright. Encyclopædia Britannica, Volume 11, 1911.*

[213] *The fraternity of female friendly societies. Daniel Weinbren. In: Máire Fedelma Cross (ed). Gender and Fraternal Orders in Europe, 1300-2000. Palgrave Macmillan, 2010, p 205.*

the work of the club, and after that long term of service those interests and aids remained unabated. The chairman concluded by handing Mr Birley a purse of gold.

'Mr S Birley responded in feeling terms, expressing his heartfelt gratitude.'[214]

The incredible attention to detail which Samuel applied to marble inlaying had also been brought to bear on the affairs of the Men's Friendly Society. During his half-century of service, he had taken upon himself the task of investigating the accounts since the Club's inception on January 6th 1769. In so doing he had discovered that, in its early history, it might appear (at least to a cynic) that it had existed primarily to benefit its committee, by way of extravagant feasting and drinking, at the expense of its members. Whilst its motto was:

'To help the afflicted is a glorious plan,
It soothes their woes, and dignifies the man' ...

... it was suggested that it should rather have been:

'Professing to help and relieve the afflicted,
But to spending our money in ale are addicted.'[215]

In its defence, this may be due in part to the challenges faced by such societies in attempting to define by trial and error the magnitude of the risks against which they hoped to insure; and how much the members should contribute to meet those risks.

In 1871 Samuel reported that he had reviewed 35 years' worth of the Club's records, analysing the sickness, mortality, contributions, donations, interest, fines, and entrance fees of its members, as well as the cost of its management. This information was entered into what was effectively a table of actuarial data, which Samuel charitably felt should be shared not only with members of his own club, but with other friendly societies as well – there being 'little definite knowledge on the subject of the statistics of sickness and mortality of friendly societies'.

The statistics were duly communicated (less helpfully, perhaps, in prose rather than in tabular form) by the local newspaper's Peak representative, who commented 'it is not astonishing, then, that one of the oldest members of one the oldest friendly societies in the Peak of Derbyshire should be honoured.'

---

[214] *Ashford Men's Friendly Society. Derbyshire Times & Chesterfield Herald, June 3rd 1893.*
[215] *Ibid.*

It is also perhaps not surprising, considering Samuel's ability to report factual matters with such great precision, that it was to him that Revd Luxmoore's son turned when he was compiling his notes on the history of Ashford Church. The evidence provided by Samuel of church and village history, and JS Luxmoore's meticulous transcription of his testimony, have together provided an enduring written legacy to stand alongside Samuel's 'masterpiece of executive power,'[216] revealed in his exquisitely beautiful inlaid Ashford marble table.

Revd Luxmoore officiated at Samuel's funeral service on October 6th 1906:

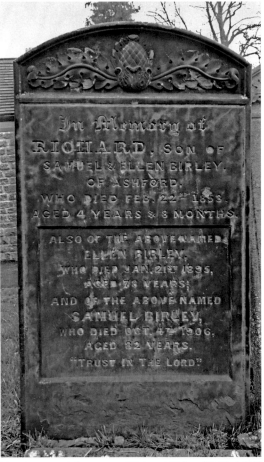

Headstone of the young Richard Birley (1848-1853) and his parents Ellen Birley, née Shaw (1817-1895), and Samuel Birley (1824-1906). Holy Trinity Church, Ashford-in-the-Water.

'In his sermon at the church, on the following Sunday, [he] made a few remarks on the exemplary life of the deceased, and the valuable work he had done in connection with the friendly societies of the village. It may be remarked that nearly every house in Ashford was represented in the churchyard when the remains were lowered to their last resting place.'[217]

That 'last resting place' is marked by a family memorial standing outside the vestry door a few yards from that of Revd John and Rosalie Luxmoore. The inscriptions to Samuel and his wife Ellen are beneath the inscription to their young child Richard.

---

[216] *Object History Note. Victoria & Albert Museum. Museum Number 157&A-1864, http://collections.vam.ac.uk/item/O18958/table-randall-j/*

[217] *Derbyshire Advertiser & Journal, October 12th 1906.*

The Nadaulds and the Brushfields

The origin of the rare Brushfield surname is the tiny agricultural hamlet of Brushfield, about 650 acres in size, set on a remote hilltop with spectacular panoramic views across Monsal Dale south-east to the ancient hill fort, Fin Cop. In Saxon times the place was known as Brihtricfeld: the 'feld' or estate of Brihtric.[218] In 1833 there were just seven houses and 40 inhabitants in this settlement.

Richard Brushfield (1747-1818) was born in Baslow. 'Although but a village blacksmith, he was a man of understanding', and had acquired some property as a result of his marriage to Hannah Blackden (1751-1826).[219] But Richard predeceased his wife, and one of her brothers, who had raised their first-born son, George Brushfield (1772-1825), ensured that George would be disinherited; indeed, he 'cut him off with a shilling'. This was possibly because he was conceived out of wedlock.[220] George, nevertheless, successfully 'rose above the disappointment and became the counsellor and friend of his poorer neighbours.'[221]

The Nadauld family name arrived in Ashford with the Huguenot Protestant refugee, Henri (Henry) Nadauld (1653-1723), who, towards the end of the 17th century, had fled from persecution by the French Catholic government.[222] Born in Île d'Oléron near the Huguenot community of La Rochelle, he was a 'gentleman' shipbuilder, and also a talented amateur sculptor. He escaped with his wife and three children in a fishing boat, concealing some family jewels within his eldest son's clothing. He commenced his new life in England –

---

[218] *The origin of the surname of Brushfield. TN Brushfield. The Reliquary, Vol 26, Bemrose & Sons, Derby & London, 1885-1886, pp 121-128.*

Letter, TN Brushfield. The Reliquary, Vol 1 (new series), J Charles Cox (ed). Bemrose & Sons, Derby & London, 1887, p 115.

[219] *Thomas Brushfield: A Memory. Llewellynn Jewitt. The Reliquary, Vol 16. Llewellynn Jewitt (ed). Bemrose & Sons, Derby & London, 1875-1876, p 210.*

[220] *Richard Brushfield and Hannah Blackden were married by licence on August 22nd 1772; their eldest son George was christened in Sheldon on December 6th 1772. A marriage by licence for a fee, rather than by the calling of banns in church on three successive Sundays, allowed them to marry quickly and with a greater degree of privacy. This was frequently the choice of a couple (or their parents) when the bride was pregnant. George's mother's will was clear that only her 'lawful children' would inherit - it appears that this may have been at the insistence of one of Hannah's brothers.*

[221] *Thomas Brushfield: A Memory. Llewellynn Jewitt. Op. cit., p 211.*

[222] *The word 'refugee' derives from the French word 'réfugié', which referred to Protestants who fled France following the reversal in 1685 of the Edict of Nantes, a law that had granted religious liberty and civil rights to the Protestant Huguenots for nearly a century. Over 400,000 French Protestants left France in the following years, many coming to England. Huguenots. Editors of Encyclopædia Britannica. Encyclopædia Britannica, 2016.*

The stone carvings on Chatsworth's Cascade House are by Henry Nadauld and Heanor-born Samuel Watson (1662-1715).

in Piccadilly, London – making decorative features for houses and gardens, including Hampton Court Palace. In the early 1700s he was attracted by opportunities at Chatsworth House and Castle Howard, by which time he was 'already at the top of the tree … [his] legacy at Chatsworth is magnificent'. His work at Chatsworth includes the stone carvings on the house of the Cascade waterworks. In 1705 he started work at Castle Howard, where 'he spent four and a half years executing much of the vigorous decoration which so enlivened both the inside and outside of Lord Carlisle's house. He was paid a massive £863 13s [an equivalent labour earnings today of £1.8 million].'[223] His financial success is clear from the fact that he purchased considerable property

---

[223] *A Biographical Dictionary of Sculptors in Britain, 1660-1851. Ingrid Roscoe, Emma Hardy & MG Sullivan. The Henry Moore Foundation, Yale University, 2009.*

Chatsworth: The House. The Duchess of Devonshire. Frances Lincoln, London, 2002, p 16.

Thomas Brushfield relates that, at Chatsworth, Henry Nadauld also 'executed the ornaments of the great frieze for the front; he was paid, in 1703, £114 for the ornaments of the great frieze, friezes over the door, cyphers, coronets, &c. He also carved 22 heads for the galleries in the inner courts, for which, and for six vases, he was paid £107 10s. In 1704 he was paid £112 16s for similar work.' The Family of Nadauld. Thomas Brushfield. The Reliquary, Vol 10, Llewellynn Jewitt (ed). Bemrose & Sons, Derby, 1869-1870, pp 116-118.

Creating Paradise: The Building of the English Country House, 1660-1880. Richard Wilson and Alan Mackley. Hambledon, London, 2000, p 167.

For further details of Henry Nadauld's works at Chatsworth and Castle Howard, and payments received, see: Huguenot Artists, Designers and Craftsmen in Great Britain and Ireland, 1680-1760. Tessa Violet Murdoch. Westfield College, University of London, 1982, pp 111-115.

in Ashford-in-the-Water, his chosen place of retirement.

The Brushfield and Nadauld families became linked in 1795 when George Brushfield married Ann Nadauld (1774-1855), the daughter of Revd Thomas Nadauld, who, in turn, was the grandson of Henry Nadauld. Revd Nadauld (1727-1807) was ordained deacon in 1751 and priest in 1752, and became Perpetual Curate of Belper and Turnditch simultaneously and continuously from 1765 until his death.[224] These two parishes are four miles apart and close to Kilburn, his home village.

Richard Nadauld Brushfield (1796-1871)

Richard Nadauld Brushfield, the eldest son of George Brushfield and Ann Brushfield (née Nadauld), was a bachelor liv-

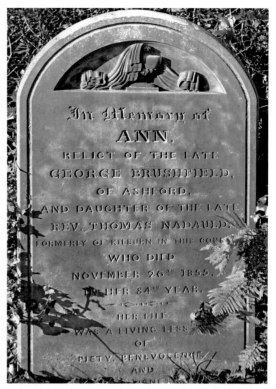

Headstone of Ann Brushfield, née Nadauld (1774-1855). Holy Trinity Church, Ashford-in-the-Water. The inscription ('literally a true one' according to Llewellynn Jewitt, a friend of her son, Thomas Brushfield) reads: 'Her life was a living lesson of piety, benevolence and usefulness.'

ing in the parental home until the age of 63, when he married 36-year-old Elizabeth Hawley – previously a servant in his family's household – in Bakewell Parish Church. A grocer and a farmer, he owned two shops in Ashford-in-the-Water: one at the corner of Church Street and Greaves Lane (still the village shop), and another further west on Church Street (now the Aisseford Tea Room). These he leased to Elizabeth's brother Henry Hawley and, subsequently, Henry's son Joseph.[225]

---

[224] *Clergy of the Church of England Database 1540-1835, https://theclergydatabase.org.uk*

Some records (including the Notes of JS Luxmoore) suggest that, during his curacy at Belper and Turnditch, Revd Thomas Nadauld may have also served variously at Great Longstone ('1755, Thomas Nadauld, curatus.' Longstone Registers. In: The Family of Nadauld. Thomas Brushfield. The Reliquary, Vol 10, Llewellynn Jewitt (ed). Bemrose & Sons, Derby & London, 1869-1870, p 118); Brewood, Staffordshire (where he was married to Elizabeth Emery in 1763); Kilburn 1801; and Horsley.

[225] *A record of changes in Ashford during the 20th century. Compiled by John F Hollingworth. Ashford Time Capsule, 2000.*

He died at the age of 74, and Revd Luxmoore officiated at his funeral service on March 17th 1871. After his death, Elizabeth continued to run the family business, and when she retired at the age of 66 she moved around the corner into a house in Fennel Street. A Brushfield family home on Church Street – Brushfield House[226] – is currently inhabited by descendant relatives of the Hawley family.

The antiquarian Brushfields

Richard Nadauld Brushfield's younger brother, Thomas Brushfield (1798-1875), was also born in Ashford-in-the-Water. Thomas, and his son Thomas Nadauld Brushfield (1828-1910), were antiquarians and 'two able contributors' to Llewellynn Jewitt's (latterly, Revd J Charles Cox's) *Reliquary* journal.

The father-and-son's voluminous writings in *The Reliquary*, and other books, pamphlets and journals, embrace many subjects of local interest, including *Derbyshire Funeral Garlands;*[227] *On Norman Tympana, with especial reference to those of Derbyshire;* [228] and three articles describing *Customs and Notions at Ashford-in-the-Water.*[229] Some 'beautiful lines ... written by Thomas Brushfield on the occasion of the Celebration of Peace' at Ashford, and read by the incumbent of the time, Revd James Burrow, 'elicited much applause'. This was part of a nationwide series of town and village parties that followed the signing of the 1856 Peace Treaty of Paris, which settled the Crimean War.[230]

The enthusiasm of these Victorian antiquarians was infectious and inspired many others. George Thomas Wright, JP, of Longstone Hall, was sufficiently 'animated by such feelings' that were espoused by the elder Brushfield's

---

[226] *'Joseph Brishfield (sic) begun to build his house, that next to the Chandlehouse'. Transcripts of the Diaries of J James Middleton of Ashford (1812-1856). Derbyshire Record Office, D307/H/38/5, entry for February, 1834.*

[227] *Derbyshire Funeral Garlands. TN Brushfield. British Archaeological Association, Vol 6 (new series), Bedford Press, London, 1900, pp 54-74. (Read at the Buxton Congress, July 19th 1899.)*

[228] *On Norman Tympana, with especial reference to those of Derbyshire. TN Brushfield. Journal of the British Archaeological Association, Vol VI, Bedford Press, London, 1900, pp 241-270.*

[229] *Notices of Some Customs and Observances at Ashford-in-the-Water. Thomas Brushfield. The Reliquary, Vol 4, Llewellynn Jewitt (ed). Bemrose & Sons, Derby & London, 1863-1864, pp 206-208.*

Customs and Notions at Ashford-in-the-Water Sixty Years ago. Thomas Brushfield. The Reliquary, Vol 5, Llewellynn Jewitt (ed). Bemrose & Sons, Derby & London, Vol 5, 1864-1865, pp 11-14.

A Second Notice of Customs and Notions at Ashford-in-the-Water Sixty Years ago. Thomas Brushfield. Op. cit., pp 152-155.

[230] *Ashford-in-the-Water and its Church. John Norman, 1961.*

Derbyshire Advertiser & Journal, June 13th 1856.

'many interesting effusions', that he was as a result moved to create his own work, *Longstone Records*, which he completed just one year before his death in July 1907.[231] I have taken the liberty of requoting George Wright's choice of Thomas Brushfield's words for my own epigraph to this book.

John Stonhouse Luxmoore cites many publications by the Brushfields in his historical notes and, as we have seen (see p10), Revd Luxmoore invited Thomas Nadauld Brushfield to present a history of Ashford Church, in the church itself, to the British Archaeological Association.

Thomas Brushfield (1798-1875)

In addition to being a published antiquarian, Thomas Brushfield was 'a self-made man … the architect of his own fortune', which he made after leaving Ashford-in-the-Water for London.

The period from 1670 to 1717 had seen about half of the 50,000 Huguenot refugees in England settling in London after Charles II had offered them sanctuary. Thomas' uncle, William Emery Nadauld (1775-1835), had gone to London in 1788 to be apprenticed to a master clockmaker and, in turn, had become a master clock and watchmaker himself. In 1814 Thomas' brother, Joseph Blackden Brushfield, became apprenticed to William, and when, a year later, the 17-year-old Thomas decided to follow them to London, he stayed initially with Joseph.

After only three weeks Thomas had found work with a tradesman in the oils and pigments business in Covent Garden, and after six years he had learnt enough to go into business on his own account at Union Street in Spitalfields, having 'made up [his] mind to win fortune'.[232] During this time he 'took considerable interest in theatricals … and was ultimately invited to join the Covent Garden company, but declined.'

At the age of 28 Thomas married Susannah Shepley at Horsley Church in Derbyshire, returning to London the same day. His 'theatrical predilections returned to him, and he took up performances under an assumed name, at the City of London Theatre, and was much extolled in the public prints.' But he again chose to forgo the prospects of a life in the theatre in favour of pursuing his business interests, in which he was now assisted by Susannah.[233]

---

[231] *Longstone Records, Derbyshire. GT Wright. Prologue. Benjamin Gratton, Bakewell, 1906.*

[232] *Although Thomas' brother, Joseph Blackden Brushfield, was apprenticed in 1814 to become a clock and watchmaker, he subsequently also became an 'oil and colour man', as (per the census of 1911) did Thomas' and Joseph's great stepnephew, William Hollis Bramwell, nearly a century later.*

[233] *Thomas Brushfield: A Memory. Llewellynn Jewitt. The Reliquary, Vol 16, Llewellynn Jewitt (ed). Bemrose & Sons, Derby & London, 1875-1876, pp 209-216.*

Although there had already been some silk making in the Spitalfields area, the arrival of the Huguenots brought new fashions and highly advanced weaving and patterning skills. Being outside the city walls, they enjoyed the advantage of being free of the restrictive jurisdiction of the city guilds, and Spitalfields became known as 'Weaver Town'. But by the time Thomas Brushfield set up shop there, the silk industry was in severe decline and the East End had become synonymous with urban deprivation. A hotbed of disease, crime and prostitution, it had become an embarrassment to the grand city of London.[234]

Living as a young man in this melting pot, Thomas would have witnessed waves of immigrants from many nations constantly flowing into the area through the docks, bringing with them different languages, ideas, religions, and politics. They made the East End of London not only their physical home, but also their spiritual home: in the temples of the Huguenots; the Roman Catholic churches of the Irish; the synagogues of the Jews; and the Protestant churches of the Danes, Germans and Swedes. Indeed, the building that in 1887 became the church hall of Christ Church, Spitalfields, was, when constructed in 1719, a Huguenot church; between times it had been occupied by Lutherans, Baptists and Methodists.[235]

For its part, the Anglican Church believed that the underlying social problems were due to a lack of moral guidance, and numerous young clergy, many of them followers of the high church Oxford Movement, descended on the East End, whilst the Evangelical William Champneys was drawing an evening congregation of 1,500 to his services at St Mary's, Whitechapel.

Thomas therefore had a fertile hotbed within which to exercise his innate passion for discovering the 'truth' – whether that meant questioning and sifting evidence in his spare time to substantiate his antiquarian researches; discussing and debating religious belief systems and doctrines; or – in what was to become a major focus of attention in his later life at Spitalfields – determining the causes of, and developing social, legal and moral responses to, the challenges of poverty and ill health.

His impulse to engage with different world views was acknowledged in his friend's assessment,[236] that 'Thomas Brushfield went in for Reform and

---

[234] *Later in the 19th century (between 1888 and 1891), 11 unsolved murders of women were to be ascribed to the notorious 'Jack the Ripper'. Flower and Dean Street in the heart of Spitalfields, associated with these murders, was 'perhaps the foulest and most dangerous street in the metropolis'. Spitalfields: The History of a Nation in a Handful of Streets. Dan Cruickshank. Random House Books, 2016, p 467.*

[235] *This is Hanbury Hall. Charles Dickens was a regular visitor in the 1800s and used the building for public readings of his works. Today it continues to serve Shoreditch as a multipurpose community venue.*

[236] *Thomas Brushfield: A Memory. Llewellynn Jewitt. Op. cit., p 213.*

Liberalism' and 'began to imbibe very loose religious and other notions … to become almost a freethinker'.[237]

In his youthful naïvety, this compulsion could get him into trouble, as when he engaged in debate with 'The Devil's Chaplain', Revd Robert Taylor.[238] An Anglican priest and founder of the Christian Evidence Society, Taylor had lost his faith, flouted church authority, and become a freethinker. Following a public meeting in which Taylor, the featured speaker, had been introduced by Thomas Brushfield, they and several others ended up being brought before the court charged with blasphemy and conspiracy to blasphemy. Taylor was found guilty and was imprisoned (just one of several such occasions).[239]

Thomas also participated in political meetings for the furtherance of Catholic Emancipation, a movement that involved reducing and removing many of the restrictions on Roman Catholics, and that also resulted in an undermining of the Anglican supremacy.

Despite these early flirtations with 'very loose religious and other notions' and his dalliances with 'The Devil's Chaplain', he quickly became the quintessential establishment figure: a diligent and successful London businessman endowed with a strong sense of civic duty. But he never completely lost his radical streak.

The year 1832 saw the establishment of a Royal Commission into the Operation of the Poor Laws. This had the goal of replacing a collection of laws introduced from the 16th-18th centuries, that had essentially morphed into a compulsory tax administered at the parish level. The authors of the associated Poor Law Commissioners' Report – Nassau William Senior and Edwin Chadwick – took the view that poverty was the result of the poor embracing their dependent status, expecting relief as their right, rather than it being related to prevailing economic and social conditions; and that benefits recipients had been inappropriately exploiting the 'rules of the welfare game'

---

[237] *A person who holds the viewpoint that truth can be formed only on the basis of logic and reason, and who is sceptical of religious dogma.*

[238] *A Joseph Brushfield, most likely Thomas Brushfield's brother Joseph Blackden Brushfield (1799-1849), along with other supporters 'drawn overwhelmingly from the respectable 'middle sort': ambitious artisans, small shopkeepers and lesser professionals', helped fund in 1826 Robert Taylor's purchase of the 'Areopagus' (named in reference to a sermon delivered by the Apostle Paul in Athens), or Salters' Hall Chapel; it became the headquarters for the Christian Evidence Society. Radical Underworld: Prophets, Revolutionaries and Pornographers in London, 1795-1840. Iain McCalman. Clarendon, 1993, p 190.*

Radical Spaces: Venues of Popular Politics in London, 1790-ca.1845. Christina Parolin. ANU E Press, 2010, pp 199-200.

[239] *Trials of the Reverend Robert Taylor and Others. The Lion, January 18th 1828.*

at local ratepayers' expense.[240] Their evidence comprised selected responses to questionnaires that supported these pre-existing views, including anecdotes provided by the 34-year-old Thomas Brushfield:

'In the pauper's habitation you will find a strained show of misery and wretchedness; and those little articles of furniture which might, by the least exertion imaginable, wear an appearance of comfort, are turned, as it were intentionally, the ugliest side outward ... the clothes of both parents and children, in nine cases out of ten, are ragged, but evidently are so for the lack of the least attempt to make them otherwise.'

'I can decidedly state, as the result of my experience, that when once a family has received relief, it is to be expected that their descendants, for some generations, will receive it also.'[241]

The Royal Commission's report led to the enacting of the Poor Law Amendment Act of 1834, which effectively divided the poor into those who deserved help; and those who did not. The former were those who worked diligently with the aim of supporting their families without the need for financial benefits from the state; the latter would be offered no assistance unless they agreed to enter the workhouse, within which conditions were made harsh to discourage claimants.

Although it is now widely accepted that not all institutions were as bad as contemporary critics such as Charles Dickens portrayed, entering the workhouse nevertheless usually struck terror into working-class communities throughout the latter half of the 19th century.

The New Poor Law in general, and the workhouses in particular, were administered by local Boards of Guardians. Thomas Brushfield was elected in 1836 to the newly-formed Whitechapel Board of Guardians, which included his parish of Christ Church, Spitalfields. Nine months later he was elected vice-chairman and, two years later, chairman – a role he held for nine years. This particular Board was regarded as a model union, regularly cited in government reports.[242]

Brushfield was seen by some as a strong leader, but by others as domineering: it is said that he snapped out his orders 'often before the applicant had stated

---

[240] *Wanting and Having: Popular Politics and Liberal Consumerism in England, 1830-70.* Peter Gurney. *Manchester University Press, 2014, p 68.*

[241] *Poor Law Commissioners' Report of 1834. Nassau William Senior & Edwin Chadwick. HM Stationery Office, Darling and Son, 1905.*

[242] *Finance, Philanthropy, and the Hospital: Metropolitan Hospitals 1850-1898. Keir Waddington. University College London, 1995, pp 32-33.*

his case, or the guardians had had any opportunity of giving their opinions'.[243]

His uncompromisingly unforgiving view of the 'undeserving' poor did not soften with age:

> 'It is impossible, however, to pass over Mr Brushfield's career as a poor-law administrator, for it is in that particular vocation that he will be longest remembered ... Like many so-called self-made and self-confident men, Mr Brushfield could not swallow able-bodied pauperism – could not believe in poverty without infirmity or age or ill health. He regarded pauperism as a crime, and, to use his own words at laying the foundation of the empty workhouse in South Grove, in 1872, 'pauperism should be dealt with by a man without a smile on his face, but firm, inflexible, and with a sort of cast-iron face.' This was the true portrait of Thomas Brushfield, drawn by himself. He regarded pauperism as a thing without sympathy or affections, and its pastures and generating hotbeds he pointed out to be almsgiving and indiscriminate charity – things that came, he admitted, from kind hearts, but which were as great an evil as wickedness.'[244]

However, he had not reached this perspective by speculating from a safe distance on the true need or otherwise of those seeking relief, or by accepting the verbal entreaties of benefit applicants without question. When he first became a parish officer in 1831 he sought personally to verify the facts, devoting 'much exertion (which had never been undertaken before)' to establish an evidence base to support his decision-making.

He would typically receive 40-50 applications for relief within a space of about four hours. Whilst it had been normal practice to give money based simply on the representations and appearance of the claimants, Thomas Brushfield refused to rely on this alone: he requested the names and addresses of the applicants so that he could visit them in their homes.

During such prearranged visits he often found ample evidence that nominally supported their claims – 'the scenes of distress were quite frightful'. But his tactical research approach went further as he made subsequent unannounced visits the following day. This typically revealed quite different pictures with, for example, clear evidence of ample food on the table and clumsy attempts to

---

[243] *This was related by the wife of Canon Samuel Barnett, Vicar of St Jude's Whitechapel. The Canon was a campaigner against the 1834 Poor Law but was nevertheless a confirmed advocate of self-help, and was to join the Board in 1873 after the conclusion of Thomas Brushfield's tenure. Quoted in: Waddington. Op. cit., p 201.*

[244] *The Late Thomas Brushfield, JP. East London Observer, 11th September 1875.*

hide it upon his surprise arrival. He exposed other, equally unsubtle, fraudulent claims when, for example, requests for double relief for a single child had been made by presenting the child in contrasting clothing on two different occasions in the same day.

As a result of this work, he concluded that about a third of claimants provided false addresses and that, overall, only about one in 20 claims was truly 'deserving'.[245]

The 1832 Royal Commission's highly selective evidence base undoubtedly served to produce a prejudiced outcome, and the resulting New Poor Law was consequently severely flawed. But the solution to the 'welfare problem' remains elusive even today, and continues to require judgements of matters that are financially, politically and morally complex.[246]

With the benefit of around 150 years' hindsight, Thomas Brushfield's legacy of Poor Law administration is seen today in a positive light:

> *'Thomas Brushfield ... was responsible for a long period of excellent local governance and many local works in the 19th century, which raised the area's profile and improved the lives of its poorest inhabitants.'[247]*

Nevertheless, the New Poor Law was viewed nationally as an attack on the working class; together with other parallel social injustices, including the treatment of trade unionists, it catalysed a new movement of protest which gained massive support and fuelled the fires of Chartism.[248] In 1840 there was considerable concern throughout London because of the apparent intention of Chartists to resort to violence and the destruction of public property in pursuit of their cause. Anxiety was at its highest in the Tower Hamlets district, including Spitalfields, Whitechapel and Bethnal Green – the principal Chartist meeting places in the city.[249] Large numbers of 'special constables'

---

[245] *Frauds of Paupers. Devizes and Wiltshire Gazette, April 18th 1833.*

[246] *The deserving or undeserving poor? Chris Bowlby. BBC News, November 18th 2010.*

[247] *A bit of history about our vibrant neighbourhood. The Spitalfields Society, est 1992, https://spitalfieldssociety.org/project/a-bit-of-history-about-our-vibrant-neighbourhood/*

[248] *In 1832 voting rights were given to the property-owning middle classes in Britain. Chartism, a reform movement that was most active between 1838 and 1848, had the goal of gaining political rights and influence for the working classes as well.*

[249] *This was the territory of the Metropolitan Police's H Division, later to be the home of the BBC's Ripper Street. In 1846, Thomas Brushfield supported a fundraiser for the otherwise destitute widow of William F Pierse, Superintendent of H Division at the height of the Chartist uprising, who had died and been buried at Christ Church, Spitalfields. East London Record, Colm Kerrigan (ed). East London History Society, 1984, pp 29-31.*

were sworn in to protect local shopkeepers against angry boycotters.[250] Having again taken a central organising role, Thomas Brushfield received a letter of thanks from the Home Secretary.[251]

He became a prominent figure in many other business, civic and church organisations during his lifetime. He was elected a magistrate of Tower Hamlets at 61; a director of the East London Bank at 65; and a Trustee of the London Dispensary – a charitable organisation, founded in 1771, that provided health services for the residents of East London, and that operated until the passage in 1946 of the National Health Service Act.

The 1735 Richard Bridge organ at Christ Church, Spitalfields. The crown over the central tower and the bishops' mitres on the outer towers are indicative of high-church associations.

As well as managing his own oils and paint enterprise, in 1842 Thomas became a director, and subsequently chairman, of the Commercial Gas Company, which had been established in 1837. This was to be his most profitable undertaking: the enterprise was incorporated in 1847 as the Commercial Gas Light & Coke Company. By 1873 it was one of nine companies supplying gas to London, and in 1882 one of only four, ultimately serving Poplar, Stepney, and parts of Bethnal Green and Essex. In 1949 it was nationalised as a part of the North Thames Gas Board.[252]

---

[250] *It is claimed that on April 10th 1848 Charles Dickens enrolled himself as a special constable. Reynolds' Newspaper, June 8th 1851.*

[251] *The Life and Death of Llewellynn Jewitt. William Henry Goss. Henry Gray, London, 1889, p 285.*

[252] *Commercial Gas Company. In: Grace's Guide to British Industrial History, https://www.gracesguide. co.uk; A-Z business listing, London Metropolitan Archives Collections Guide, 2016, p 101.*

At the age of 57 Thomas transferred his Union Street oils and paint business to his younger son Richard, which, more than 20 years later, 'he still honourably and successfully continues'.[253]

Thomas Brushfield was elected churchwarden of Christ Church Spitalfields when he was 37. His work in this capacity was notable almost immediately in the context of a fire that broke out on February 17th 1836 – the day after his 38th birthday:

'The roof of the church was partially destroyed, the magnificent organ damaged to require reconstruction,[254] the finest set of chimes in the kingdom, together with the clock and bells, were destroyed, as well as the whole interior fabric of the massive steeple. Just prior to this calamity, an expenditure of nearly £8,000 had been incurred in repairing and beautifying the church, and the active responsibility cast upon the senior churchwarden of the parish at such a time can be more easily imagined than described. The task of raising the necessary funds was deemed almost impossible, but the word was not in Mr Brushfield's dictionary, and he set to work with that steady business perseverance for which he was remarkable and converted the impossibility into a fact, and the church was repaired and reopened within a comparatively short time, mainly due to the untiring exertion and restless determination of our churchwarden. Corroboration of this circumstance will be found on the tablet recording the fire, and on which his name is inscribed under the massive portico of Christ Church.

'A singular instance of Mr Brushfield's business capacity occurred after the fire just mentioned. The bells were so shivered in pieces by the fall, or fused by the heat, that many of them were not recognisable, but the larger shapeless masses and pieces were removed from the rubbish. Mr Brushfield, passing over the heap one day, examined some of the dirt, and, having some knowledge of the mineral processes in his native

---

[253] *Thomas Brushfield: A Memory. Llewellynn Jewitt. Op. cit., p 216.*

[254] *'Only four large organs could be found in English churches in the 18th century. Those at St Paul's Cathedral, Salisbury Cathedral and St Mary Redcliffe, Bristol have long since disappeared – only the organ at Christ Church remains, and almost the only instrument that bears witness to the vibrant and rich musical life of Georgian London ... After a fire in the steeple in 1836, HC Lincoln was brought in the following year to make repairs necessitated by extensive water damage.' The Friends of Christ Church, Spitalfields. Organ: History, https://www.christchurchspitalfields.org/organ/history.aspx.html*

'One of the most important musical events in London in 2015 was the long-awaited opening of the 1735 Richard Bridge organ (restored by William Drake) in the [Nicholas] Hawksmoor-designed Christ Church, Spitalfields. For many decades it was the largest organ in the UK, and its musical importance is immeasurable.' Andrew Benson-Wilson, https://andrewbensonwilson.org

county, detected the presence of bell metal in the debris, and at once set the men to wash for the metal in accordance with his knowledge, and thus a large quantity of almost infinitesimal particles of metal were saved and a large amount added to the funds. The present eight bells were cast by Messrs Mears at the celebrated bell foundry in Whitechapel[255] and they each bear the name of Thomas Brushfield, as well as that of William Sykes, his co-church-warden.'[256]

Christ Church Spitalfields, along what is now Brushfield Street. 1815.

In March 1870, when Thomas was 72 years old, the Metropolitan Board of Works, together with 36 owners and occupiers of property in Union Street and Union Street East in Spitalfields, unanimously passed an order to rename those streets 'Brushfield Street':

'The name is a well-deserved compliment to a gentleman of strong views in local matters, from whom, consequently, many persons often differ, whose opinion, especially upon matters concerned with the treatment of the poor, have never commanded our unfailing adhesion; but to whose length of service to his parish and district, to whose vigorous common sense, energy, and industry, no sane person at the East of London would think of denying a need of acknowledgement.'[257]

As Thomas looked back on his transformation from a radical youth into a venerated Victorian gentleman, he contemplated on how his former idealism

---

[255] *The sale of the bell metal produced £690 2s and £899 was paid to Thomas Mears of Whitechapel for a new ring of eight bells; one of the bells of this ring was cast in 1836 and the other seven in 1837. Christ Church Spitalfields. Society of Royal Cumberland Youths, https://srcy.org.uk/towers/spitalfields.php*

[256] *The Late Thomas Brushfield, JP. East London Observer, September 11th 1875.*

[257] *East London Observer, March 5th 1870.*

had given way to realism and perhaps a little cynicism:

> *'Like most young thinkers, I thought 'reform' meant really some improvement, true reformation in the proper sense of the word, as I thought 'liberal professions' meant liberality in action; mature years and experience dispels the vision!'*

This reflection was recounted in the contexts of 'the furtherance of Catholic Emancipation', and the 'reform of the 'Representative System'' (no doubt a reference to numerous parliamentary efforts made during the 19th century to tackle the problem of electoral corruption).[258] But it more broadly reflects the hard-headed pragmatism that grew from Thomas Brushfield's deep personal experiences of the extremes of inner-city squalor and rural arcadia; wealth and poverty; ambition and apathy; and radical Dissent and establishment respectability. His disenchantment with the 'liberal professions'[259] has resonance with a specific controversy between his elder brother, Richard Nadauld Brushfield, and Revd Luxmoore, to which we will turn shortly. Thomas Brushfield never excused Revd Luxmoore's attitude in this matter.

In his final tribute to his friend, Llewellynn Jewitt writes, 'Mr Brushfield, ever to the latest moment of his long, useful and successful life, entertained a love, an undying and fervent love, for his native village and its surroundings.'[260]

Dissenting perspectives

The concept of the Nonconformist 'chapel' has long suggested more than a building, and even more than a Dissenting doctrinal and theological perspective. In the 19th century it was allied stereotypically with social class. The Anglican parish church was the 'establishment' place of worship that would serve the gentry and higher class professional ('the Tory party on its knees'), whereas the chapel would serve the labouring and servant classes who 'knew their place'. However, in practice the boundaries were less clear: it was not only the privileged class that paid for pews in the parish church – they were just as likely to be occupied by shopkeepers; villagers might attend 'chapel' in the morning and 'church' in the evening; Methodists might send their children to the parish church school. And perhaps above all in small communities, powerful or charismatic local personalities could

---

[258] *Thomas Brushfield: A Memory. Llewellynn Jewitt. Op. cit., p 213.*

[259] *In the 19th century, the 'liberal professions' were medicine, the law and divinity. The Ritual Culture of Victorian Professionals – Competing for Ceremonial Status, 1838-1877. Albert D Pionke. Routledge, 2016, p 7.*

[260] *Thomas Brushfield: A Memory. Llewellynn Jewitt. Op. cit., p 215.*

significantly influence these stereotypes one way or the other.[261]

Among a bewildering array of Dissenting sects in England, the number of Wesleyan Methodist, Baptist and Congregational chapels alone increased by more than 600 per cent during the first half of the 19th century.[262] Locally, the Religious Census of 1851 showed that about 17 per cent of Derbyshire's population attended Anglican services, and 25 per cent attended a wide variety of Nonconformist places of worship. In Ashford, the percentage of residents attending the parish church on the day of the census was higher than the county average, with 192 people (25 per cent) attending the morning service and 217 (28 per cent) attending the evening service. Eleven per cent of the villagers attended either the Unitarian Chapel (20) or the Wesleyan Methodist Chapel (64). In Sheldon, percentage attendances were roughly similar, with 42 people attending the Anglican service in the old church, and 20 attending the morning service and 40 the evening service at the Primitive Methodist Chapel.[263]

The notion of a single English religious identity had therefore been abandoned, and the Anglican Church no longer had any expectation of privilege or control.[264]

Although boundaries between Anglicanism and Nonconformism were softening towards the end of the 19th century, the seeds of a formal ecumenical movement had yet to be planted. Interdenominational – and, indeed, *intra*denominational – conflict could therefore still generate societal tension.[265] Some examples will show how this was manifested in Ashford-in-the-Water: firstly, through the consequences of the heated national controversy regarding burial laws (p 114);[266] secondly, through the religious sentiments of the village's Huguenot descendants and their family members – especially the Nadaulds and the Brushfields (p 118); and thirdly, through the impact of High Court proceedings brought by the son of a key benefactor of Cliff End Chapel on the operation of Ashford's Thomas Roose charity (p 125).

---

[261] *The Derbyshire Returns to the 1851 Religious Census. Margery Tranter (ed). Derbyshire Record Society, 1995, p xxxv.*

[262] *Ibid., p xiii.*

[263] *Ibid., pp 172, 174, 175.*

[264] *Living Heritage: Religion and Belief – Religion in the 19th century. UK Parliament Website, https://www.parliament.uk/about/living-heritage/transformingsociety/private-lives/religion/overview/religionc19th-/*

[265] *Conflict. James D Davidson and Ralph E Pyle. Encyclopædia of Religion and Society, Chapter 110. William H Swatos, Jr, (ed). Hartford Institute for Religion Research, AltaMira Press, 1998, http://hirr.hartsem.edu/ency/conflict.htm*

[266] *'The living and the dead.' Burial Reform Discourse in Victorian England (ca. 1830-1880). Kelly Mayjonade-Christy. Paris-Sorbonne University, 2019.*

Through these observations, we will catch a glimpse of Revd Luxmoore's reactions to the shifting sands of religious doctrine and practice, including his controversial response to an ostensibly benign provision in the will of Richard Nadauld Brushfield. We will also witness the efforts invested by an aged John Stonhouse Luxmoore – Revd Luxmoore's son – in his attempts to respect Thomas Brushfield's entreaty to care for the grave of his Calvinist maternal great-great-grandfather, Henry Nadauld; a commentary on the extent to which relations between the denominations had improved by the 1930s.

Burial and funeral practices and polemics

The Victorians were preoccupied with death and its associated rituals – not least the question of burial, which was particularly vexing in the context of the Christian doctrine of the resurrection of the body.[267]

Ashford was perhaps unusual for a small 19th-century rural community, in that it had a separate Baptist burial ground: in small villages, it was more typical that the parish church would effectively have exclusive control over local burial sites and practices.

In prior centuries, burial within the church building itself had been common, including at Ashford (see p 178), but by the mid 19th century, health campaigners – notably Edwin Chadwick, who was also an author of the Poor Law Commissioners' Report (see p 105) – argued that this practice and, indeed, burial anywhere close to a densely-populated area, was detrimental to public health. This was hotly disputed by some, however, including the Archdeacon of London, William Hale Hale, who asserted that the abolition of 'intramural' burials (i.e., those within church buildings or their adjacent churchyards) would be 'injurious to religion and morals'.[268]

In towns and cities, the context of the argument was a rapid proliferation of commercial 'extramural' cemeteries beyond their outskirts, but in more sparsely populated villages, concerns had more to do with the purported pros and cons of interments within the church walls, versus outside in the churchyard. In either case, it was alleged that the motives of the various factions sometimes

---

[267] *Death and Funerals. Cynthia Carlton-Ford. In: Sally Mitchell (ed). Victorian Britain – An Encyclopædia. Routledge, Abingdon, Oxfordshire, 2011, p 211.*

Cremation was not pronounced legal until 1884, and it remained essentially a curiosity until the passage in 1902 of the Cremation Act. Even then, growth in the practice remained slow, with only about 9,600 cremations (1.8 per cent of all deaths) taking place annually a third of a century later. By this time, however, episcopal pronouncements in favour of cremation were beginning to be heard. The Cremation Society, Kent, https://www.cremation.org.uk

[268] *Intramural burial in England not injurious to the public health. WH Hale. Addressed to the Clergy of the Archdeaconry of London. Rivingtons, London, 1855.*

went beyond questions of public health, or noble sentiments such as those espoused by Archdeacon Hale. J Charles Cox, for instance, suggested that 'the odious custom' of burials within the church might have been advocated because receipt of the associated 'pit money' from the family of the departed was 'an easy way of adding to church funds'.[269] And some city cemetery companies (albeit a minority) were charged with profiteering from death – most infamously, the London Cemetery Company, which flourished by selling a 'luxury burial service' at its new Highgate Cemetery.[270]

Cox noted that, even in the parish church of the small town of St Neot in Cornwall, 'the number of intramural interments from 1606 to 1708 was 548'. He calculated that 'the whole area of the church must have been stocked with corpses considerably more than twice over within a century. And the process was considerably increased within many town churches.'[271] Indeed, between 1984 and 1986 nearly 1,000 interments were excavated from the burial vaults during the restoration of Christ Church, Spitalfields.[272]

Whether or not this practice was a health hazard, the repeated disturbance of interior paving for burials could lead to subsidence and dangerously uneven flooring: the churchwarden's accounts at Ashford Church refer to repairs having to be made to a vault in the central aisle.[273] Aware of this problem, Sir Christopher Wren created the burial vaults at St Paul's Cathedral with separate access, 'that the pavement above may be preserved'.[274]

People in Bakewell could recall churchyard burials in 1860 where the body, wrapped in a burial shroud, would be transported to the graveside in a reusable parish coffin. However, uncoffined burials were not common by that time. Whether within or without a coffin, the Burial in Woollen Acts of 1666, 1678 and 1680 made it illegal to clothe a body for burial in anything not manufactured from sheep's wool, the goal being to create a new market for woollen cloth. Excepted from this rule were the destitute, for whom wool would have been unaffordable, as well as victims of the plague. The parish

---

[269] *Churchwardens' accounts from the 14th century to the close of the 17th century. J Charles Cox. Methuen & Co Ltd, London, 1913, p 169.*

[270] *The Origins and Progress of Cemetery Establishment in Britain. Julie Rugg. In: The Changing Face of Death. PC Jupp et al (eds). Palgrave Macmillan, London, 1997, pp 105-106.*

[271] *Churchwardens' accounts. J Charles Cox. Op. cit.*

[272] *The Spitalfields Project. Vol 1, The Archaeology: Across the Styx. Jez Reeve & Max Adams. Council for British Archaeology, York 1993.*

[273] *This was the vault of the infant, Mary Swann Bullock, see pp 178-179. John Stonhouse Luxmoore. Derbyshire Record Office, D7672/Lx.C-30.*

[274] *His Invention So Fertile: A Life of Christopher Wren. Adrian Tinniswood. Pimlico, London, 2002, p 190.*

priest was required to maintain a register of affidavits confirming adherence to the law, but, notwithstanding, it was essentially impossible in practice to prove compliance, and the statutes were for the most part ignored. There is one affidavit recorded in the Ashford parish registers in 1718, but against no specific burial entry. After that, no affidavits are documented until October 7th 1729, in respect of the burial of William Stone. There were then nine others, the last being on March 6th 1739 (Joshua Brettnor of Nether Haddon). The Burial in Woollen Acts were repealed in 1814.[275]

The Faculty[276] for Revd Luxmoore's restoration of Ashford Church appropriately required that 'any bodies or remains there may be found shall be decently and properly reinterred' (see p178). The last burial within the walls of Ashford Church had taken place more than 20 years earlier, in 1846; thereafter, burials were in either the churchyard or the Baptist graveyard, until the latter closed in the early 20th century.[277] In 1933, when the churchyard reached capacity, land was acquired by the Parish Council for a new cemetery adjacent to Hall Orchard (see p204).

Dissenters across the nation objected vociferously to being required to adhere to Anglican traditions and rituals for burials in church-controlled graveyards.[278] Indeed, the burgeoning growth of municipal cemeteries in Britain in the 1820s and 1830s was substantially a result of the fact that they were beyond the control of the Church of England; in addition, the cemetery companies were frequently owned by Nonconformists.[279] The Dissenters' protestations were reaching a climax when, on March 3rd 1876, the Liberal MP Sir George Osborne Morgan introduced a motion in the House of Commons that would permit burials to be performed in churchyards by people other than the incumbents themselves, and even without the requirement for burial services. His resolution passed with a small majority (Ayes 279; Noes 248)[280] and a new Burial Act came into law in 1880. This protected the right of any

---

[275] *John Stonhouse Luxmoore. Derbyshire Record Office, D7672/Lx.C-30.*

[276] *Faculty jurisdiction is the process that allows the Church of England to care for alterations to its buildings outside the secular listed building system. The legal document that confirms approval for such works to proceed is known as a faculty. The Glossary. Church of England Alphabetical Companion, https://www.churchofenglandglossary.co.uk/dictionary/d_to_g*

[277] *Based on the surviving gravestone inscriptions, the last burial in the Baptist graveyard was in 1904; see grave no. 13, p 250.*

[278] *'The living and the dead.' Burial Reform Discourse in Victorian England (ca.1830-1880). Kelly Mayjonade-Christy. Paris-Sorbonne University, 2019, pp 4-5.*

[279] *The Origins and Progress of Cemetery Establishment in Britain. Julie Rugg. Op. cit., pp 109-110.*

[280] *Burial Services in Parish Churchyards – Resolution. Hansard. House of Commons. Volume 227, March 3rd 1876.*

relative, friend, or legal representative to take responsibility for the burial of a deceased person, with or without any associated religious service.

Even before the passage of the Burial Act, however, different members from Ashford families could be found buried in both the churchyard and the Baptist graveyard: George Brushfield (1772-1825) was buried in the latter, where his son Thomas Brushfield 'placed there a gravestone to his memory' with the 'lines of his own composing'.[281] However, Thomas Brushfield himself, his brother Richard Nadauld Brushfield, and even George's wife, Ann Brushfield, née Nadauld (see p 101), were all buried in Holy Trinity churchyard. Similarly, the master marble inlayer Samuel Birley and his wife, Ellen, buried their young son, Richard, in the churchyard. However, Samuel's parents, Samuel Birley, Sr (1795-1870) and Ann Birley, née Mawrey (1794-1870), were buried in the Baptist graveyard, as were his two sisters, Mary Ann (1814-1831) and Mary (1837-1849) – see grave no. 17, pp 250-251. Samuel and Ellen themselves were subsequently buried in the churchyard, in the same grave as their son (see p 98).[282]

As was noted earlier in the case of Revd Luxmoore's great-granduncle, Charles, funerals could be elaborate affairs even before the Victorian era – at least for those who had the money (see p 48). But for those who didn't, and who had to be buried at the expense of the parish, the survivor's family could be destined to bear a lifelong stigma. The funeral had become society's final judgement on a person's life and his relationship to society, where social standing could depend more on acquired attributes and wealth, than on any sense of inherent worth.[283]

Although this picture may, more often than not, have been true in the most rapidly growing urban areas, there is increasing evidence that in rural areas the situation could be less stark, the pressure of local conventions and expectations dictating the scale and form of pauper funerals. Indeed, it was not unusual for paupers to be laid to rest in decorated coffins with appropriate ceremony, the parish authorities responding with benevolence and feeling.[284]

---

[281] In 1876 George's gravestone was 'now ruthlessly broken to pieces and scattered about.' Thomas Brushfield: A Memory. Llewellynn Jewitt. Op. cit., p 211. However, it was at some subsequent time replaced with a new stone. See grave no. 4, p 247; Additional Note 3, p 252.

[282] Ashford-in-the-Water, Holy Trinity Monuments. Revd Clive Thrower, http://www.thrower.org.uk/ashford/monuash.htm

The Nadauld Family. The Reliquary, Vol 16. Llewellynn Jewitt (ed). Bemrose & Sons, Derby & London, 1875-1876, p 225.

[283] Bodies, Death, and Pauper Funerals. Thomas Laqueur. Representations, No 1, University of California Press, 1983, pp 109-131.

[284] 'Begging for a Burial': Form, Function and Conflict in 19th-Century Pauper Burial. Elizabeth Hurren & Steve King. Social History, Vol 30. Taylor & Francis, Ltd, 2005, pp 321-341.

Towards the close of Revd Luxmoore's ministry most villagers in Ashford would be paying about 1s per week to the Friendly Society, to help defray the cost of future medical and funeral expenses. There is also certainly the sense that generous villagers, such as Alice Mary Dawson's grandmother, Fanny Thorpe, would rally round at times of need:

'Life began and ended in the home and my grandma was there to assist. ... She used to carry a black bag with ... in the case of death, lavender water and eau de cologne to sprinkle in the room and on the body ...

'When laying out she carried a coffin-shaped board to prepare and lay the body on, until the coffin arrived. Later she assisted the undertaker in placing the body into the coffin ... Grandma was paid around 2s 6d to 5s for her services [a labour value today of around £40 to £80].'[285]

The religious sentiments of Huguenot families

The Calvinist convictions of Henry Nadauld were sufficiently intense that he risked a dangerous journey from France in the hope of finding a more spiritually tolerant society in England (see p 99). He, and some of his fellow refugees, wishing to retain elements of their Huguenot religious identity, naturally attached themselves to one of England's Dissenting sects. Over time, however, some of Henry's descendants were to become associated with the Established Church, including his great-granddaughter, Ann Brushfield, who was buried in Holy Trinity's churchyard (see p 101). Ann's father, Revd Thomas Nadauld, had even become a minister in the Anglican Church, and his case was not unique amongst Huguenots and their descendants.

Many families from the nobility were quick to employ Huguenot refugees as tutors for their children, or in other important capacities. Thus, we find Monsieur Huet – a Huguenot who was Henry's supervisor at Chatsworth – acting as a steward to William Cavendish, 1st Duke of Devonshire. Like Revd Thomas Nadauld some 50 years later, Huet had aspirations of becoming an Anglican clergyman. He wrote in 1700 that he would, however, find it difficult to take up a living that had been offered to him – because of his struggles with the English language, rather than anything related to his Calvinist heritage.[286]

Another family of Huguenot descent – the Olivier family – 'is remarkable for

---

[285] *My Ashford: A Century Past. Alice Mary Dawson. Robert Dawson (ed). Peak Advertiser, Bakewell, 2017, pp 8-9, 33.*

[286] *Huguenot Artists, Designers and Craftsmen in Great Britain and Ireland, 1680-1760. Tessa Violet Murdoch. Westfield College, University of London, 1982, pp 12-13.*

a profusion of clergymen'.[287] Revd Jourdain Olivier (1643-1709), a Huguenot pastor from Pau in south-western France, fled to Holland in 1683, and in 1688 became chaplain to the champion of Protestantism, William of Orange, at the commencement of the *Glorious Revolution*. The consequent successful deposition of the Catholic King James II by William and his wife Mary (the daughter and heir to James II) resulted in William and Mary becoming joint monarchs; and in William – a Calvinist from the Dutch Reformed Church – becoming a Nonconformist head of the Church of England. To reward Nonconformists for their support of William and Mary, and to demonstrate unity between the Church and Nonconformists, the 1689 Toleration Act allowed them freedom of worship, albeit with limited doctrinal flexibility.[288]

Seven generations later we find a direct descendent of Revd Jourdain Olivier – William Herbert Olivier (1904-1992) – living at Ashford Hall with his wife Kitty. William and Kitty are memorialised in the stained-glass 'Olivier window' in the north aisle of Holy Trinity Church (see p 187).

As well as Revd Jourdain Olivier – who was William Herbert Olivier's fifth great-grandfather – William's grandfather, Henry Arnold Olivier (1826-1912); second great-grandfather, Daniel Stephen Olivier (1755-1826); and fourth great-grandfather, Jerome Olivier (1687-1724), were also clergymen, as were other close relatives.[289]

The burial and reinterment of Henry Nadauld

Henry Nadauld retained his Dissenting views. He was buried not in the parish churchyard, but, in what appears to be a unique case, in the Presbyterian Chapel at Cliff End[290] (see p 239). A funeral sermon was delivered by Revd John Ashe, and the epitaph on the plain stone that covered Henry's remains, read,

> *'Here lies the body of Henry Nadauld, carver,*
> *who departed this life July 3rd 1723, aged 70 years.'[291]*

---

[287] *Laurence Olivier: A Biography. Donald Spoto. Harper Collins, New York, 1992, p 2.*

Olivier. In: Protestant Exiles from France, Vol 2. David CA Agnew. 1886, Book 3, Chap 18, Sec 15.

[288] *William was not successful, however, in also obtaining parliamentary approval for toleration for Catholics, who he was hoping to recruit as allies against Louis XIV of France; Catholic Emancipation would not be delivered until the passage in 1829 of the Roman Catholic Relief Act.*

[289] *Revd Daniel Stephen Olivier was Rector of All Saints' Church, Clifton, Bedfordshire, as was his son, Daniel Josias Olivier (1789-1858), who was William Herbert Olivier's great-granduncle. Revd Henry Arnold Olivier was Rector at St Peter's Church, Poulshot, Wiltshire.*

[290] *Henry Nadauld: A Biographical Dictionary of Sculptors in Britain, 1660-1851. Ingrid Roscoe, Emma Hardy & MG Sullivan. The Henry Moore Foundation, Yale University, 2009.*

[291] *The Family of Nadauld. Thomas Brushfield. The Reliquary, Vol 10, Llewellynn Jewitt (ed). Bemrose & Sons, Derby & London, 1869-1870, p 117.*

Thomas Brushfield provided in his will for the Ashford Men's Friendly Society to 'maintain in decent order … [the grave of] … my maternal ancestor, the late Henry Nadauld (in the Chapel at Cliff End).' Circumstances made this impossible when the chapel became disused and finally collapsed in 1937, 62 years after Thomas had died. JS Luxmoore immediately took it upon himself to notify the vicar, Revd Henry Ernest Sherlock, who was then on holiday. In his reply, Revd Sherlock anticipated the difficulty of disposing of the property whilst at the same time treating Henry Nadauld's grave with due respect.[292]

Demolished by Vibration

Mr. H. C Hill, of Watcombe-circus, Nottingham, told me last night that during the day he drove along the Manchester-Bakewell road and spent his last film on photographing the ruins of the 200-year-old Unitarian Chapel at Ashford which had collapsed in the morning.

"It was a strange sight," he said, "to see an arched window lying by the side of the road and several pews sticking up out of the debris.

"Rumblings were heard by nearby residents on two occasions the night before. At 9.30 this morning a big lorry passed and the building collapsed.

"I was told the chapel was founded by the French Huguenots. It was last used as a chapel 23 years ago."

Report of the collapse of Cliff End Chapel in 1937.

JS Luxmoore also contacted promptly an old acquaintance, James William Wylde, who informed him that, when he had bought the chapel some years previously, he had not been permitted to have the building converted to another use whilst Henry Nadauld's body was still there. Mr Wylde had engaged a solicitor to advise him as he pursued this and 'other proceedings' with the Home Secretary, at a personal cost of more than £20. The 'other proceedings' included exhumation of the body and its reinterment in the churchyard of Holy Trinity Church. However, it did not include removal and reinstatement of the gravestone; Mr Wylde confirmed that he would be happy for JS Luxmoore to arrange for this, but cautioned him that he would be unable to contribute any further costs. Mr Wylde died 15 months later, apparently never having recovered from the shock of the chapel's collapse.[293]

By December 1938 Ashford Parish Council was anxious to remove the remains of the chapel to the village tip, prompting a comment that this would be a 'queer resting place for consecrated material'. The following month

[292] Letter from Henry Sherlock to JS Luxmoore, August 7th 1937. Derbyshire Record Office, D7672/Lx.C-47/39.

[293] Letter to JS Luxmoore from JW Wylde, dated September 6th 1937; Letter to JS Luxmoore from Jane Wylde, dated December 28th 1938. Derbyshire Record Office, D7672/Lx.C-47/39.

JS Luxmoore stepped in again. Although by then aged 75 and living in Sheffield, he obtained a quotation of £7 0s 0d, not only to remove four feet of accumulated rubble from the chapel, but also to recut the lettering on the gravestone and to relocate it. Anticipating that he would be unable to bear the cost himself, he had earlier inquired whether Archibald Nadauld Brushfield, the son of Thomas Nadauld Brushfield, might wish to make a contribution. Notwithstanding the latter's own apparently worsening financial situation, he indicated that he would be willing to help support the expense of moving the stone. JS Luxmoore had also contacted the Huguenot Society of London, who hinted that help could possibly be forthcoming.[294]

On the day that he received the quotation for the removal of the gravestone, JS Luxmoore had travelled from Sheffield to Ashford and was told that Henry Nadauld's body had been found to be lying not directly beneath the stone, but a short distance from it. He therefore started working immediately to confirm that the body now reinterred in the churchyard was indeed that of Henry Nadauld.[295] However, he was to die himself the following year, and we have no record of whether this burning question has ever been fully resolved.

The burial of Thomas Brushfield

As we have seen (see p 105), Thomas Brushfield at one time came close to becoming a freethinker. Although he served as a steadfast churchwarden of Christ Church, Spitalfields, his religious opinions remained controversial to the end. He was keenly aware of the ongoing burial law arguments, making his own position clear in a codicil to his will written three months before his death. He stated his desire that 'my Executors if and so far as they may find it practicable (having regard to the Ecclesiastical and State Law in force at the time of my decease) to cause to be omitted *The Order for the Burial of the Dead* as contained in the Book of Common Prayer either in the church or churchyard [of Holy Trinity, Ashford-in-the-Water].' Osborne Morgan's resolution was not passed until six months after Brushfield's death, and the new Burial Act four years after that, so we do not know whether Revd Luxmoore acceded to Thomas' request not to use the Anglican burial service.[296]

---

[294] *Letter to JS Luxmoore from Jane Wylde, op. cit.; memo from Ebenezer D Gregory to JS Luxmoore, January 10th 1939; letter from AN Brushfield to JS Luxmoore, January 26th 1938; letter by JS Luxmoore, January 11th 1939 (unsigned). Derbyshire Record Office, D7672/Lx.C-47/39.*

[295] *Letter by JS Luxmoore, January 11th 1939, op. cit.*

[296] *The officiating minister at Thomas Brushfield's funeral on September 7th 1875 was Revd Luxmoore's friend, Revd William H White. This, together with the fact that Revd Laxon E Sweet, Vicar of Great Longstone, officiated at subsequent funerals on September 9th and 10th, suggests that Revd Luxmoore may have been away from home, or ill, at the time.*

The Richard Nadauld Brushfield memorial controversy

Thomas Brushfield's brother, Richard Nadauld Brushfield, would have been dismayed to know that in 1874, three years after his death, a stipulation in his will would trigger a very public and emotionally charged dispute between the vicar and the villagers of Ashford. To the consternation of many, Revd Luxmoore rejected what they believed to be a quite reasonable request: that a memorial tablet be placed in the church, detailing Richard's bequest to the 'most needy and deserving' of the village residents.

Directly contrasting this refusal to Rochester Cathedral's permission to mount a brass plaque in honour of Charles Dickens,[297] 'A Lover of Truth' wrote to the *Derbyshire Times & Chesterfield Herald,*

> *'This curate, or vicar, or whatever he calls himself, cannot have much of his master's spirit in him to refuse so reasonable a request; and, seeing what has taken place at Rochester, it strikes me forcibly that some petty, spiteful feeling, which should never have a place in the breast of a minister of Christ, has caused the unholy, unchristian and unjust deed to be done ... I am told that our Member of Parliament, who resides at Ashford, countenances and defends the vicar ... I have great regard for Lord Cavendish and voted for him at the last election, but he must satisfy me that he is in no way a party to this folly and injustice respecting the tablet at Ashford – a subject now widely discussed – or I cannot support him again.'[298]*

Moreover, a decade later, in announcing the funeral of Benjamin Bretnor (1811-1884) – once the village's butcher, the largest landowner in the village (apart from the Duke of Devonshire), and 'a strong supporter of Dissent' – it was said that,

> *'on more than one occasion [Benjamin Bretnor] found himself in direct opposition to the clergyman of the village, especially in the opposition of the latter to the erection of a monument in the church in memoriam of Mr Brushfield, who was a large donor to the local charities, &c.'[299]*

---

[297] *Dickens' religious views might today be characterised as 'liberal Christian': he 'disliked and mocked displays of piety, but he maintained a reverential attitude towards the idea of God throughout his life'; although 'happy with Christian prayers and precepts [he] did not care about denominations and was determined to avoid heavy preaching, heavy moralising and calls for penitence'. Charles Dickens: A Life. Claire Tomalin. Penguin Books, 2001, pp 137 and 204.*

[298] *Letter to the Editor dated January 5th 1874. Derbyshire Times & Chesterfield Herald, January 17th 1874.*

[299] *Notice of the Funeral of Mr Benjamin Bretnor. Derby Daily Telegraph, March 27th 1884.*

In 1831, Benjamin Bretnor's brother, Joseph (1801-1835), almost certainly a Unitarian, had been elected trustee of the Thomas Roose Charitable Trust. See Attorney-General v Samuel Shore, p 125.

Although the parish record for Benjamin Bretnor's burial in Ashford churchyard is written in Revd Luxmoore's hand, he did not officiate at the ceremony. It was not unusual for a visiting clergyman to officiate at burials at Ashford Church, but in this case the burial was 'certified by Richard Bramwell of Ashford', a joiner. In accordance with the provisions of the new Burial Act that had become law four years earlier, this could not be refused by Revd Luxmoore.

Richard Bramwell (1849-1919) was born into a family of Dissenters. But – as is the case for other Ashford families – his forebears are found buried in both the churchyard and the Baptist cemetery. He was the grandson of Frances Bramwell (née Brushfield), the only child from George Brushfield's first, short-lived marriage, prior to his second marriage to Ann Nadauld.[300] Frances, her husband William and six of their children (four of whom died young), are all buried – as was Frances' father George Brushfield – in the Baptist cemetery (see graves no. 4, 12 & 13, pp 247, 249, 250). However, their first-born son, George Bramwell (1815-1888),[301] and his wife Leah, née Hollis (1819-1875), are buried in Ashford churchyard – notwithstanding the fact that the Baptist cemetery was still in use at the time of their death. In fact, it was George Bramwell's brother, Robert Bramwell (1830-1904), who was the last to be buried there, 16 years later.[302] George and Leah's son (Richard the joiner) is buried in the churchyard in the same grave as his parents.

Richard Nadauld Brushfield's memorial tablet controversy even gets a mention in John Norman's history of the parish, and is reprinted in the current church guidebook:

'Don't be misled into thinking that life in Victorian Ashford was always idyllic, however. The following excerpt is from a letter written in dialect in 1874 from Tommy of Sheldon to Sammy of Ashford, and later printed. The robust sentiments it contains were inspired by the refusal of the vicar to allow a memorial to the prominent Methodist, Thomas Brushfield (sic – see footnote 303), to be placed in church ...'

In this letter, Tommy seems to be attempting to help pour oil on troubled waters as he writes diplomatically to Sammy:

---

[300] *Mary Bretnor, Benjamin Bretnor's mother, was a witness to the marriage of William Bramwell (1788-1845) and Frances Brushfield (1790-1843) on October 31st 1814.*

[301] *George, a tallow chandler, was the stepcousin of Thomas Brushfield, and was an Executor and Trustee of Thomas' will.*

[302] *It will be recalled that the chairman at the May 30th 1893 Men's Friendly Society meeting honouring Samuel Birley was William Hollis Bramwell (see p 96); William Hollis Bramwell (1846-1918) was the elder brother of Richard Bramwell.*

'A deed loik ar owd friend Brushfilt's conna be smuthert ... ber moind-lad we munna be hard on parsons – they're only flesh and blood loik ourselves ... en however weak they are or stupid they seemen, su as thay downe theor best – accordin to their powers – pay them always proper respect'.[303]

We do not know whether the reason for Revd Luxmoore's refusal to accommodate the tablet in church was a result of Richard Nadauld Brushfield's religious beliefs (or lack of them). Perhaps it was because the vicar objected to the explicit requirement, inscribed prominently on the memorial, that the income from Richard's bequest should be distributed to the villagers 'without reference to their religious sentiments and opinions'; this was a clear challenge, designed to deter any future incumbent from attempting to restrict the beneficiaries of Richard Nadauld Brushfield's generosity for the reasons of religious belief.[304]

When Richard's younger brother, Thomas Brushfield, died in 1875, one year following the memorial tablet controversy, he left a bequest to the Ashford Men's Friendly Society, which was conditional on the stipulation that the Society would ensure that 'the tablet prepared under the direction contained in my late brother Richard's will has been permitted to be permanently affixed in the Parish Church, Ashford-in-the-Water.' This ultimately had its intended effect, as the memorial tablet now sits prominently on the west wall of the vestry.

THIS TABLET
*is placed here
in accordance with the Will of*
RICHARD NADAULD BRUSHFIELD
an old Inhabitant of this Village,
who died on the
13th March 1871.
and who left the sum of
Two Hundred and Fifty Pounds;
THE NET INCOME FROM WHICH TO BE DISTRIBUTED IN THE MONTH OF JANUARY IN EACH YEAR AMONG SUCH OF THE INHABITANTS OF THE TOWNSHIP OF ASHFORD AS THE TRUSTEES OR TRUSTEE FOR THE TIME BEING OF THE MONIES SO INVESTED SHALL IN HIS OR THEIR JUDGMENT DEEM TO BE MOST NEEDY AND DESERVING, "WITHOUT REFERENCE TO THEIR RELIGIOUS SENTIMENTS AND OPINIONS".

Richard Nadauld Brushfield's generous bequest for the support of Ashford villagers is memorialised on a tablet mounted on the west wall of the vestry in Holy Trinity Church, Ashford-in-the-Water.

---

[303] *Holy Trinity Church, Ashford-in-the-Water, 1996, pp 15-16. The comment that Thomas Brushfield was the subject of the memorial is incorrect; the error also appears in John Norman's earlier editions, i.e., Ashford-in-the-Water and its Church. John Norman, 1961, 1979.*

[304] *There is a little further evidence that Revd Luxmoore was clearly a man of strong principles, that may on occasion have verged on the dogmatic: he was criticised for not permitting an 'artificial memorial' to be laid on the grave of a young man, John Gregory. The 'natural resentment' of the villagers was all the more unforgiving because the artificial wreath in question had been paid for by subscriptions from his colleagues at his employer, the grocers Messrs Orme & Co of Bakewell. Derby Daily Telegraph, July 28th 1905.*

Thomas Brushfield had also penned for Richard's tombstone the inscription:

> *Farewell dear friend – thy spirit now is free:*
> *Thy deeds – though found not on the scroll of fame –*
> *By grateful hearts shall long remembered be,*
> *And all who knew thy worth shall bless thy name.*[305]

Could Thomas' controversial desire, that *The Order for the Burial of the Dead* should not be read at his own funeral, be a final protestation against Revd Luxmoore's apparent intransigence regarding Richard's memorial tablet?

Attorney-General v Samuel Shore and the Thomas Roose Trust

As well as ongoing conflicts between the Anglo-Catholic and Evangelical wings of the Established Church, and between the Established Church and Dissenters, there were also long-standing frictions between Trinitarian and Unitarian Dissenters, and frustration with legislation that prohibited Unitarian worship. Only with the passage of the Doctrine of the Trinity Act of 1813 was a requirement of the 1697 Blasphemy Act rescinded, under which Christians had been required to uphold the doctrine of the Holy Trinity. The Trinity Act also overturned a requirement of the Toleration Act of 1689 that had allowed Dissenting worship only if a Trinitarian theology was adhered to. Under the 1813 Act, therefore, Unitarianism became legal, and Unitarians were free to practise their religion without fear of prosecution.

In 1704 and 1705 the Dissenter and heiress Lady Sarah Hewley (1627-1710) arranged that income from her estate should support 'poor and godly preachers for the time being of Christ's holy gospel.' By the end of the 18th century, all the trustees managing her bequest were Unitarian, and other Dissenting orders were concerned that the income was not being distributed fairly.[306] In 1830 legal proceedings were brought in the High Court of Chancery by the Unitarian Samuel Shore and other Dissenters to settle the matter.[307] The ruling of 1833, upheld in 1836 and 1842 following two appeals, went against the Unitarians, and endorsed the view that a Trinitarian commitment was necessary in order to benefit from the Hewley Trust. The Unitarian trustees were duly replaced with three Congregationalists, three Orthodox Presbyterians, and one Baptist.[308]

---

[305] *Thomas Brushfield: A Memory. Llewellynn Jewitt. Op. cit., footnote, p 210.*

[306] *York Civic Trust, http://yorkcivictrust.co.uk/heritage/civic-trust-plaques/lady-sarah-hewley-1627-1710/*

[307] *Attorney-General v Samuel Shore and others. Chancery, information filed June 30th 1830, and House of Lords, National Archives, Kew, Ref. TS 11/789/2547.*

[308] *The Unitarians Defeated. Substance of the Judgment Delivered December 23rd 1833. James Fraser, London, 1834.*

As a direct response, the Unitarian Dissenter Edwin Wilkins Field (1804-1871) pressed for the introduction of legislation that resulted in the passage of the Dissenters' Chapels Act in 1844. This Act ruled that the right of possession of a chapel could not be challenged on doctrinal grounds, as long as the congregation had worshipped there for 25 years.[309]

The Samuel Shore (1761-1836) of the eponymous High Court proceedings was the son of the Samuel Shore (1738-1828) who, together with Robert Newton, 'had practically rebuilt the [Ashford Cliff End] Chapel, and invested £300 in 3 per cent consols for the benefit of the minister', who at that time was a Revd Evans (see p 240).

The elder Samuel Shore, who lived latterly at Meersbrook Hall, had been born into one of Sheffield's most wealthy families. He was to become a prominent Dissenter, and a key member among the Manchester and Sheffield abolitionists.[310] The Shores were founder members of Sheffield's Upper Chapel on Norfolk Street, which was built in 1700 for the use of Dissenters.[311] At that time the Shores were Presbyterians, but, swept up in a powerful trend across England, their allegiance gradually shifted towards Unitarianism,[312] as did that of Revd Evans and succeeding ministers at Cliff End Chapel.[313]

Within a year of the initiation of the High Court action, a deed was executed to appoint new trustees to Ashford's 1761 charitable bequest from Thomas Roose (see p 166). The Roose Trust stipulated that a sum of 40 shillings a year should be paid to 'the minister of the Presbyterian Dissenting Chapel of Ashford', and that an additional sum of 20 shillings per year should be paid to the 'curate of Ashford'. This deed transferred responsibility for administering the Roose Trust to Revd John Browne, then the incumbent of the parish

---

[309] *Nonconformist Places of Worship. Christopher Wakeling. Historic England, Paul Stamper (ed). 2016, p 6.*

[310] *The mobilisation of public opinion against the slave trade and slavery: Popular abolitionism in national and regional politics, 1787-1838. Mark Jones. Dissertation, University of York, 1998, pp 31, 78, 81.*

[311] *Time Walk Project: Promoting Sheffield's Heritage, https://sheffieldtimewalk.wordpress.com /2018/10/03/samuel-shore-the-quiet-reformer-1738-1828/*

[312] *Although the label 'Presbyterian' grew to be associated in England with Unitarianism, Unitarian ideology lay in the broader theology of 'Dissent', rather than in any clearly differentiated denominational beliefs. The causes and conditions for Unitarianism were less to do with denominational factors, than with socio-economic matters such as congregational wealth and educational status of the clergy. Did the English Presbyterians Become Unitarian? Russell E Richey. Church History, Vol 42, 1973, pp 58-72.*

[313] *Transactions of the Congregational Historical Society, Vol VI, 1913-1915, pp 349-350.*

church, and a roster of new trustees.[314] This roster included none other than the younger Samuel Shore. Revd Browne – there to protect the interests of the 'curate of Ashford' – was now likely the sole Trinitarian trustee and, as of August 24th 1831, Cliff End Chapel was 'in the hands of the Unitarians'.[315]

Four months later, on December 30th 1831, another deed was entered into, this time by the trustees of Ashford's Methodist Chapel, one of whom was George Oldfield. George was a descendant of Jane Oldfield, the mother of Revd William Bagshawe, for whom Cliff End Chapel had originally been built (see pp 241-242). The Methodists were possibly unhappy with the Unitarian 'take-over' of what had theretofore been a Presbyterian chapel; their own legal arrangement was perhaps put into effect, at least in part, to help ensure that the Methodist Chapel could not also come under the control of the Unitarians.

As soon as the case of *Attorney-General v Samuel Shore* had commenced, the new trustees of the Roose Trust decided to discontinue payments to the minister of Cliff End Chapel. This may have been because they felt that they were legally constrained by the 1761 Trust to make payments only to a Presbyterian minister (the minister at the time being Unitarian), or perhaps because they wished to await the outcome of the High Court proceedings. In the event, the minister went without this income for a long time, because *Attorney-General v Samuel Shore* – in the manner of *Jarndyce v Jarndyce* in Charles Dickens' *Bleak House* – was not definitively concluded for a further 12 years.

Three years after the last and final decision had been handed down, (by which time the Dissenters' Chapels Act had come into force), the Unitarian minister of the Cliff End Chapel sought an opinion from a barrister of the Honourable Society of Lincoln's Inn, still having not received any income from the Roose Trust since the new trustees had been appointed. He asserted that 'he has an undisputed right to the 40 shillings a year and the arrears thereof, and threatens to take proceedings against the trustees for the arrears remaining unpaid.'[316]

The barrister deliberated whether the Roose Trust was legally associated with the physical chapel building on Cliff End Lane, and whether the references in the Roose Trust's deed to a 'Presbyterian' minister could be enforced in the context of the new Dissenters' Chapels Act – especially since the Roose Trust deed did not prescribe that the minister should preach any particular doctrine.

---

[314] *Per the deed dated August 24th 1831, the new trustees appointed to manage Thomas Roose's 1761 charitable legacy were: Revd John Browne, John Green, Thomas Cooper, Robert Lees, Joseph Bretnor, Joseph Blackden Brushfield, Samuel Shore, Offley Shore and Henry Malkin.*

[315] *Transactions of the Congregational Historical Society. Op. cit., p 350.*

[316] *Case as to the right of the minister of Presbyterian Chapel of Ashford to the sum of 40 shillings a year. January 31st 1845. Derbyshire Record Office, D747/A/PF/1/4.*

The barrister was unable to give a definitive opinion, because he could not predict with certainty whether the terms of the Roose Trust or the Dissenters' Chapels Act would prevail. But he was very clear that, under the terms of the latter, 'the trustees are not justified in withholding the 40 shillings per annum', in which case 'the present minister is entitled to the 40 shillings per year which have accrued since his incumbency.'

He was also asked to consider – in the event that the minister should choose to act on his threat to initiate a legal case against the trustees – which party might be responsible for paying the costs of the court, this clearly being a critical factor in deciding whether to take such an action. Again, he could not give a definitive answer if the suit turned on the Dissenters' Chapels Act, 'considering the difficulties which have been raised by the decision in Lady Hewley's case', i.e., *Attorney-General v Samuel Shore*.

The Shore family scandals

At around the time Revd Luxmoore arrived in Ashford in 1861, Offley Shore (1797-1870), the son of the younger Samuel Shore, was (or had been) living at Churchdale Hall.[317] Thirty years earlier, Offley, together with his father, had been elected new trustees of the Roose Trust. But, even if there had been no regular rotation of trustees since that time, Offley would not have been holding this position in 1861, because he had emerged only one year earlier from a 17-year bankruptcy. His ill-advised business dealings had lost the Norton Hall estate in Sheffield, which had been the family seat since the 17th century. Among other things, Offley had joined the family bank, Parker Shore & Co of Sheffield, in 1818, on the retirement of his granduncle, William.[318] The bank had been in business for more than 70 years, and had been hailed 'a legend of trustworthiness': 'As Sure as Shore's Bank'. But in 1843 it failed, and all the partners were bankrupted.[319]

---

[317] *History, Gazetteer and Directory of the County of Derby. Francis White & Co, 1857, p 490.*

[318] *A Sheffield Banking Scandal: The Fall of the House of Parker Shore. Neville Flavell. Transactions of the Hunter Archaeological Society, Vol 25, 2009, pp 45-52.*

[319] *There were multiple bank failures in the mid 19th century. We were reminded of this at the time of the 'credit crunch' in 2008, when, coincidentally, Andrew Davies' TV adaptation of Charles Dickens' 'Little Dorrit' was released. Dickens based his doomed character, Mr Merdle – the Man of the Age: the richest man in London – on the infamous Irish financier and MP, John Sadleir, who caused the collapse of the Tipperary Bank.*

Credit crunch classic: It's the new BBC blockbuster. And with its tale of greed, crooked bankers and ruined families, 'Little Dorrit' could never be more relevant. AN Wilson & Sarah Chalmers. Mail Online, October 24th 2008.

'At the time Dickens was engaged in the writing of 'Little Dorrit' [1855-1857], an epidemic of sordid financial scandals seemed to be shaking the confidence of the public'. Secret Pockets and Secret Beasts: 'Little Dorrit' and the commercial scandals of the fifties. Barbara Weiss. Dickens Studies Annual, Vol 10. Penn State University Press, 1982, pp 67-76.

The year Offley Shore emerged from bankruptcy, his son, Offley Bohun Shore (1839-1911), became a doctor of medicine. Offley B Shore was cousin to the father of Florence Nightingale (1820-1910), and that 'founder of modern nursing' became godmother to his daughter, Florence Nightingale Shore (1865-1920).[320] Offley B Shore was no better than his father at managing his financial affairs and, in 1878, he also became bankrupt, mainly because his interest in 'various collieries ... have suffered largely by the depreciation of that description of property'. His insolvency necessitated the sale of the Meersbrook estate, which his great-grandfather, the elder Samuel Shore, had acquired 90 years earlier – the same Samuel Shore who had rebuilt Ashford's Cliff End Chapel.

In the same year that Offley B Shore was declared bankrupt, his wife succeeded in obtaining a divorce for his 'adultery coupled with desertion'. Nine years later, at the age of 48, Offley remarried: his new wife – an illegitimate servant girl – was, at the time, two years younger than his daughter, the then 22-year-old Florence.

Despite what must have been a tumultuous childhood, Florence Nightingale Shore lived up to the ideals of her namesake. She became a well-respected nurse, who was decorated for service in France in the First World War. Tragically, in 1920 she was bludgeoned to death in a railway carriage, and in spite of the best efforts of the local police, Scotland Yard and the famous forensic pathologist, Bernard Spilsbury, the crime was never solved. Nearly a century later, new theories are still being proposed.[321]

The Stonhouse family tragedies

The unhappy case of Revd Luxmoore's Uncle Charles in 1851 (see p 39), and the loss of a child in infancy in 1870 (which we will turn to on pages 140 and 195), were not John and Rosalie's only family tragedies.

Rosalie's sister, Alice Edith Stonhouse, was still living in her father's vicarage in 1871 when she was 26, but had left there by the time she gave birth in Wimbledon to an illegitimate son, on approximately March 28th 1877. Her baby, Henry James Charles Stonhouse, was baptised on April 21st 1877, but died a few days later at the age of four weeks, and was buried on April 27th 1877. Five days after the burial, Alice was admitted to the Peckham House Lunatic Asylum.[322]

---

[320] *The Heathcotes (the family of Rosalie Luxmoore's Aunt Clara Rosalie and her husband Revd Gilbert Heathcote) were also great friends of Florence Nightingale. The Heathcote Memorial Stone. Ash and District Local History Museum Society, Ash, Surrey GU12 5DP, http://www. ashmuseum.org.uk/heathcot.htm*

[321] *The Nightingale Shore Murder: Death of a World War One Heroine. Rosemary Cook. Matador, Beauchamp, Leicestershire, 2015.*

[322] *UK Lunacy Patients Admission Registers. Case 31033, date of admission May 2nd 1877.*

In the second half of the 19th century, childbirth was believed to be a quite common cause of a particular form of mental illness. Whilst 'baby blues' – today recognised as a common problem – was then remarked upon rarely, severe 'puerperal insanity', or 'puerperal mania', attracted a great deal of attention. The illness caused previously calm women to strike out physically and verbally at both themselves and those around them; it was no respecter of class or status, affecting paupers and those from highly respectable backgrounds equally; and at its most severe it could result in infanticide and suicide.

Today, puerperal psychosis occurs about once in every 1,000 labours, but it appears that the frequency of diagnosis in the 19th century was much higher: it was estimated in 1872 that 10 per cent of all female lunatic asylum admissions were attributed to puerperal insanity. There is a strong impression that there were real differences in the nature and extent of the disease compared to today.[323]

If Alice had indeed developed this condition, her case was complicated by the huge stigma of being an unmarried mother. She died in the asylum less than two years later at the young age of 35: was this a result of the combination of both unbearable mental and societal stresses?

Revd Luxmoore had gone 'in a hurry' to Richmond, Surrey, about two months before the birth of Alice's baby. He had stayed at Friar's Stile Road, the home of Alice and Rosalie's elder sister, Isabella Harriet Stonhouse.[324] Surrey was also home to Rosalie's uncle, Revd Charles Stonhouse (1807-1883), Rector of St Peter's, Frimley, and her aunt, Clara Rosalie Heathcote, whose husband was Rector of St Peter's, Ash. These two churches were just five miles apart, and about 25 miles south-west of Friar's Stile Road.

Revd Luxmoore would have made advance arrangements whilst in Richmond to ensure that Henry would be baptised according to the appropriate Christian rites. Indeed, a note in the margin of the register of Holy Trinity

---

[323] *Puerperal insanity in the 19th century. I Loudon. Journal of the Royal Society of Medicine, Vol 81, 1988, pp 76-79.*

Lunatics, Imbeciles and Idiots: a history of insanity in 19th-century Britain and Ireland. Kathryn Burtinshaw & John Burt. Pen & Sword Books, Ltd, Barnsley, South Yorkshire, 2017, pp 197-203.

[324] *Per letters dated January 31st 1877 to Revd Luxmoore from Whitehall, and February 7th 1877 from Rosalie Luxmoore to the Chatsworth Estate, regarding the proposed new school at Sheldon. This Remote Little School. Brian Greasley. Country Books, 2013, pp 14-15 (see p 81).*

Rosalie Luxmoore's nephew, Charles Cecil Gordon Stonhouse, lived in Richmond with his aunt, Isabella Harriet Stonhouse, from 1877 until his death. However, he may not have taken up residence in Friar's Stile Road by the time of the birth in March 1877 of his cousin, Henry James Charles Stonhouse.

Church in Wimbledon indicates that a private baptism had been arranged. This practice – in which the child would be baptised in the home – was ubiquitous in London, typically for infants who were sickly and unlikely to survive long enough for a baptism at the church font to be arranged; or for those born in conditions of secrecy due to illegitimacy; or in situations where no suitable sponsors were forthcoming. Although the first two scenarios certainly fit this case, Revd Luxmoore was not to know when he returned to Ashford some weeks before the birth that the baby would live for only a short time.

The address given in the register for baby Henry's burial is seven miles from Friar's Stile Road, across Richmond Park and Wimbledon Common. This is likely to be the house where Alice stayed, not only during her confinement in her final weeks of pregnancy, but probably also for several months beforehand. This would have enabled her father, Revd Arthur Stonhouse-Vigor, to keep quiet the fact of his unmarried daughter's pregnancy whilst, at the same time, it would have provided Alice with the comfort of knowing that her sister Isabella was nearby, and that an aunt and an uncle were also not too far distant.

Some mothers suffering from puerperal insanity did commit infanticide, but there is no evidence that this was the case here. Notwithstanding the stigma of Henry's illegitimacy, Alice's family seem to have supported her to the extent that societal norms would allow: she had been sent to live close to her elder sister; her brother-in-law had visited to make arrangements for the christening; and, following her tragic death in the asylum at Peckham, she had been buried in her father's churchyard in Walford.

A further indication that her family had not abandoned her is that they had paid privately for her care – an indulgence that it had not been possible to extend to Revd Luxmoore's uncle, Charles Luxmoore. The fees for private patients at Peckham were one to 1½ guineas per week, for which superior accommodation and a private garden separated from the paupers were furnished. A higher fee of five guineas per week would provide 'every comfort'. A published review of a guided tour in 1874 praised the care bestowed: 'The unfortunate patients are treated with the utmost kindness and attention'; and 'nothing that can tend to ameliorate the medical condition of the patient is left undone.'[325]

The family's apparent empathy may derive from their prior experiences with the challenges and emotional strains of mental illness: the youngest of Rosalie's siblings, Edward Huntingford Stonhouse (b.1851), had been admitted three years earlier to Brislington House Asylum near Bristol, also on a

---

[325] *Peckham House. Lost Hospitals of London, http://ezitis.myzen.co.uk/peckhamhouse.html*

The Story of Peckham House. The Peckham Society, https://www.peckhamsociety.org.uk/?page_id=1078

private basis.[326] The diagnosis was 'mania' which, like puerperal insanity, had a rapid onset of symptoms, including extreme 'mental exaltation and bodily excitement'.[327] Edward died there in 1907, aged 56.

Thomas Nadauld Brushfield (1828-1910)

Thomas Brushfield's son, another high achiever, has relevance to Revd Luxmoore beyond their shared interest in ecclesiatical history. This Brushfield was a polymath: a renowned antiquarian and noted authority on the life of Sir Walter Ralegh;[328] he also had a distinguished medical career as an alienist, devoted to the study and treatment of mental diseases.[329] He was Medical Superintendent at Chester County Asylum for 14 years, and then at Brookwood Asylum, Surrey:

> *'He was a first-rate asylum superintendent and practically introduced a new era in the treatment of the insane ... [and promoted] schemes for their entertainment which have been adopted in every asylum since that time.'*[330]

He was therefore in the vanguard of a remarkable improvement in the treatment and care of the mentally ill. New legislation in the latter half of the 19th century ushered in enormous advances in both care and comfort: accommodation; food; clothing; hygiene; opportunities for employment; access to churches and libraries; and a wide range of leisure and outdoor activities, including dancing, parties and concerts. All these became *de rigueur* as asylums were built and operated as 'palaces rather than prisons'; 'moral therapy', based on a humane approach to treatment, became the norm:[331]

> *'A pleasant feature of life ... is the Fancy Dress Ball which Dr Brushfield and his assistants get up ... The patients, four hundred in number, had it all to themselves from half past seven to half past nine o'clock, after which two hundred visitors were admitted ... The spacious Recreation Hall was beautifully decorated with exotic plants, flags, wreaths, statuettes,*

---

[326] *UK Lunacy Patients Admission Registers. Case 30967, date of admission April 4th 1874.*

[327] *Lunatics, Imbeciles and Idiots. Op. cit., p 211.*

[328] *Dr Brushfield always spelled the name 'Ralegh', noting that Sir Walter never spelled it 'Raleigh'. However, as discussed in Dr Brushfield's 1886 note, 'Sir Walter Ralegh; a Plea for a Surname', family members themselves seem to have spelled it in a variety of ways. Lunacy to Croquet: The Life and Times of Dr Thomas Nadauld Brushfield. Roger Bowen. 2013, pp ix and 128.*

[329] *An alienist was the name used in Victorian times for what we would now call a psychiatrist or psychologist. The term is still sometimes used to describe a forensic psychiatrist.*

[330] *Obituary. Thomas Nadauld Brushfield. The British Medical Journal, December 31st 1910, p 2054.*

[331] *Lunatics, Imbeciles and Idiots. Op. cit.*

mirrors, and Chinese lanterns. Refreshments were provided for the patients at twelve o'clock; but the visitors, among whom were many officers, and ladies and gentlemen of the neighbourhood, kept up the ball several hours after midnight'.[332]

Even though light relief within workhouses may have been slow coming, there was a similar level of celebration in the Bakewell Workhouse by the time of the New Year of 1884 – a remarkable contrast with Dickens' earlier shocking workhouse portrayals:

'During the evening the inmates partook of tea and a good supply of cake ... an entertainment was given in the Dining Hall, which consisted of music, singing, and dancing ... quadrilles, lancers, polkas, and country dances, were admirably executed ... young and old were compelled to dance ...

TN Brushfield as the hunchback – 'The Ruling Spirit' – in the Fancy Dress Ball at the Brookwood Asylum, Surrey.

An inmate, well known by the name of 'Garibaldi,' played a piece on the piano, and received a well-merited encore. At eight pm a Christmas tree ... was tastefully decorated by Mrs W Bramwell and Miss Nelson ... in this they had succeeded admirably. Gaily painted toys, lit up with Chinese lanterns, presented quite a feast to the eyes of the youngsters .... Paper hats and aprons were floating about in all directions ... Mr Swain then proposed a vote of thanks to Mr W Bramwell, Mrs Bramwell, Miss Nelson, Miss Bramwell, and Mr Hudson, for their kindness in procuring toys for the children, and ... to those kind friends, tradesmen and inhabitants of Bakewell, who had so cheerfully given their contributions for the purchase of toys, &c. ... Miss Calder sang several Scotch [sic] songs during the evening with considerable warmth and feeling

... the singing of 'God Save the Queen' by the children brought the entertainment to a close.'[333]

However humane and professional were the underlying philosophies and motivations, provision of psychiatric care in asylums, rather than in the community, tended to isolate patients from the general public. A consequence of this 'out of sight, out of mind' approach was that the stigma of mental illness was not fully addressed, as remains the case to some extent today.

Thomas Nadauld Brushfield retired to Devon, where he became a founder of the Devon & Cornwall Record Society, and died at Budleigh Salterton. Two of his sons also trained as physicians, Thomas Brushfield (1858-1937) becoming Medical Superintendent of the Fountain Hospital for Imbeciles in Tooting.[334]

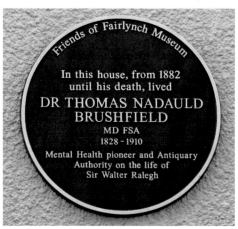

Blue plaque at TN Brushfield's house in Budleigh Salterton, Devon.

Dr Thomas Nadauld Brushfield and Revd John Reddaway Luxmoore were born less than a year apart; they shared deep personal connections with both rural Devon and rural Derbyshire; their lives spanned the entire 63-year reign of Queen Victoria; they both had an interest in ecclesiastical architecture and history; and they had both been intimately close to mental illness, albeit from dramatically contrasting perspectives. We are left to wonder whether Revd Luxmoore, with multiple experiences of mental illness in his extended family, felt comfortable to discuss with Dr Brushfield – one of the country's most respected psychiatrists – the tragedies of his Uncle Charles Luxmoore's life, and the illnesses that had afflicted his wife's sister Alice and brother Edward.

50th Jubilee as priest at Ashford

In 1911 Revd Luxmoore celebrated two major anniversaries: January 17th marked the golden anniversary of his marriage to Rosalie, but this was a quiet affair – at least as far as the village was concerned – because there was

---

[333] *Buxton Advertiser, January 5th 1884.*

[334] *Anna Shepherd. Institutionalizing the Insane in 19th-Century England. Pickering & Chatto Ltd, London, 2014, note 16, p 187.*

'no demonstration in honour of the event'.[335] In contrast, the parishioners were determined to commemorate his 50 years as priest of Holy Trinity. Indeed, the preparations and celebrations for this latter great occasion were reported in considerable detail:[336]

> *'His parishioners came to the conclusion that they ought not to allow such a unique occasion to pass without demonstrating in a tangible form how highly they esteem and respect their vicar.*

> *'During his long sojourn in the parish, the Revd gentleman has always been most diligent in the performance of his duties and has ever shown a keen interest in the welfare of his flock, not only from a religious point of view, but from every standpoint.*

> *'There is not the slightest doubt he has endeared himself to everyone in the parish, of whatever creed.'*

If this last sentiment seems somewhat over-embellished given the controversy over the Brushfield memorial, the article does attempt to further justify the assertion:

> *'No more striking illustration of this can be obtained than from the fact that Churchpeople and Nonconformists were present at the meeting held on March 28th, all denominations being agreed that the village should be asked to subscribe towards a token of esteem for one who had worked so long amongst them, and who had always been backed up in his good work by Mrs Luxmoore, who, like her husband, is highly respected by all.*

> *'The question was fully discussed at the meeting, and it was eventually decided that the most suitable way of showing the general appreciation of the Revd gentleman and his wife's long period of usefulness would be by the presentation of a purse of money and an illuminated address with an album containing the names of the subscribers.*

> *'The meeting appointed collectors, and an appeal was issued asking for donations, pointing out that there could only be a very few residents in the village who had not, at some time or another, benefitted by their vicar's ministrations, and by both his and his wife's practical sympathy and kindly help in times of sickness and need.*

---

[335] *Derbyshire Times & Chesterfield Herald, January 21st 1911.*

[336] *Derbyshire Times & Chesterfield Herald, June 3rd 1911. Also reported in: Derbyshire Times & Chesterfield Herald, March 25th 1911; Derbyshire Courier, June 6th 1911.*

'The response to the appeal was so spontaneous and so general that the promoters' most sanguine expectations were more than realised. Not only did the present residents show a desire to give evidence of their appreciation of the vicar's good works, but former residents were to the fore also, and consequently the committee of which Mr Frederick Lees, of Ashford Hall, was chairman and treasurer, and Mr WR Stubbs secretary, were in the happy position of having a splendid sum to hand over to the Revd gentleman at the presentation, which took place in the Schoolroom on Thursday [June 1st 1911].'

Attending the presentation, in addition to Revd Luxmoore and his family, were local clergy and representatives from nearby villages. Numerous letters of congratulation and telegrams had been received, including apologies from the 9th Duke of Devonshire, who 'would have liked to personally voice my strong support for Mr and Mrs Luxmoore'; and from Dr Charles Thomas Abraham, Bishop of Derby,[337] who noted that '50 years is a long time to put in as vicar … there was no one in the deanery who could come within 20 years of Mr Luxmoore.'

Lord Kerry[338] commented that he was 'delighted to join and should not have liked to have been left out, because I know what an institution Mr Luxmoore is in Ashford'.

In his presentation address, Col JC Cavendish (a son of Lord George and Lady Louisa Cavendish of Ashford Hall) noted that, 'prior to his coming they could not get a clergyman to stay, but they found one in Mr Luxmoore. (Applause.)' William Blackwell (a committee member) 'spoke of the kindness the vicar had extended to him in marrying him twice and christening his 16 children. (Laughter.)'

The gifts were 'a beautifully designed album … bound in full levant morocco' that included the names of the approximately 250 subscribers; and 'a purse containing £360 for himself and Mrs Luxmoore.'

'Great applause greeted Mr and Mrs Luxmoore on their receiving the testimonial, and in reply the Revd gentleman said words failed him to express what he felt on that occasion. Mrs Luxmoore and himself thanked them most heartily for their generous gift, and for their kind remarks. The

---

[337] *Charles Thomas Abraham (1857-1945) was Vicar of Bakewell from 1897-1918, and the second suffragan Bishop of Derby from 1909 to 1927. He was the son of Charles John Abraham (1814-1903), Bishop of Wellington, New Zealand.*

[338] *Henry William Edmund Petty-Fitzmaurice (1872-1936), 6th Marquess of Lansdowne, styled Earl of Kerry until 1927, was a Member of Parliament for West Derbyshire from 1908 to 1918.*

Revd John Reddaway Luxmoore and Rosalie Luxmoore on the occasion of the 50th Jubilee of Revd Luxmoore as priest at Ashford in 1911.

beautiful album would be prized very much, and he was sure it would be treasured by their sons and daughters when they were grown. He did not know whether his wife would like him to say that she had been a hard worker, and without her help the work that he had done in the parish could not have been completed. For himself, during the 50 years he had been there, he had received much kindness and support from all classes.'

With a value in today's money of about £36,000, the amount in the purse was truly remarkable. By way of comparison, on April 1st 1850, the occasion of the departure of one of Revd Luxmoore's predecessors,

'A subscription was made by the people of Ashford to purchase a silver inkstand to give to the Revd WG Giles, as a token of respect for the good he had done. The sum of £22 [£2,370] was collected.'[339]

And at a farewell presentation on May 26th 1964 for one of his successors,

'The sum of £50 [£1,020] had been presented to Mr and Mrs Norman, together with a standard lamp.'[340]

Three weeks later, Revd Luxmoore was involved in celebrating another landmark occasion – the Coronation of King George V on June 22nd 1911. Street parties and festivities were once again organised by numerous villages and towns and, on this special day, Ashford's villagers were invited by Mr George Jobson Marples to celebrate

Ashford.

Divine service was held in the parish church, and in this all religious denominations in the village joined. The Rev. J. R. Luxmoore officiated. After service the village children were entertained with milk and buns, and dinner was provided for all persons over 16. After dinner a procession was formed, and the whole marched off to Thornbridge House and Grounds, where they were entertained during the afternoon and evening by Mr. G. J. Marples. The Coronation arrangements for the village were carried out by a committee consisting of Messrs. W. Daybell, W. Twigg, J. R. Widdowson, F. Cox-Wilson, S. Furniss, W. R. Stubbs, W. Cox-Wilson, T. W. Wilson, W. Hurst, G. Hambleton, E. Gregory, G. Oldfield, with Mr. H. Buchanan as chairman. The whole of the Ashford Coronation arrangements were admirably carried out, but the committee were considerably relieved by Mr. Marples' generosity in inviting the people over to Thornbridge to partake of his hospitality.

Report of the celebrations in Ashford of the Coronation of King George V.

at Thornbridge Hall.[341] And Sheldon had been making its plans, too:

---

[339] *Transcripts of the Diaries of J James Middleton of Ashford (1812-1856). Derbyshire Record Office, D307/H/38/5, entry for April 1st 1850.*

[340] *PCC Minutes, July 13th 1964. Derbyshire Record Office, D747/A/PC/1/2.*

[341] *Derbyshire Advertiser & Journal, June 23rd 1911.*

Coronation Day on Church Street, Ashford-in-the-Water, June 22nd 1911. Returning to Ashford Hall following the church service are Fred Lees (centre) with 'Bertie' Lees and Claude Ratcliffe. The village constable, John Webster, is on their right; John Revel Widdowson is outside his shop with his wife, Diana (white skirt).

'The residents in the little hamlet of Sheldon do not intend to be outdone by their larger neighbours in regard to the celebration of the Coronation. A definite programme has not yet been decided upon, those who have the arrangements in hand being desirous of 'cutting their coat according to their cloth.' To that end they are making a collection first, and from what we hear the response is satisfactory.'[342]

Family and household

Rosalie bore six children in the vicarage in the space of nine years, but the Luxmoores did not live to see their two grandchildren.

- Mary Luxmoore was born on January 9th 1862, and died unmarried on February 26th 1952, aged 90, in Buxton.

- John Stonhouse Luxmoore ('Johnny') was born on August 1st 1863. He left home at 17 to study at Trinity College School, Stratford-upon-Avon. He was further educated at Exeter College Oxford, gaining a BA in 1888 and MA 1898. He had obtained some teaching experience in the 1890s[343] at Ashford School, before being ordained priest at Chester Cathedral in

---

[342] *Derbyshire Times & Chesterfield Herald, May 27th 1911.*

[343] *John Stonhouse Luxmoore is recorded as a schoolmaster in the 1891 census.*

1900 and licensed to St Peter's Church, Rock Ferry, on the Wirral. He was later Curate of Tarvin, Cheshire, for 11 years and then Vicar of Edale from 1916 until his resignation in 1924 'owing to considerations of health', after which he became Diocesan Chaplain to the Bishop of Sheffield. He died, aged 77, in Sheffield on August 9th 1940.

- Edith Rosalie Luxmoore was born on February 22nd 1865, and died unmarried on March 14th 1942, aged 77, in Buxton. She is buried in All Saints' Churchyard, Ecclesall, Sheffield.

- Margaret Sophia Patience Luxmoore was born in 1868, and died unmarried on December 4th 1927, aged 59, in Sheffield.

- Arthur Samuel Luxmoore was born on or about March 22nd 1870. He was christened on June 17th 1870 at Holy Trinity Ashford by the Bishop of Lichfield, who that same day formally reopened the church for public worship following Revd Luxmoore's extensive renovations. Arthur Samuel died on or about August 9th 1870, aged just over 4 months. Revd Edward Balston, of Bakewell Parish Church, officiated at his funeral at Holy Trinity Church, on August 13th 1870.

John Stonhouse Luxmoore, ca.1900.

Edith Rosalie Luxmoore, ca.1933.

- William Cyril Luxmoore was born on July 13th 1871. He was schooled at Repton (1882-1888) and Winton House School, Winchester (1889-1890), and then at Keble College Oxford, where he obtained a BA in 1893 and MA in 1897. He was ordained deacon on December 28th 1899 by the Bishop of London. His first curacies were at St Mary's Church, Haggerston, in Hackney (ca.1902-1905); St Barnabas' Church, Hove (ca.1906-1909);[344] and St Helen's Church, Ashby de la Zouch (ca.1911-1913), after which he entered service as a chaplain during the First World War. He was later assistant clergyman at St Matthew's Church, Northampton, and at St Peter's Church, Leicester, and an interim priest-in-charge at St Mary's Church, Stafford. He was appointed Vicar of St James' Church at Boroughbridge, near Harrogate, in 1923. He also took responsibility for the nearby St Mary's Church, Dunsforth, when it became vacant four years later. In 1938 he was appointed Private Chaplain to the Marquess of Zetland at Aske Hall, near Richmond, north Yorkshire. He married 29-year-old Constance Evelyn Shoesmith in 1921, at the age of 49, with his brother John as best man. Constance had received a medal for her service with the Voluntary Aid Detachment in Cyprus from September 1915 to April 1916. William Cyril died in Knaresborough, Yorkshire, in 1967, aged 96; Constance died in Leeds in 1979, aged 87.

William Cyril Luxmoore and Constance Evelyn Luxmoore (née Shoesmith) on honeymoon in 1921, aboard their motorcycle and sidecar.

---

[344] *Whilst at Hove, William Cyril Luxmoore was living at the same address as Mary Fenella Stanford Bolsover, née Downes, of Ashford (1877-1957), who was possibly acting as his housekeeper. Mary had previously worked as a domestic servant at Riversdale (now Riverside), which was next door to her house on Fennel Street in Ashford. The framed photomontage of Ashford Church and Revd JR Luxmoore (see p 194) was treasured by Mary Bolsover. Lillias Bendell. Private communication, 2020.*

Their elder son, Christopher Charles Luxmoore, was born in Boroughbridge Vicarage in 1926. He was ordained priest in 1953 and served successively at St John the Baptist Church, Newcastle; St Bede's Church, Newsham, near Blyth; Salibia, in Trinidad; and Headingley, Leeds. He was also Canon Precentor at Chichester Cathedral; Bishop of Bermuda (1964-1989); Archdeacon of Lewes and Hastings; and, in retirement, Assistant Bishop in Chichester. He belonged firmly to the Church of England's Anglo-Catholic wing. He died in 2014, aged 87.

Revd JR Luxmoore's grandchildren, Christopher Charles Luxmoore (left) and Robin Stonhouse Luxmoore, at Boroughbridge Vicarage, ca.1934.

Their younger son, Robin Stonhouse Luxmoore, was born in 1928, also in Boroughbridge. In 1949, following two years' National Service in the Army, he emigrated to Alberta. He worked first on the ranch of his grandmother Rosalie's nephew, Sir Arthur Allan Stonhouse, with Sir Arthur's son, Philip;[345] and then on a vast 240,000-acre ranch on the US border: 'You might imagine a young man wearing spurs and chaps and speaking in a refined English accent while surrounded by hardened cowboys.'[346] He later worked in the Arctic and was then involved in oil exploration, before moving to Kelowna, British Columbia, as a

---

[345] In 1967, following the death of his father, Philip Allan Stonhouse (1916-1993) succeeded to the title of Sir Philip, 18th Bt. of Radley. Philip Stonhouse, Alberta on Record, Archives Society of Alberta, https://albertaonrecord.ca/stonhouse-philip

[346] Personal communication. Robin Stonhouse Luxmoore, 2020.

director of a large irrigation system that served fruit growers in the area; in 1965 he was appointed chief surveyor for the city. He returned to British Columbia in 2014, having spent 25 years working to restore groundwater depletion and soil erosion in Central Mexico.

For a period of 20 years between them, brothers John Stonhouse Luxmoore and William Cyril Luxmoore engaged enthusiastically in that English passion: organised competitive games.[347] The public school ethos would have instilled in them the ideology of 'muscular Christianity', where physical endeavour has equal priority with high moral values and notions of Christian manliness.[348] Cricket and tennis would likely have been their chief summer entertainment in their teens and 20s: they both became members of the Wye Valley Wanderers Cricket Club, and in later years they played tennis regularly in tournaments at Darley Dale (where John was sometime Honorary Secretary) and at Matlock. However, they never made much progress beyond the second round![349]

Rosalie's mother had died in 1868, aged only 59. Therefore, upon the death of her father in 1883, Rosalie's sister, Sophia Stonhouse (1846-1926), then aged 37 and unmarried, would have had to move out of the vicarage in Walford. Consequently, by 1891, Revd Luxmoore and Rosalie had invited Sophia to live in the vicarage in Ashford, where she remained for at least another ten years, before moving to live in Richmond, Surrey, with the eldest sister in the family, Isabella Harriet Stonhouse.

In 1871 the Luxmoores were employing three servant girls, reducing to two in the 1880s, and one in the 1890s and thereafter, as the children had grown up and left home.

The longest-serving of the Luxmoores' servants was Elizabeth Gyte (1851-1929), who worked at the vicarage for at least 13 years until she was married to William 'Billy' Naylor in November 1883 by Revd Luxmoore, at St Michael and All Angels' Church Sheldon – the church that her father, Anthony Gyte, had built 20 years earlier.

Elizabeth's younger brother (also Anthony Gyte) was the husband of Maria

---

[347] *For example: Derbyshire Times & Chesterfield Herald, August 25th 1888; Derbyshire Times, August 13th 1908.*

[348] *Sport, religion and English national identity. Andrew Parker & Nick J Watson. In: Sport and English National Identity in a 'Disunited Kingdom'. Tom Gibbons & Dominic Malcolm (eds). Routledge, London, 2017, Chapter 10.*

The worldwide Young Men's Christian Association was founded on the principles of 'muscular Christianity'.

[349] *Miss Fenton – who helped in 1884 to tastefully decorate the church (see p 84) – was on occasion John Stonhouse Luxmoore's partner in the Ladies' & Gentlemen's Doubles tennis tournaments. Derbyshire Times & Chesterfield Herald, August 13th 1898.*

Gyte, whose poignant war diaries have been painstakingly edited by Ven Gerald Phizackerley. As the Priest-in-Charge of Ashford with Sheldon and Archdeacon of Chesterfield, he was a resident of Ashford Vicarage from 1978 to 1991.[350]

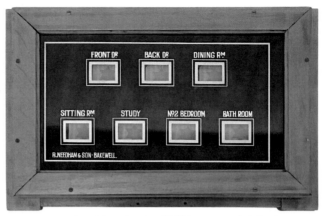

The servants' bell box in the Old Vicarage, Ashford.

Retirement and death

Revd JR Luxmoore preached his farewell sermon at Ashford on September 29th 1912[351] and formally retired the following day to live in Buxton, with a church pension of £50 per annum.[352] Five weeks later, on the afternoon of November 6th, he paid a final visit to the school he had established in Sheldon.[353]

Revd Luxmoore may have wished to be remembered for rebuilding the dilapidated village church, but one local newspaper chose (not inappropriately) to highlight his rare 'distinction' as having been Vicar of Ashford 'for the long period of 52 years'.

✚ ✚ ✚

There are not many instances of a living being held for over half a century by one clergyman. The Rev. J. R. Luxmoore claims this distinction, as he has been the Vicar of Ashford, near Bakewell, for the long period of 52 years. The aged clergyman has now retired from his parochial labours, and preached his farewell sermon last Sunday. He will spend the winter of his life in Burton, and the members of his old flock, by whom he was greatly revered, as most of them he had watched grow up from childhood, will wish him a peaceful and happy retirement, and the health to enjoy a well-earned rest.

✚ ✚ ✚

Report of Revd JR Luxmoore's retirement.

---

[350] *The Diaries of Maria Gyte of Sheldon, Derbyshire, 1913-1920. Gerald Phizackerley (ed). Scarthin Books, 1999.*

[351] *Derbyshire Courier, October 5th 1912.*

[352] *The London Gazette, October 25th 1912.*

[353] *This Remote Little School. Brian Greasley. Country Books. Little Longstone, Derbyshire, 2013, p 116.*

At a Vestry Meeting on April 14th 1917, Revd Sherlock made 'sympathetic reference' to 'the serious illness of the Revd JR Luxmoore'. Less than a month later, on May 11th 1917, he died in Buxton, aged 88.

That same day, FW (Fred) Brocklehurst of Sheldon, having been posted back to England when the wound he sustained during the Somme offensive had failed to heal, wrote from Chelsea Barracks:

May 11th. I wish I was at home again, it seems such a waste to me, marching up and down all day when I might be helping at home.

Fred's aunt, Maria Gyte, wrote in her diary four days later:

May 15th. Bitterly cold. Our men working on moor and spreading manure. Ethel and Evelyn[354] walked to Bakewell to get the wreath for Mr Luxmoore. On getting it, they took it to Ashford and was in time for the funeral. The inscription on the wreath was as follows: In loving

LATE VICAR OF ASHFORD.

The funeral of the late Rev. John Reddaway Luxmoore, who was for fifty-two years Vicar of Ashford-in-the-Water, near Bakewell, and died at Buxton, where he had lived in retirement for the past five or six years, took place in the Ashford Churchyard yesterday. The clergy present were: The Bishop of Derby and Vicar of Bakewell (Dr. Abraham), Canon Scott-Moncrieff, Vicar of Buxton, Canon Kewley, of Matlock; the Revs. C E. Harris, St. Ann's, Buxton; H. E. Sherlock (Ashford), and T. F. Salt (Curbar). The principal mourners were the Revs. John S. Luxmoore, Vicar of Edale, and Cyril Luxmoore (Market Drayton), deceased's sons, and the Misses Edith and Margaret Luxmoore (daughters).

Report of the funeral of Revd John Reddaway Luxmoore.

remembrance of our late Pastor and friend. From the people of Sheldon. Evelyn had been to ask a few in Sheldon to subscribe for wreath and she got 23 shillings. The wreath cost a guinea, the box one shilling, and the other shilling is being used to buy flowers for altar. Mr Luxmoore's funeral took place at 2.30. There were many present, 8 clergymen, the Bishop of Derby and many local people. Anthony and Thos Wm Brockley joined and led the procession with Ashford churchwardens. The Ashford choir walked and the hymn Abide With Me was sung. (Our milk cows lay in tonight as it was so cold.)[355]

Armistice Day 1918 came 18 months after Revd Luxmoore's death, by which time 24 young sons from the villages of Ashford and Sheldon where he

---

[354] *Ethel and Evelyn were Maria Gyte's daughters.*

[355] *The Diaries of Maria Gyte of Sheldon, Derbyshire, 1913-1920. Gerald Phizackerley (ed). Scarthin Books, 1999, entry for May 15th 1917, p 131.*

Entry in the Ashford Church Registers for the burial of Revd John Reddaway Luxmoore.

had served as vicar had been killed, including three nephews of his one-time domestic servant Elizabeth Naylor (née Gyte), and the cousin of Alice Mary Dawson's grandmother, Fanny Thorpe (née Wildgoose).[356]

John Richard Birley of Staveley, near Chesterfield, grandson of Samuel Birley's brother and sister-in-law John and Hannah Birley, was also killed in action, in 1917. A Lance Corporal in the 9th Battalion of the Sherwood Foresters (Nottinghamshire and Derbyshire Regiment), he is buried with his parents in a grave adjacent to that of Samuel and Ellen Birley's four-year-old son, Richard (see p 98), who would have been John Richard Birley's uncle had he survived beyond childhood. The soldier had received his middle name in memory of that young child, whose life had also been cut short so tragically.

Rosalie lived to see the return of peace: she died on January 16th 1921 at the age of 84, four years after her husband. The following day would have been their 60th wedding anniversary:

'Mrs Luxmoore was not long in following her husband to rest. A long, long life they had together, helping and serving each other and the common cause. It was beautifully significant that they should be reunited in Paradise on the anniversary of their wedding day. Ashford and Sheldon owe much to her as to him for the self-denying work she did for 52 years. A vicar's wife occupies no easy or enviable position in the parish where her lot is cast. It oft-times means hard work, and sometimes not much recognition of it; but there is a warm corner in many hearts, especially amongst the older folk who were her contemporaries in Ashford and Sheldon, for Mrs Luxmoore.'[357]

---

[356] *Elizabeth's nephews, John ('Jack') Brocklehurst, Thomas A ('Tant') Brocklehurst and Anthony ('Tony') Gyte, and Fanny Thorpe's cousin, Alfred Wildgoose, are all named on a memorial in St Michael and All Angels' Church in Sheldon.*

[357] *Derbyshire Record Office, D747/A/PC/1/2. Rosalie Luxmoore actually died one day before the anniversary of her wedding day. The same error is reflected on the inscription of John and Rosalie's memorial at Ashford Church (see p 150).*

In November of the following year, Nancy, the eldest of the Mitford sisters, was to 'come out' in a grand debutante ball. She was one of the aristocratic 'Bright Young Things' who would help launch the modern cult of celebrity. It was the beginning of the 'Roaring Twenties': Rosalie – and certainly her husband – would have been aghast at the decadence and flamboyance that ushered in this new era, and which would have been so completely alien to their Victorian sensibilities. Women over 30 had been given the vote in 1918 and were beginning to feel more confident, empowered and independent. Their dresses were shorter, and they started to smoke, drink and (at least if sufficiently wealthy) drive motor cars.

However, in their roles as vicar and vicar's wife in two Chatsworth villages, Revd Luxmoore and Rosalie had themselves benefitted from their relationships with, and the generosity of, the aristocracy – specifically, four of the Dukes of Devonshire. The 6th 'Bachelor Duke' had given the land for their new vicarage; the 7th Duke donated land for St Michael and All Angels' Church, Sheldon, contributed to the renovations of Holy Trinity Church, Ashford, and worked with Revd Luxmoore on the plans for Sheldon School; the 8th Duke had entertained them at the 1899 Chatsworth Ball and also during the visit of King Edward VII and Queen Alexandra in 1904; and the 9th Duke had sent his personal congratulations to Revd Luxmoore in 1911, on the occasion of his 50th Jubilee as Vicar of Ashford.

Upon her marriage to Andrew Cavendish in 1941, Nancy's sister Deborah – who had been born in the year before Rosalie's death – lived in the Rookery in Ashford. In 1950 they inherited the Chatsworth estate and, notwithstanding the mammoth task of managing an 80 per cent inheritance tax liability, succeeded in making it one of Britain's most successful stately homes. It is a wonderful thing that this outstanding estate is now accessible to everyone.

Bequests and legacies

In his will, Revd Luxmoore mentions that his 'sons John Stonhouse Luxmoore and William Cyril Luxmoore are already provided for' via their interests in 'the West Week Estate in the Parish of Lifton … and … the farm known as East Risdon in the parish of Jacobstowe' respectively. He requests that 'my Hatherleigh land [inherited from his Aunt Elizabeth at her death in 1874] shall not be sold unless it be clearly to the advantage of my family.'

After Rosalie's death, the income from her husband's residual estate passed to their daughters – Mary (59), Edith Rosalie (55) and Margaret (52). When her son, John Stonhouse Luxmoore, died in 1940, his residuary estate and personal effects passed to 75-year-old Edith Rosalie.

In addition to these mid-life inheritances from their parents, the Misses Luxmoore were to thank certain of their mother's family members for helping to ensure their financial independence. In particular, a bequest from their granduncle, Charles James Fox Bennett, when they were 21, 18 and 15, would likely have formed the bulk of their lifetime income.

Charles Bennett (1793-1883), it will be remembered (see p 61), was the one-time Premier of Newfoundland, in whose home in Clifton the parents of the Misses Luxmoore had stayed on their honeymoon. After various individual bequests (some substantial) to his wife, family members and friends, Charles left 2 per cent of the net income derivable from the remainder of his general estate to Rosalie Luxmoore, 'in aid of the education and maintenance of her children of their marriage as she may deem fit, requesting her special care for her unmarried daughters'. Since Charles was said to be one of Newfoundland's wealthiest citizens, even this small fraction of his estate may have been a considerable sum.[358] Being thus financially self-sufficient, they may have felt that marriage was less of an imperative than did most other ladies of their age.

In 1929, the two then-surviving sisters were to receive a final legacy. By this time, Mary was 67 and Edith Rosalie 64.

Rosalie's elder brother, James Stonhouse (1835-1872), had left England for colonial India, where he married Corinne Louisa Grace Reade, a native of Mangalore – a major port city on the Arabian Sea on India's western coast. Their son, Charles Cecil Gordon Stonhouse (1859-1929), was born in Visakhapatnam, a port on the Bay of Bengal on the eastern coast used by the East India Company, which the colonial British had named Waltair. When Charles Cecil was about 12, his father had returned to the family home, the

---

[358] *The will of Charles James Fox Bennett is a holograph (i.e., entirely handwritten). Available copies may be incomplete or inaccurate, but a decision of the Supreme Court of Newfoundland regarding particular aspects of the will provides certain facts that may be relied upon. It appears that, after paying his funeral expenses, Charles bequeathed £600 per year, plus a separate one-time lump sum of £500, to his wife Isabella, Rosalie's aunt. Some of his other friends were to receive a total of approximately £500. Of the net income derivable from the remainder of his general estate, 90 per cent was left to certain other named relatives and a friend; 5 per cent to his sister-in-law Harriet Josephine Brettingham; and 5 per cent to the then-surviving daughters of his wife's late sister, Sophia Stonhouse; i.e., Rosalie Luxmoore and her sisters. Of this 5 per cent, 60 per cent was to be shared amongst Rosalie's living female siblings, i.e., Isabella Harriet, Amy Bertha, Sophia, and Josephine Emily; and 40 per cent to Rosalie to aid the education and maintenance of her children – in particular, her unmarried daughters.*

Estate of the late Charles Fox Bennett. Decisions of the Supreme Court of Newfoundland, EP Morris (ed). JW Withers, St John's, Newfoundland, 1897, pp 36-38.

Will of Charles JF Bennett. Transcribed by Judy Benson & Ivy Benoit. Newfoundland Will Books Vol 8, probate year 1904, pp 155-162.

vicarage of Revd Arthur Stonhouse-Vigor in Walford, where he died soon thereafter at the age of 37.

As a teenager, Charles Cecil had become an apprentice indentured to the Merchant Navy, but was reported to have deserted the ship *Star of the North* on December 20th 1876. Soon thereafter, he had made his way back to England, where he worked for 40 years for the Board of Trade. He lived in Richmond at the homes of his aunt, Isabella Harriet Stonhouse (1833-1921),[359] for at least 48 years until his death in 1929.[360]

Charles Cecil was predeceased by all of his uncles and aunts except for Amy Bertha Stonhouse, to whom he left £50 plus an annuity of £80 per year, but Amy died two years later. He left his personal household effects to John Stonhouse Luxmoore, and bequeathed the rest of his estate to the two surviving daughters of Revd Luxmoore and Rosalie. The net value of Charles Cecil's estate was £9,093 4s 8d [£557,000].

Memorial

A cross standing outside the vestry door of Holy Trinity Church, Ashford-in-the-Water, memorialises both Revd John Reddaway Luxmoore and Rosalie Luxmoore. In 1961 William Cyril Luxmoore, then aged 90, wrote to the then incumbent, Revd John Norman, expressing his concern at the state of his parents' grave.[361] Revd Norman replied suggesting that the Church would be willing to share the cost of repairing the cross and generally tidying the grave. Revd Norman had remarked to the Parochial Church Council that 'it was exactly 100 years since Mr Luxmoore came to Ashford in 1861'. Repair of the memorial had been completed by January 1962 at a cost of £5, after which the vicar received a letter of appreciation from William Cyril Luxmoore.[362]

---

[359] *Successively on Richmond's Friar's Stile Road, Dynevor Road, and Sheen Road.*

[360] *At various times, other sisters of Rosalie Luxmoore also lived with Charles Cecil Gordon Stonhouse and Isabelle Harriet Stonhouse; i.e., Sophia Stonhouse (1846-1926), Amy Bertha Stonhouse (1848-1931), and Josephine Emily Rocke, née Stonhouse (1843-1906), widow of Revd Thomas Owen Rocke. Charles Cecil was to become a close and trusted friend of his Aunt Rosalie and Uncle John Reddaway Luxmoore and their children: John himself appointed Charles Cecil as an Executor of his will, and Charles appointed his cousin John Stonhouse Luxmoore as an Executor of his will. Charles Cecil had also been an Executor of the substantial estate of Rosalie's aunt, Clara Rosalie Heathcote.*

[361] *PCC Minutes, May 9th 1961. Derbyshire Record Office, D747/A/PC/1/2.*

[362] *23 years earlier, William Cyril Luxmoore's brother, John Stonhouse Luxmoore, had obtained a quotation of 10 shillings for cleaning their parents' grave. Derbyshire Record Office, D7672/Lx.C-47/39.*

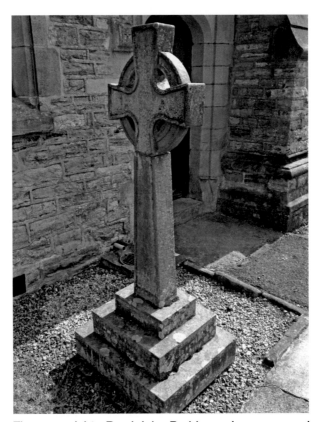

The memorial to Revd John Reddaway Luxmoore and Rosalie Luxmoore that stands outside the vestry door of Holy Trinity Church, Ashford-in-the-Water. The inscription reads:

JOHN REDDAWAY LUXMOORE
PRIEST
ENTERED INTO REST MAY 11 1917
AGED 88 YEARS
RIP
FOR FIFTY-TWO YEARS VICAR OF THIS PARISH
ROSALIE
WIFE OF THE
REVD JOHN R LUXMOORE
AT REST, JANUARY 16 1921
AGED 84 YEARS
JESU, MERCY
REUNITED ON THEIR WEDDING DAY

III

Renovation of Holy Trinity, Ashford-in-the-Water

Victorian ecclesiastical architecture

Victorian church architecture was influenced by shifting and conflicting theological doctrines and, externally, by revolutionary developments in the arts, science and society. Nineteenth-century buildings therefore became vehicles for different constituencies to promote their various religious and secular notions as they were advanced.[363] One persistent driver within the 19th-century Anglican church, however, was the high church Oxford Movement's desire to counter the rise of Nonconformism.

Iconographical phase

Mediaeval architectural styles that were being revived across the western world at the time were appropriated by the Established Church in support of its ambition to reinforce its continuity with its pre-Reformation Catholic past. The early 'gothic revival' style, including the adoption of sentimental iconographical symbols to represent spiritual themes and stories, was explicitly reinforced in the requirements associated with Parliamentary Grants for new buildings and for restoration: money was available only on the condition that the preferred

---

[363] *What do Victorian Churches Mean? Symbolism and Sacramentalism in Anglican Church Architecture, 1850-1870. Michael Hall. Journal of the Society of Architectural Historians, Vol 59, No. 1, 2000, pp 78-95.*

Competing theologically-inspired design philosophies were, of course, nothing new, but the 19th century seems to have adopted less pragmatic and more dogmatic approaches to ecclesiastical architecture. In the 17th century, for example, whilst 'Anglicanism feared both Catholic ritual and Nonconformist dogma', the 'auditory church' design of that period sought to give prominence to all liturgical acts, 'taking what it needed from both [the Catholic and Nonconformist traditions]'. 'Nor was there any need to worry overmuch if ritual east didn't correspond to the point on the compass.' Indeed, 'there was plenty of room for variation.' His Invention So Fertile: A Life of Christopher Wren. Adrian Tinniswood. Pimlico, London, 2002, pp 215, 219.

The high pulpit in Dukinfield Old Chapel, Greater Manchester, built in 1839-1840, affirms the centrality of preaching in the Nonconformist tradition.

high church style was followed. This included specifically the renunciation of the preaching-centric architectural elements of Nonconformism: John Keble, a leading light of the Oxford Movement, lamented that 'sermons are far too much thought of, in comparison with common prayer, the administration of the sacraments, and other parts of the public worship of God.'[364]

In most types of Nonconformist chapel, the pulpit would have been placed centrally and in an elevated position facing the pews, with the communion table beneath. The sermon would thereby be prioritised symbolically above the raising of the Host as practised in Anglican high church ritual. The Nonconformist minister, by descending from the pulpit to celebrate the communion, would therefore metaphorically reject the idea that priests are from a group spiritually distinct from lay people, but rather belonged to 'a priesthood of all believers'.

Architects in the 19th century who wished to appropriate the gothic revival style in Nonconformist chapel architecture therefore found themselves likewise constrained by religious ideology:

---

[364] *Sermons, Academical and Occasional. John Keble. John Henry Parker, Oxford, 1847, p 47.*

'The Nonconformist architect was in even greater difficulties than his Anglican brother; he was obliged to retain the traditional type of chapel, and could not dispense with the galleries and central pulpit, or elongate his building into any semblance of mediaeval form. All he could do was to point his windows and fill them with tracery ... and attach pinnacles and battlements to the exterior.'[365]

The gothic revival style became further entrenched as the English national style when, in 1836, Sir Charles Barry's gothic design was accepted for the rebuilding of the Palace of Westminster (Houses of Parliament).

By the 1840s, the design principles of the Church Building Acts had been effectively superseded by those of the Ecclesiological Society, which promoted a particularly dogmatic architectural philosophy to restoration, teaching that the only true gothic style was that represented by the middle pointed or decorated styles of the late 13th to mid 14th century.[366]

Metaphorical phase

The argument for a uniform, static and backward-looking architectural style was eventually lost in the face of a society that was progressive in almost every other way. There was a growing acceptance that creation stories were not literally true, and that the physical world (particularly as evidenced in geological formations) had been, and was, in a state of continuous change. In the 1850s, buildings therefore started to incorporate a wide range of natural geological materials and ornaments, and ushered in a fashion for 'structural polychromy', characterised by bands of black and red brickwork and coloured marbles and tiles, whilst narrative spiritual symbols in stained glass were replaced by individual figures of saints and prophets. The deeper goal of this 'high Victorian gothic' style therefore became the reconciliation of science and art and, in the eyes of the Church, naturalism became a metaphor for God's divine plan, and a reminder of his involvement in the process of creation.

Sacramental phase

In the 1860s the concept of a divine, continuous creation receded with the advent of Darwin's theory of natural selection, leading to the abandonment

---

[365] *Nonconformist Church Architecture. Ronald P Jones. The Lindsey Press, London, 1914, pp 36-37.*

[366] *The original Ecclesiological Society, established in 1839 as the successor to the Camden Society, was 'a highly-effective pressure group for the gothic style, together with a rigid set of 'laws of church arrangement'. These views had been transmitted with verve, sarcasm and cast-iron certainty through its famous Journal, The Ecclesiologist.' The Ecclesiological Society closed in 1868, and a society with the same name was established in 1879, with a less trenchant, broader, perspective. The non-professional study of Ecclesiology: a brief history of the Ecclesiological Society, http://ecclsoc.org*

of modernism and a retreat back into historicism, with confidence in the union of art and science suffering as a result. In the high Anglican church, the notion of temporal architectural development became contrary to the dogma that Christianity was a revelation of supernatural truth, not a progressive science. Moreover, change over historical time was perceived as redolent of Nonconformism, the Reformation itself being a consequence of change. The high Victorian gothic style rapidly declined and, after the 1870s, a view was ushered in that the church building should embody the fact of the supernatural Eucharist and a supreme and eternal God, and architecture should therefore emphasise timeless abstract ideas that embodied an inherent spiritual meaning.

These phases were not clearly demarked: architecture lagged behind artistic and scientific scholarship; strong-willed ecclesiastical architects wished to express their own voice rather than imitating rules laid down by others, even when this put them at risk of castigation by their contemporaries; and the realities of funding and the availability of skilled artisans mandated pragmatic decision-making, especially in rural areas.

Against this backdrop of a vigorous, albeit turbulent, architectural revival following three centuries' worth of neglect of England's churches and cathedrals,[367] the Victorian restoration movement gathered steam: it is estimated that around 80 per cent of all Church of England churches were affected in some way, from minor repairs to complete demolition and rebuilding.

The suppression of the concepts of time and change in the last significant phase of the gothic revival was inconsistent with the new secular philosophy of historically-informed restoration, driven by the view that the value of old buildings as historical documents should supersede any spiritual function. It is without doubt that many 'restorations' were over-enthusiastic, destroying much of value in their path. In 1877 William Morris, one of the most noteworthy cultural figures of Victorian Britain and a key figure in the Arts and Crafts movement, was appalled when he visited Tewkesbury Abbey, and wrote a letter to the *Athenaeum* denouncing the work being performed there:

> *'My eye just now caught the word 'restoration' in the morning paper, and, on looking closer, I saw that this time it is nothing less than the Minster of Tewkesbury that is to be destroyed by Sir Gilbert Scott. Is it altogether too late to do something to save it – it and whatever else beautiful and historical is still left us on the sites of the ancient buildings we were once so famous for?'*[368]

---

[367] *This neglect was spectacularly illustrated when the spire of Chichester Cathedral collapsed on February 17th 1861.*

[368] *Letter to Athenaeum, March 10th 1877.*

This was the catalyst for the establishment, by Morris and others in that same year, of the Society for the Protection of Ancient Buildings. His commitment to this cause was expensive, not only in the time he devoted to it, but also in lost income: he pledged never to supply stained-glass windows for church restorations that did not meet his standards, thereby ending what had previously accounted for a third of his commissions.[369]

Morris was not the first to voice his concern for the sometimes destructive loss of a valuable architectural

The whole of the chancel floor in Tewkesbury Abbey is covered with polychromic tiles made by William Godwin in the mediaeval style.

heritage. Thirty-seven years earlier, in 1840, All Saints' Church in Bakewell was in a 'dilapidated and dangerous' state. Much to the dismay of the parishioners, the diocesan architectural consultant, Thomas Johnson, had recommended renovations that included rebuilding the tower but without a spire, notwithstanding the fact that a spire had adorned the church in the 14th century, before it was removed in 1825 for fear of its collapse.

The Vicar of Bakewell, Revd HK Cornish, fought in the first year of his incumbency against Johnson's plan, in favour of a more conservative approach,

'to preserve the present fabric, as far as it may be possible so to do. The valuable and excellent specimens of architecture which it contains, from early Norman downwards, render it most desirable that this should be accomplished, rather than that a style of restoration should be adopted not in character with the present building.'

[369] *An Illustrated Life of William Morris 1834-1896. Richard Tames. Shire Publications, 2003.*

Revd Cornish and his local architect prevailed and a new spire was erected, albeit 16 feet shorter than its predecessor.

Thomas Johnson's additional recommendation that the Norman nave should be stripped out and rebuilt in the gothic style was, however, adopted in 1852. At least a prior adviser's recommendation in 1824 that the church be totally demolished was never acted on.[370]

Revd Giles' renovations (1837-1850)

We now focus on what was to become a 50+ year building programme at Ashford Church, started by Revd William Galley Giles (1807-1854), and reaching its climax in Revd Luxmoore's restoration.

Revd Giles was licensed Perpetual Curate of Ashford Church on March 9th 1837[371] (the year Queen Victoria ascended the throne at the age of 18) and remained until he was appointed to a living in Dungarvan, Ireland, in 1850.

A necessary first project under his stewardship was the remediation of some rather urgent structural defects:

'The church walls was getting into a very dilapidated state when he came, the outer walls giving way owing to the flat [slightly pitched] roof and the heavy oak timbers and the lead roof.'[372]

In an attempt to resolve this problem,

'a new square stone pillar to support the roof next to the octagon archway pillars opposite the pulpit was put in.'[373]

Further work included the building of a vestry with a new entry door in the north wall, the cost of which was 'chiefly raised by a church rate';[374] and,

'the greater part of the high pews were lowered, yet a few of them were left remaining in their original condition, owing to the opposition of one or two who claimed possession of theirs, and objected to any alteration being made in them.'[375]

But Revd Giles' most visually conspicuous change – the symbolic removal

---

[370] *Bakewell: The Ancient Capital of the Peak. Trevor Brighton. Halsgrove, 2005, pp 58-60.*

[371] *Clergy of the Church of England Database 1540-1835, https://theclergydatabase.org.uk*

[372] *Mr S Birley's Remarks on the Church Copied Verbatim, Jan 1900, Derbyshire Record Office, D7672/Lx.C-33.*

[373] *Ibid.*

[374] *Ibid. The door in the west wall of the vestry into the north aisle was not inserted until 1950. Letter of Licence dated April 24th 1950, Derbyshire Record Office, D747/A/PI/8/4.*

[375] *John Stonhouse Luxmoore. Derbyshire Record Office, D7672/Lx.C-30.*

of a 'triple-decker' pulpit – effectively initiated the process of restoration broadly along the lines espoused by the Anglican high church.

The contempt in which the Nonconformist 'preaching' architectural style was held is apparent in Revd George S Tyack's article in Andrews' *Antiquities and Curiosities of the Church*:

'When the sermon came to occupy a more prominent place in public estimation, the pulpit naturally grew in importance ... the people ceased to take much part in the service except as listeners, and prayer and praise were left to the parson and the clerk, and the 'three-decker' came into being.

Illustration of a three-decker pulpit, from Revd George S Tyack's article on pulpits.

'In the lowest of the three pulpits sat the clerk, monotonously mouthing the responses to the prayers read by the parson in the second pulpit just above his head. And at the close of the duet, the latter, donning black gown and bands, ascended to the 'upper deck' to deliver his sermon of an hour or more.

'This hideous abomination in the way of ecclesiastical arrangements generally stood in the centre of the church, towering like Babel up to heaven, and completely shutting out the altar from sight, proclaiming itself the only feature of importance in the House of God ...

'The destruction of the acoustic properties of an old church by the introduction of galleries and high-backed pews, and the ignorance of many of the later architects of the rules governing those acoustic properties, resulted in the invention of the sounding-board as an *assistance to the preacher's voice. These are seldom introduced now, but not a few instances remain.'[376]*

Revd Giles accordingly de-emphasised the architectural primacy afforded to the sermon by replacing the old pulpit, as recounted by JS Luxmoore:

'Before Mr Giles came in 1837, and when the old high pews existed, the pulpit, reading-desk, and clerk's desk were of the 'three-decker' order, painted in oak colour, and stood where the present pulpit does.

'Mr Giles, probably in 1843, had this 'three-decker' taken down, and a new hexagonal pulpit made, with clerk's desk below, the panels being carved oak ones of the Jacobean period. These panels Mr Giles had collected from old furniture soon after he came to Ashford. The pulpit had a door to it. There was over it a sounding-board, now in the vestry. The reading-desk was, at this time, placed in the chancel (sic nave?), next to the Hall pew.

'Since this pulpit was made for Mr Giles by George and Peter Milnes, the following entry in the churchwardens' accounts may refer to it: '1843. Feb 11. Pd George Milnes ... joiners bill £1 2s 2d.'[377]

Revd Giles also installed the chandeliers that appear in the 1875 photo-montage of Ashford Church (see p 194),[378] and that were first lit seven months after his arrival.

Revd Luxmoore's restoration (1868-1870), with reference to the Faculty Document of 1868

Revd Luxmoore and his churchwardens, John Francis Green and Abel Tomlinson, voted in favour of plans for the restoration of Holy Trinity Church, Ashford-in-the-Water, at a Vestry Meeting on April 25th 1868, and approval for the work to proceed was granted by Bishop George Augustus Selwyn of the Diocese of Lichfield on September 15th 1868. The diocesan

---

[376] *Pulpits. Revd George S Tyack. In: Antiquities and Curiosities of the Church. William Andrews (ed). William Andrews & Co, 1897, pp 128-131.*

    ASIDE: Revd Tyack was a prolific writer at the end of the 19th century on a wide range of mainly ecclesiastical subjects, including the rather gruesome 'Human Skin on Church Doors', in The Church Treasury of History, Custom, Folklore. William Andrews (ed). William Andrews & Co, 1898, pp 158-167.

[377] *John Stonhouse Luxmoore. Derbyshire Record Office, D7672/Lx.C-30.*

[378] *'The first time of lighting the shabdeliers (sic) in Ashford Church'. The Diaries of J James Middleton of Ashford (1812-1856), entry for Sunday October 1st 1837.*

    Personal communication. Lillias Bendell, 2020.

seal was printed on the Faculty Document the following week, at the diocesan office in Stafford.[379]

The text of the Faculty provides the rationale for the renovation, summarises the main changes that were to be made, and highlights some practical matters that were to be considered as the work progressed. The Faculty also effectively ensured that the resulting building would reflect the architectural philosophies promoted by the Oxford Movement.

Each of the main aspects of the renovation are introduced below by relevant quotations from the Faculty Document.

'THE PARISH CHURCH OF ASHFORD AFORESAID IS IN GREAT NEED OF RESTORATION AND REPAIR'

Holy Trinity Church was almost completely rebuilt between 1868 and 1870 under Revd John Reddaway Luxmoore's governance. The sad state of the building as it had existed beforehand is stated succinctly in a building and architecture periodical:

> 'The old building ... [was]... in so dilapidated a condition that recon-struction had become a work of necessity.'[380]

Apart from the tower, the tower arch, and the three 16th-century arches and octagonal pillars that separate the nave from the north aisle, most of the rest of the structure, and major interior fittings and furniture, were all replaced.

The plans were prepared by the Manchester architectural firm James Medland & Henry Taylor,[381] and the building contract was won by Mr Joseph Brown & Co of Matlock Bridge.[382] The principal financial supporters of the project, that had an overall cost of about £2,000, were Lord George and Lady Louisa Cavendish.

---

[379] *Faculty for the Restoration of Ashford Church, 1868. Derbyshire Record Office, D747/A/PI/8/1.*

[380] *Building Intelligence. Building News and Engineering Journal, July 1st 1870, p 13.*

[381] *Church of Holy Trinity, Church Street, Ashford-in-the-Water, Derbyshire. A Biographical Dictionary of the Architects of Greater Manchester, 1800-1940. Manchester Group of the Victorian Society, https://manchestervictorianarchitects.org.uk/buildings/church-of-holy-trinity-church-street-ashford-on-the-water-derbyshire (sic)*

[382] *Tenders had been provided by Gyte & Thorpe (£1,195 16s 5d) and J Brown & Co (£960 2s 10d). Trade News. Building News and Engineering Journal, February 12th 1869, p 147.*

The contract had been won by J Brown & Co. Building Intelligence. Building News and Engineering Journal, July 1st 1870, p 13.

Matlock Bridge refers to the area situated around the Crown Square, Matlock, and its 13th-century bridge. Derbyshire Dales Planning. Conservation Areas: Matlock Bridge, https://www.derbyshiredales.gov.uk/planning-a-building-control/conservation/conservation-areas/matlock-bridge

A photograph of the south elevation of Ashford Church before the 1870 restoration.

It is said of the architect James Medland Taylor that,

'He was proof that not all Victorian architects were mere imitators in their ecclesiastical architecture. Although individual elements can easily be traced back to period precedent, their mixture with completely original ones results in an unprecedented whole. It is curious that attributes such as flair and imagination, now highly prized, should still be considered a failure on the part of some Victorian architects reluctant to meekly follow the herd.'

One has to assume that it was this 'flair and imagination' that was responsible for him being berated by some of his perhaps less adventurous contemporaries as an 'arch rogue architect'.[383]

'REBUILD THE NORTH AND SOUTH WALLS OF THE CHURCH'

Consistent with the remark in the *Building News and Engineering Journal* about the dilapidated state of the church (see p 159), Mr Birley's recollections indicate that Revd Giles' prior remedial work on the north aisle pillar had

---

[383] *James Medland Taylor. A Biographical Dictionary of the Architects of Greater Manchester, 1800-1940. Manchester Group of the Victorian Society, https://manchestervictorianarchitects.org.uk/ architects/james-medland-taylor*

merely postponed an inevitable need for a comprehensive rebuild. They also suggest that the new arch in the north wall of the chancel, which abuts obliquely on the face of the skewed arch in the outer vestry's old southern wall, was constructed during this 1868-1870 restoration:

> *'Nearly the whole body of the church has been rebuilt on the old foundations, the tower, the octagon pillars and arches, and part of the wall next to the chancel was left remaining, but this wall was so much pressed out by the weight of the old roof, it was refaced and made straight at the restoration.'*[384]

The 1868-1870 restoration therefore not only eliminated the structural instability, but also straightened the chancel wall, as corroborated by TN Brushfield.[385]

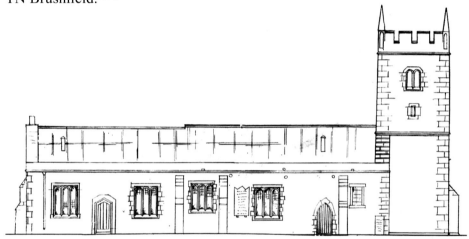

The north elevation of Ashford Church before the 1870 restoration.

Prior to its restoration, the church had a shallow-pitched roof, as can be seen in the pre-restoration photograph opposite. At the time of the restoration, this was replaced with a double-gable, high-pitched roof that covered the north aisle and nave, to a design that is consistent with the Victorian gothic style.

We have no direct evidence of changes that may have been made to the building before the pre-restoration photograph, but there would have been many, given the length of time that a church has existed in this particular location. There are specific suggestions, however, that at some time predating the photograph an older roof may have had a high pitch.

[384] *Mr S Birley's Remarks on the Church Copied Verbatim, Jan 1900, Derbyshire Record Office, D7672/Lx.C-33.*

[385] *Ashford Church. TN Brushfield. Journal of the British Archaeological Association, Vol VI, Bedford Press, London, 1900, p 283.*

Firstly, John Norman opines that the decorative stones currently situated around the upper periphery of the tympanum were previously the supporting blocks for a corbel table.[386] This architectural feature, which typically consists of a narrow stone shelf located just below the eaves of a high-pitched roof, was popular in early mediaeval churches, and particularly in Romanesque buildings.[387] Secondly, Thomas Nadauld Brushfield is confident in his assertion that 'we may fairly assume the early roof to have been an open and high-pitched one'.[388] Thirdly, buildings of the Tudor period (1485-1603), as well as those of mediaeval churches, were typically characterised by steeply-pitched roofs.

'BUILD A NEW PORCH ON THE SOUTH SIDE'

Representing the 'gateway to Christian life', a porch with an elaborately decorated tympanum would have been given great prominence in churches of the Norman period. And so, in the 1870 restoration, a new south porch was built by Revd Luxmoore, and the Norman tympanum was placed above a new (internal) door. In fact, this was most likely the original position of the tympanum, but in the interim it had been removed and affixed to the exterior south wall, a little to the east of the main south entrance:

'This stone had undoubtedly once served as the tympanum or top stone of the semicircular doorway of the Norman chapel erected here in the early

The south entrance of Ashford Church before the 1868-1870 restoration. The semicircular profile of the tympanum can be seen to the upper right edge of the entrance archway (arrow).

---

[386] *Ashford-in-the-Water and its Church. John Norman, 1961.*

[387] *Architecture: Corbel Table. Editors of Encyclopædia Britannica. Encyclopædia Britannica, 1998.*

[388] *Ashford Church. TN Brushfield. Journal of the British Archaeological Association, Vol VI, Bedford Press, London, 1900, p 281.*

part of the 12th century, and it has now been happily restored to its proper position'.[389]

In 'an attempt to give a scriptural interpretation to the carving' on the tympanum (see the drawing on p 21 and the photograph on p 164), either Revd William Boyd (incumbent from 1850-1852) or Revd James Burrow (1852-1861) had placed beneath it a tablet with text from Psalm 80, verse 13:

'The boar out of the wood doth waste it, and the wild beast of the field doth devour it.'

However, JS Luxmoore concurs with J Charles Cox's view that this was 'an interpretation of the stone which had probably never occurred to the mind of the fanciful sculptor.'[390]

It was when the tympanum was resited inside the new porch that the decorative blocks were added as voussoir stones around its arched periphery:[391]

'Around the tympanum are placed five small square blocks of stone, with grotesque heads carved upon them. These were found embedded in the old walls at the time when they were taken down, 1869-70.'[392]

This portrayal of the designs on the stone blocks as 'grotesque heads' does not describe what we see today. A recent and more apt suggestion is that the carvings may once have been part of a chain motif.[393] When the architect James Medland Taylor reviewed the restoration project records for Revd Luxmoore, he could unfortunately find no written evidence that these stones had in fact been 'embedded in the old walls',[394] and it remains unproven that – as per John Norman's suggestion – they were previously the supporting blocks for a corbel table. However, the two propositions are not mutually exclusive.

---

[389] *Notes on the Churches of Derbyshire, Vol II, The Hundreds of the High Peak and Wirksworth. J Charles Cox. Bemrose & Sons, Derby & London, 1877, p 45.*

Confirmed in: On Norman Tympana, with especial reference to those of Derbyshire. TN Brushfield. Journal of the British Archaeological Association, Vol VI, Bedford Press, London, 1900, p 247.

[390] *Notes on the Churches of Derbyshire, Vol II. J Charles Cox. Op. cit.*

[391] *Voussoir stones are wedge-shaped blocks used to construct a circular arch. Architecture: Arch. Shiveta Singh, rev editors of Encyclopædia Britannica. Encyclopædia Britannica, 2002.*

[392] *Ashford Church. TN Brushfield. Journal of the British Archaeological Association, Vol VI, Bedford Press, London, 1900, p 278.*

[393] *Holy Trinity, Ashford-in-the-Water, Derbyshire. The Corpus of Romanesque Sculpture in Britain and Ireland. Registered Charity No: 1168535, visit date 2014.*

[394] *'Nor is there any record of where the carved stones placed around the 'wild boar' came from'. Letter from James Medland Taylor to Revd JR Luxmoore, June 9th 1899. Derbyshire Record Office, D7672/Lx.C-29/16.*

The south porch of 1870 replaced what had previously been a simple arched entrance at about the same location on the south wall (see p162). But it is argued that this former simple entrance had in fact replaced an earlier south porch:

The tympanum at Holy Trinity Church, Ashford, with decorative voussoir stones around its periphery.

'That there had been a porch before the entrance, seems to be proved by the fact that a square-flagged floor remained in front of the south entrance, for many years previous to the restoration ...

'According to local tradition, one of the villagers, having, for some unknown cause, quarrelled with his relations in the church porch, left the place, vowing that he would never return, until the porch was removed to the top of Hill Cross. The story says, and with apparent truth, that the farm buildings at the top of the hill [now Highfield Farm] were partly reconstructed with the materials of the old porch. A variant states that the cottage just below the farm was the building the materials were used on. Of course, the whole story may be one of those which originate after the occurrence.'[395]

JS Luxmoore further relates that it was said by 'old inhabitants' that, before the old porch was removed, the tympanum had indeed been situated over the south entrance, giving credence to the satisfactory conclusion that we now find it 'happily restored to its proper position'.

'TAKE DOWN AND REMOVE THE GALLERY AT THE WEST END OF THE CHURCH'

The comprehensive internal reordering included the removal of what Revd George S Tyack contemptuously referred to as 'monstrous galleries ... reared around the church',[396] which were architectural features found frequently before the Victorian restoration era.

---

[395] *John Stonhouse Luxmoore. Derbyshire Record Office, D7672/Lx.C-30.*

[396] *Pulpits. Revd George S Tyack. In: Antiquities and Curiosities of the Church. William Andrews (ed). William Andrews & Co, 1897, p 128.*

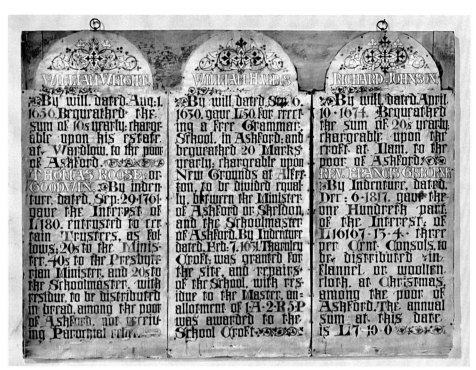

A list of charities associated with the village of Ashford-in-the-Water. Prior to the 1870 restoration, this board was hung on the front of the west gallery of the church. After the gallery was removed, it was relocated to the wall of the north aisle.

Before Revd Luxmoore's renovations, access to Ashford's 40-seat west gallery had been via a winding staircase, which had filled up the space under the tower arch and which, along with a wooden partition, had cut off the tower from the nave.

The cost to remove the gallery was £9 17s 6d. At the same time, an exterior door on the south wall of the tower was blocked up; this had previously provided the only access to the tower.

The old gallery, panelled on the front and sides and extending eastwards to the first pillar in the nave, had been erected in 1735. An inscription to John Greatbatch, who had given £5 towards its construction, had originally featured prominently on the front-facing panels.[397] However, sometime during the incumbency of Revd James Burrow, this inscription was moved to a less conspicuous place on the north panel of the gallery, and was replaced with a set of three wall panels that itemise several other charitable givings to the parish. These panels now hang at the west end of the north aisle wall.

The charitable contributions listed on this panel are:

---

[397] *Struggling to interpret the date on John Greatbatch's inscription, JS Luxmoore argues with himself whether the date was 1755 or 1735, but decides '1735 is the more likely'.*

- 1630: **William Harris**: left £50 for the erection of a free grammar school[398] and gave a piece of land (1½ acres), called Thornley Croft, for the support of the schoolmaster. He also bequeathed £13 6s 8d out of his estate at Alfreton, with £6 13s 4d to be paid to a minister for preaching 20 sermons in the Chapel of Ashford or in the Chapel of Sheldon, and the residue to be appropriated to the benefit of the free school.

- 1656: **William Wright**: donated 10 shillings yearly out of his estate at Wardlow to the poor of Ashford.

- 1674: **Richard Johnson**: provided 20 shillings yearly from the rent charged on a croft at Ilam for the poor of Ashford.

- 1761: **Thomas Roose or Goodwin**: left the interest on £180 per annum, 20 shillings thereof to be paid to the curate of Ashford, 40 shillings to the minister of the Presbyterian Chapel, 20 shillings to the schoolmaster of the free school, and £2 8s to be laid out in bread and distributed amongst the poorest inhabitants. [It is said that the loaves for many years were laid out on [Thomas Goodwin's] tombstone when the distribution was made.][399] See p 125.

- 1817: **Revd Francis Gisborne**: provided an annual sum (£7 10s in 1817) to be distributed in woollen or flannel cloth amongst the poor of Ashford.

'West Gallery Music' was the tradition in many 19th-century village churches, notwithstanding the Calvinist prohibition of musical instruments in worship that still prevailed in some localities. And so we find that, fastened on the old gallery at Ashford, 'there was a revolving box, with moveable letters (sic), for posting up the numbers of the hymns'.

Choirs at this time would typically be accompanied by the village band, comprising whatever players and instruments happened to be available. Musicians had been known, for example, to include a thatcher and a shepherd, shoemakers, weavers, farmers, tailors, and shipwrights.[400] When the choir and instrumentalists started to play, the congregation would then turn around to face west to be led in the singing; hence the expression 'to face the music'.[401]

---

[398] 'Sir John Coke, Secretary of State to King Charles I, gave the close in which it [the school] stands'. Magna Britannia, a concise topographical account of the several counties of Great Britain, Vol 5 (Derbyshire). Daniel & Samuel Lysons. T. Cadell & W Davies, London, 1817, p 31.

[399] John Stonhouse Luxmoore. Derbyshire Record Office, D7672/Lx.C-30.

[400] The music that the Church lost. Rollo Woods. Church Times, August 25th 2017.

[401] The instrumentation and music of the church choir-band in eastern England, with particular reference to Northamptonshire, during the late 18th and early 19th centuries. Stephen J Weston. University of Leicester, 1995, pp 28-29.

In the Ashford gallery, the seats were divided into two blocks by a passageway: 'a few seats' on the north side were open to any of the congregation, and the south side was occupied by the choir and musicians ('bases, fiddle and flute'[402] or 'hautboy [oboe], flutes, fiddles, basses, etc.').[403]

These independent instrumentalists and singers had a reputation for being rebellious, and in the eyes of the Oxford Movement were 'the worst members of the parish. The radicalism of singers and bell-ringers is notorious.'[404] Indeed, music-making at Ashford was not always an orderly and harmonious affair; JS Luxmoore recounts the story of a strike by the Ashford choir:

Church Choirs – the Old Style, 1891.

'*On a certain Sunday, when the hymn was given out, the instruments did not begin to play as usual, but a slate was hung out on the front of the gallery to the effect that the instruments would not play until someone was expelled from, or readmitted to, the choir*'.

---

[402] *Mr S Birley's Remarks on the Church Copied Verbatim, Jan 1900, Derbyshire Record Office, D7672/Lx.C-33.*

[403] *John Stonhouse Luxmoore. Derbyshire Record Office, D7672/Lx.C-30.*

[404] *John Mason Neale (1818-1866). Neale helped found the Camden Society, precursor to the Ecclesiological Society. He is remembered today for his Christmas hymns, including 'Good Christian men rejoice' and 'Good King Wenceslas'.*

The Tideswell singers were paid £10s 0d to sing at Ashford Church on June 12th 1832, but there was no payment to the Ashford singers: this may have been a consequence of the strike.

As time went on, instrumentalists were replaced with barrel organs, pipe organs or harmoniums. In addition to the fact that this was a less expensive option, it was easier for a vicar to control one organist than a whole band. Such a change is a principal plot strand in Thomas Hardy's 1872 novel *Under the Greenwood Tree*, which the author had originally planned to call *The Mellstock Quire*.[405]

It was during the incumbency of Revd William Galley Giles that 'the stringed instruments and flute [were] put aside' and a 'barrel' or other type of 'small organ' was placed at the front of the gallery:

'Mrs Giles [the vicar's wife] played the organ and attended to the choir and girls of the Sunday School, who sat behind the choir in the gallery.'[406]

The excitement at the arrival of such an instrument in a rural Wiltshire church (St Peter's, Langley Burrell) in 1874 is captured in the diary of Revd Francis Kilvert:

'This morning was an epoch in the history of Langley Church and the first sound of an instrument within the old walls, an event and sensation not soon to be forgotten.'

And the following Sunday:

'All has gone off well. Fanny played the harmonium nicely and the singing was capital. The congregation were delighted and some of them could hardly believe their ears.'[407]

Ashford's small organ was relocated during the renovation, from the old gallery to the north-eastern end of the chancel. It was placed just outside the vestry door, as can be seen on the post-restoration floor plan (see p177).

---

[405] *From around 1801, Hardy's father and grandfather had played stringed instruments in the church band in his own parish of Stinsford, the model for the fictional Mellstock. Music and Thomas Hardy. Phil Scowcroft. Classical music on the web, 2001, http://www.musicweb-international. com/classrev/2001/May01/Hardy.htm*

[406] *Mr S Birley's Remarks on the Church Copied Verbatim, Jan 1900, Derbyshire Record Office, D7672/Lx.C-33.*

[407] *Selections from the Diary of Revd Francis Kilvert, 1870-1879. Jonathan Cape, 1944, p 264.*

The existing, larger, organ – installed in 1926[408] – now occupies space in an outer vestry, which replaced a section of the new congregational pews that had been instated at the time of the 1870 restoration.

'REMOVE THE FONT FROM ITS PRESENT POSITION AND REFIX THE SAME UNDER THE TOWER AT THE WEST END'

According to the Ecclesiological Society's principles, the font should be at the west end of the nave. It was already so located before Revd Luxmoore's restoration, but removing the gallery allowed it to be moved a few yards further west into an area now made available under the tower arch and belfry.

John Norman's pamphlet[409] mentions how the present font had for some years been used as a garden ornament. JS Luxmoore provides further details: around the end of the 18th or beginning of the 19th century,

> *'In spite of protest, the churchwardens disposed of [the font] to Mr Thornhill of Stanton Hall'.[410] Fortunately, when Mr Thornhill was 'appealed to by the vicar and asked to restore it to the church … he generously acceded, and the font was brought back from Stanton to Ashford.'*

In the interim,

> *'A plain, ugly, Grecian, alabaster font, about 1 foot in diameter, was put in the church, in place of the old stone font …*

---

[408] ASIDE: *A potential new organ is mentioned in the Parochial Church Council Minutes of June 3rd 1921. Made by J Housley Adkins, its installation was finally completed by October 29th 1926, at a cost of £462 13s 0d. It was, of course, hand-blown. The first mention of obtaining an electric blower was in June 1942, and the subject appears in the Minutes on 14 further occasions over the next 4½ years, until a new electric blower was installed in October 1946 at a cost of £55. During that long period, the organist, Mr Broomhead, 'said how very difficult it was to get anyone to blow the organ' and how 'at the moment [April 1945] an electric blower was quite unobtainable' – no doubt mainly due to wartime constraints. A donation from the family of a prior organist covered the entire cost and, as a result, the vicar, Revd Reginald Absell, immediately suggested that the monies that had been set aside for the electric blower be transferred to the bells fund. All agreed, and a subcommittee was formed to enquire into the details of the bells. This began an eight-year process of planning and further fundraising, so that in 1954 the three existing bells were recast; a new additional bell was cast in memory of Revd Henry Sherlock who had died in 1943; and the old oak bell frame of 1612 was replaced with a new cast-iron frame made ready to accommodate two further bells. In his 'Report on the Fabric, Goods and Ornaments of the Church' on April 14th 1955, Revd Thomas George called this 'the largest alteration probably since [Revd Luxmoore's] restoration of the church in 1869'. The final two bells were added in 1966 to complete the current peal of six. The 'good' part of the old frame now stands in the north aisle. Derbyshire Record Office, D747/A/PC/1/2.*

[409] *Ashford-in-the-Water and its Church. John Norman, 1961.*

[410] *Probably Bache Thornhill (1747-1830), the father of the similarly named Revd Bache Thornhill (1785-1827), Perpetual Curate of Ashford Church from 1812 to 1828.*

'When Mr Luxmoore came to Ashford in 1861, he found [the alabaster font] in the vestry, cracked and useless, and ordered it, in 1869, when the church was restored, to be buried in the chancel, under the altar, where it now is.'[411]

'REFLOOR THE PASSAGES AND REARRANGE AND RENEW THE APPARATUS FOR HEATING THE CHURCH'

The heating and ventilation of churches aroused Victorian passions. Advocates for the use of fresh air included Robert Boyle (1821-1878) and his son, who were both vociferous in their condemnation of lack of ventilation:

'The vitiated atmosphere usually found in imperfectly ventilated churches is the principal cause of the drowsiness with which many of the congregation are overcome before the service is over, and the fainting fits which so frequently occur in certain churches.'[412]

William Walker in 1859 suggested that heating be implemented using hot water pipes:

'The most suitable and successful arrangement for churches is to conduct hot water pipes all along the church from end to end, under the floor, with gratings over them for the escape of warmed air; the air-flues being so arranged as to cause the fresh air to impinge on them before it enters the church through the gratings.'

Alternatively, he suggests,

'A church may certainly be warmed sufficiently by a stove, (and it has frequently been done), by closing all egress openings, and heating the same air over and over again ...'

Romesse pot belly stove in St Michael and All Angels' Church, Edmondthorpe, Leicestershire.

---

[411]   *John Stonhouse Luxmoore. Derbyshire Record Office, D7672/Lx.C-30.*

[412]   *Robert Boyle & Son Ltd, ventilating engineers of London & Glasgow, ca.1900. Quoted in: The warming and ventilation of Victorian and Edwardian churches. Brian Roberts & Frank J Ferris. A Chartered Institution of Building Services Engineers Heritage Group Publication, 2012, p 18.*

However, he warns, in the manner of the Boyles,

'... but it is obviously and radically wrong; inasmuch as it is warmth without ventilation; and, if in such case the quantity of air proper for health be admitted, it will prove to be ventilation without warmth.'[413]

Whether 'radically wrong' or not, the 1867 plan drawing of Holy Trinity indicates that there were two stoves in place before the restoration: one in the north aisle at the rear of the church; and one towards the front of the main aisle, adjacent to the front pews on the south side (see p176).

Given the small amount of space available, the stove at the front would likely have been similar to an example at Edmondthorpe Church in Leicestershire. The one at the rear may have been larger, since Mr Birley recalls,

'The church was heated by a large metal stove near the north door.'

An anthracite-burning 'Gurney Stove' at Tewkesbury Abbey, Gloucestershire.

Use of warm-air stoves in churches did indeed grow considerably from the middle of the 19th century. For example, it was claimed that, by 1897, Dr Goldsworthy Gurney's anthracite-burning stove had been used to warm 22 cathedrals and over 10,000 churches, schools and other buildings.[414]

But stoves did not escape the denunciation of the Ecclesiological Society, which admonished anyone 'complaining of their church as cold or damp, or in adopting any artificial means', that 'the simplest, the best, the most Christianlike method of warming a church is to open it for daily prayers.' Stoves in particular, it was argued,

[413] *Useful Hints on Ventilation. William Walker. JT Parkes. Manchester, 1859, pp 33-34.*

[414] *19th-century Radiators and Heating Systems. Cathedral Communications Ltd,*
    https://www.buildingconservation.com/articles/heating-systems/heating-systems.htm

'are inadmissible in churches ... their unsightly and unecclesiastical character; the grievous disfigurements they generally cause to the roofs, walls, or windows; their dirt, unwholesome exhalations, liability to cause destructive conflagrations, the space they occupy, and other objections which more or less apply in every instance, render their introduction strongly to be reprobated.'[415]

At Holy Trinity, the cast-iron grilles that were installed in the floor of the aisles, and a new exterior stepped entrance at the outside north-east corner of the tower marked on the building plan 'to heating apparatus' (see p 177), indicate that a heat source was to be located in a cellar that was to be excavated beneath the new floor of the nave. This would have been a coke or coal-fired furnace, but there would have been no mechanical blowing of the air; circulation would rather have relied upon convection, and the heating would therefore have been far from adequate.

Hot-water radiators may have been introduced when they became widely available at the turn of the century. In the meantime, should the parishioners' daily prayers have been insufficiently exothermic, stoves may still have been used to provide ancillary heating.

'THE PRESENT PEWS, SEATS AND SITTING PLACES IN THE SAID CHURCH ARE INCONVENIENTLY ARRANGED AND INSUFFICIENT FOR THE ACCOMMODATION OF THE PARISHIONERS'

A 1632 document entitled, *A Perfect order how men are to Sit in the Chapel of Ashford by the Official Mr Rowlandson and the neighbours of Ashford*, shows the seating arrangements for certain named parishioners.[416] Based on the names of the occupants of each pew, it appears that most of the men sat on the south side; the women on the north; and 'under the pulpit is for the minister's wife whomsoever she is'.

Contrary to popular wisdom, the practice of renting or owning specific pews, in mainly Anglican churches but also some Nonconformist chapels, was not in the 19th century restricted to the wealthy and privileged; the primary renters were from the middle and lower middle classes, particularly small business owners. Although the practice had been largely abolished by the late 19th and early 20th centuries, this was not for philosophical or charitable reasons,

---

[415] *The Warming of Churches. The Ecclesiologist, Vols 1-3, Nos XXXIII, XXXIV, August 1844, pp 135, 137.*

[416] *Notes on the Churches of Derbyshire, Vol II, The Hundreds of the High Peak and Wirksworth. J Charles Cox. Bemrose & Sons, Derby & London, 1877, p 50.*

but because the cost and bother of administration exceeded the value of the income generated.[417]

Before Revd Luxmoore's 1870 restoration, Ashford Church was fitted with box pews that allowed the congregation to face the west gallery when singing, and the pulpit on the south side when listening to the sermon. These pews originally 'were very high and in very good condition,'[418] but, as mentioned previously (see p156), Revd Giles had lowered most of them. It was discovered at the time of the 1870 restoration that,

> 'there was no faculty for any of the old pews, and that their appropriation to this or that individual was purely a matter sanctioned by time or custom.'[419]

So Revd Giles would have been quite within his rights to reduce the height of all the pews, and therefore to ignore the objections of certain parishioners who did not want him to lower 'theirs'.

In addition to the box pews, the children from the Boys' School 'had raised seats near the door at the north-west end of the church, and a few forms placed under the gallery for those who might need them', whilst 'the girls of the Sunday School sat behind the choir in [the] gallery'.[420]

The pre-restoration floorplan of 1867 (see p176) shows that there were three main columns of box pews: one ran along the north wall; one along the south wall; and the third – a double column – ran between the other two. The north column extended eastwards up to the vestry wall; the double central column extended likewise to the vestry wall on its north side, and a little further towards the chancel on its south side; and the south column reached right up to the steps of the chancel, which occupied a considerably smaller area than is now the case. Revd Giles' new pulpit and clerk's desk were located in approximately the middle of the south column, projecting into the nave to the same depth as the pews themselves.

A 21st-century fire marshall may not have been too happy with the location of the large stove at the west end, situated as it was close to the north exit door. Worse still, the double central column of pews restricted egress from the north aisle to the alternate (south) exit door: passage would have been possible only

---

[417] *The English Anglican Practice of Pew-Renting, 1800-1960. John Charles Bennett. University of Birmingham, 1960, p ii.*

[418] *Mr S Birley's Remarks on the Church Copied Verbatim, Jan 1900, Derbyshire Record Office, D7672/Lx.C-33.*

[419] *John Stonhouse Luxmoore. Derbyshire Record Office, D7672/Lx.C-30.*

[420] *Ibid.*

by squeezing through the small gap between the pews and the stove itself. The church may therefore have been lucky that the stoves did not cause the 'destructive conflagrations' contemplated by the Ecclesiological Society.

JS Luxmoore indicates the following ownership at that time of some of the pews, with reference to the numbers pencilled in on the 1867 plan:

1	Greatbatch and/or Gyte	22	Thornbridge
2	Ashford Hall	23	Vicar's family
3 & 4	? The Hall	26 & 27	Bretnor
5	Sterndale	28	Old Parsonage
6	Morewood & Sleigh[421]	29	House above the Grange
11	Bailey (last of the Cheneys)	32	Devonshire Arms
17	Fowler	47	Churchdale
		50	Green Family

The 1851 Religious Census recorded that there was a total of 464 sittings in Ashford Church, 164 of which were free.[422] But it seems that the 164 free 'sittings' may actually have been 'standings': handwritten annotations on the 1867 floorplan indicate that, prior to Revd Luxmoore's restoration, there was actually seating for only 260 on the ground floor in the 50 box pews, plus 40 in the gallery. The incumbent who signed the census return, Revd William Boyd, stated that the average attendance for the most popular (evening) service was 300, so there may have been as many as 464 in attendance only exceptionally, e.g., for the 'standing room only' services, such as Christmas day and Easter day.

One rationale stated in the Faculty for the restoration was that the existing seating was 'insufficient for the parishioners'.[423] The proposed post-restoration seating plan seems not to support this, because further handwritten annotations indicate that the rebuilt church would have 300 sittings, 'the gallery being done away with' – exactly the same number as before. A more powerful reason for wishing to comprehensively reorder the 'inconveniently arranged' seating would have been that the church concurred

---

[421] The Morewood family (see p 186) owned Thornbridge Hall until 1859. John Sleigh was an owner for a short time until 1871. Thornbridge Hall. Historic England, list entry number 1001275.

[422] The Derbyshire Returns to the 1851 Religious Census. Margery Tranter (ed). Derbyshire Record Society, 1995, p 174.

[423] Faculty for the Restoration of Ashford Church, 1868, Derbyshire Record Office, D747/A/PI.

with Revd Tyack's disdainful observation on box pews in general: that 'the nave was cut up like a modern cattle market, into so many closed pens or pews, and the whole place was arranged for comfortable bearing rather than for devout worshipping.'[424] JS Luxmoore had a similar opinion:

> *'It was in the 16th and 17th centuries that those hideous pews which disfigured most churches until the present generation – and are to be found in many now – first came into fashion.'[425]*

And so, at Revd Luxmoore's restoration, 'all the pews were swept away, and the church fitted throughout with pitch pine seats.'[426]

'REFIT AND REPAIR THE NAVE, AISLES AND CHANCEL'

Prior to the restoration, the easternmost box pews were almost within touching distance of the altar (see p 176). Therefore, in order to give greater architectural significance to the mystery of the Eucharist, the chancel was considerably enlarged westwards and set one step above the floor of the nave, symbolically separating clergy and laity. A further visual partition was provided by a new chancel arch, supported on columns fashioned from the rare and beautiful 'Duke's Red Marble'.[427] Raising the altar by two further steps, and placing it behind a new communion rail, ensured that it became a distinctive focal point for all the congregation.

The tradition of a robed choir was virtually unknown in Anglican parish churches until the Oxford Movement sought to revive a more Catholic liturgical practice. With galleries now abolished, choirs were relocated from the west end to an elevated position in the chancel (although some in the high church did object to allowing such a large group of laity into the chancel):

> *'Before the restoration, the chancel was pewed like the rest of the church, while the choir sat in the gallery. At the restoration these pews were replaced by oak choir stalls.'[428]*

---

[424] *Pulpits. Revd George S Tyack. In: Antiquities and Curiosities of the Church. William Andrews (ed). William Andrews & Co, 1897, p 128.*

[425] *John Stonhouse Luxmoore. Derbyshire Record Office, D7672/Lx.C-30.*

[426] *Ibid.*

[427] *The Geology of Chatsworth House, Derbyshire. Ian Thomas and Mick Cooper. Mercian Geologist, Vol 17, East Midlands Geological Society, Nottingham, 2008, p 30.*

[428] *John Stonhouse Luxmoore. Derbyshire Record Office, D7672/Lx.C-30.*

(Holy Trinity Church, Ashford-in-the-Water, 1996, p6, states that the choir stalls are 20th century, but JS Luxmoore affirms that these were installed during the 1870 restoration.)

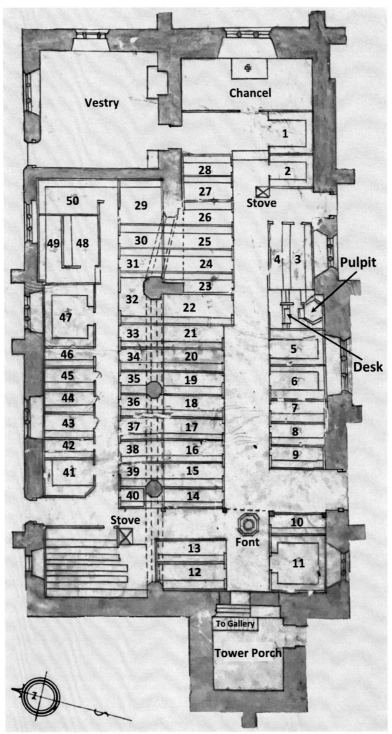

Plan of Ashford Church as of 1867, before the restoration. The box pew numbers, shown highlighted here, are lightly penciled in on the original document. The annotations have been redrawn, for clarity.

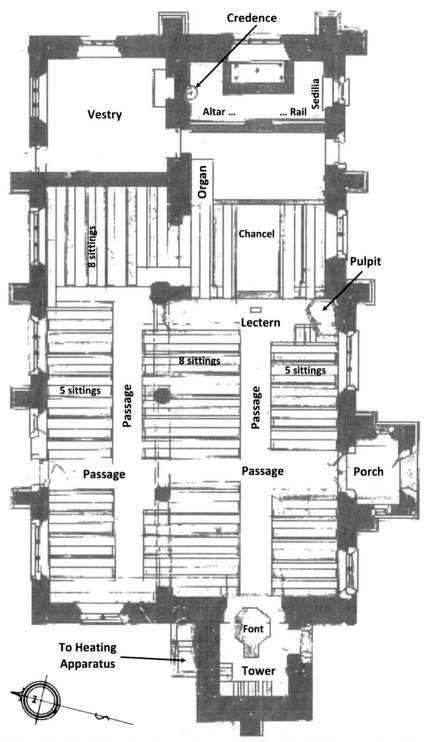

Plan of Ashford Church as it was to appear after the 1870 restoration. The annotations have been redrawn, for clarity. The 'credence' is a small niche for holding the elements of the Eucharist. The 'sedilia' are seats for the clergy.

The higher priority given to the choir and to music encouraged the introduction, even in small parishes, of substantial settings of the morning and evening canticles and anthems, by leading composers such as Samuel Sebastian Wesley. These had previously only been sung in cathedrals and the largest parish churches.

The edict to 'repair the nave aisles' included excavation work and the installation of cast-iron grilles for the new heating system. It is likely that, during these and other repairs to the flooring in the main and north aisles, the builders came across the remains of parishioners who had been buried there, for 'it is said (by Mr James Green) that burials in the church were a common thing at Ashford'[429] (see p114).

The Faculty appropriately cautioned,

'And if it shall be necessary in any case in carrying out the proposed alterations and restoration to remove or disturb any graves, vaults or tombstones, due care shall be had thereof and such graves and vaults shall be rebuilt within the churchyard of the said parish and any bodies or remains there may be found shall be decently and properly reinterred within such churchyard.'

JS Luxmoore mentions the following burials inside the church:

* *'1801. February 10th. Buried Mary Swann, an infant of John and Hannah Bullock of Cliff End, who died Feb. 6. In a vault now made under their seat in the middle aisle. ... Aged nine months.'*

* *'The Bullocks lived at the Rookery, which belonged to them, but was not then called the Rookery'.*

* *'Halls of Churchdale are buried near the north wall.'*

* *'Greens in the north aisle'.*

* *'Blackwells elsewhere.'*

* *'The last buried inside was Mr James Green, Nov. 1846, in the north aisle.'*

The Faculty gives special instructions for a particular tombstone which had to be relocated when the new porch was erected:

'To remove (in case it should be necessary for the due carrying out of the Plans) a monumental slab erected to the memory of a Mrs

---

[429] *John Stonhouse Luxmoore. Derbyshire Record Office, D7672/Lx.C-30.*

Hoole, with the railing thereunto belonging, from their present position in the churchyard near the south door three or four feet in the same direction further west – provided always, and it is hereby expressly declared, that the vault or grave over which the said slab is erected shall in no way be interfered with but that the flat stone and railing thereunto belonging shall alone be taken away and removed aforesaid.'

JS Luxmoore indicates that Hannah Hoole (1804-1852) of Sheffield was the last of the Bullock family; the tombstone confirms that she was the daughter of John Bullock (1774-1820) and Hannah Bullock, née Hoyle (1778-1820), and wife of Henry Hoole (1804-1855), a Sheffield merchant. It was her sister, Mary Swann Bullock, who, as mentioned above, had died as an infant and had been buried in the church.

A memorial to John Bullock's father, William Bullock (1735-1784), hangs on the inside south wall of the tower. William was a 'doctor of physic' and a JP for the county of Derby. In 1764 he married a Mary Swann (1740-1807), after whom their ill-fated granddaughter had been named.[430] The Ashford tablet also memorialises another John Bullock, who had been the Vicar of St Giles' Church, Hartington, from 1754 until his death in December 1789.[431]

Two wall plaques that had originally been secured on the west wall of the nave under the old gallery – one plaque each side of the wooden partition – were relocated to the south wall of what is now the outer vestry. One of these stone plaques memorialises John Harris (1692-1775) and his wife Elizabeth (1710-1772); the second memorialises John Cresswell (1721-1767), his wife Margaret (1717-1780), their sons, and other Cresswell family members.

It was probably at the time of this restoration that the 'two large stone tablets inscribed with the ten commandments, which formerly adorned the walls of the sanctuary', were relocated to their present position on the interior walls of the vestry.[432] They can be glimpsed in their original location in Revd Luxmoore's 1908 photograph of the maidens' garlands (see p 188).

---

[430] *In 1808, John Bullock erected a memorial to his mother, Mary, in Chelmorton Parish Church. Prior to her marriage to William Bullock, Mary had been married to one John Barrow. The History, Gazetteer, and Directory of the County of Derby. Part 2. Stephen Glover. Henry Mozley & Son, Derby, 1829, p 257.*

[431] *Clergy of the Church of England Database 1540-1835, https://theclergydatabase.org.uk*

[432] *Ashford-in-the-Water and its Church. John Norman, 1961.*

Other matters related to Revd Luxmoore's restoration

Screen

In the 16th century, following the English Reformation, Anglican churches were typically fitted with a wooden latticework screen between the chancel and the nave.[433] This was to separate and protect the sacramental bread and wine, physically and symbolically, from unauthorised access by lay people. Indeed, John Norman seems confident that, at Ashford, 'the rood screen and loft, on which stood a crucifix [the 'rood'], originally separated the chancel from the nave.'[434]

Dr Brushfield opines that, whilst there is no documentary evidence for or against the existence of a rood loft,

'the third pillar to the east [at the level of the current chancel step, where the nave now terminates] is considerably larger than either of the others, and is strengthened by a piece of walling on its southern aspect, 3 feet wide, which acted as a buttress. A similar projection corresponded to this on the inside of the south wall, the inner face of each being continuous with that of a contracted chancel. In the same line with these projections, a buttress was planted against the south wall. There can be little doubt as to the explanation of all this extra strength. We learn from the testimony

The 1846 Camden Society illustration of the rood screen and loft at All Saints' Church, Upper Sheringham, Norfolk, as referred to by TN Brushfield.

---

[433] *Roods, Screens and Lofts in Derbyshire Churches. Aymer Vallance. In: Memorials of Old Derbyshire. J Charles Cox (ed). Bemrose & Sons, Derby & London, 1907, p 200.*

[434] *Ashford-in-the-Water and its Church. John Norman, 1961.*

of observers, that in the angle behind the present pulpit, that is to say, at the junction of the wide part of the nave with the chancel, where the wall was originally made much thicker than the rest on the south side, ... several steps leading to the rood loft were found in situ. From this it is evident the original chancel commenced at this spot, that an arch probably separated it from the nave, and that a screen, with its upper structure of a rood loft supporting the rood and attendant figures, formed the line of demarcation between the two portions of the building. This is further corroborated by the chancel floor being elevated 6 inches above that of the nave, commencing at this spot.'

Rood lofts in smaller churches would indeed often have been supported by a transverse rood beam running across the juncture between the chancel and nave, the beam resting at each end on corbels or other structural elements. However, it seems that the 'extra strength' of the third pillar at Ashford had not been provided explicitly to support a rood loft; it seems rather that this was the 'new square stone pillar' built by Revd Giles (see p156).

The crucifix referred to by John Norman would quite likely have been illuminated on festival days by candles placed in the narrow rood loft, in which case access may have been via some narrow rood stairs as suggested by Brushfield. JS Luxmoore comments that James Medland Taylor had 'some recollection' of steps to a rood loft'[435] and also recalls that 'a native of Ashford is sure [no doubt Brushfield's 'testimony of observers'] that, at the time of the restoration, or during some previous repairs, steps were found by the south wall.'[436]

So, there seems to be good reason to believe that a rood screen and loft had at one time existed in Ashford Church. Dr Brushfield, referencing a plate published by the Cambridge Camden Society in 1846, believes that its general appearance would probably have been similar to that of All Saints' Church, Upper Sheringham, Norfolk;[437] this may be so, except that in Sheringham's case the rood beam is supported via upright posts at the north and south ends, rather than via pillars or corbels.

---

[435] *James Medland Taylor's letter of June 9th 1899 to Revd JR Luxmoore states 'my brother [Henry] says that he has a dim recollection of some indication of steps to a rood loft, but I see no office record of them.' Derbyshire Record Office, D7672/Lx.C-29/16.*

[436] *John Stonhouse Luxmoore. Derbyshire Record Office, D7672/Lx.C-30.*

Such a staircase could have been very narrow indeed: 'In Derbyshire there are to be found rood entrances as narrow as, if not even narrower than, anywhere else in the kingdom [some measuring] only 18 inches wide'. Roods, Screens and Lofts in Derbyshire Churches. Aymer Vallance. Op. cit., p 232.

[437] *Ashford Church. TN Brushfield. Journal of the British Archaeological Association, Vol VI, Bedford Press, London, 1900, p 280.*

If such a structure had once been in place, it would probably have been removed by around 1800, when the rood screen and loft had become virtually extinct in Europe.[438] Although they were frequently reintroduced in Victorian restorations, this evidently did not happen at Ashford.

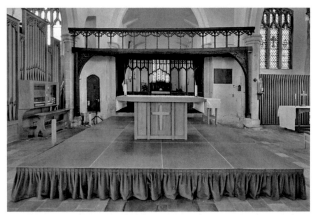

A nave altar is now situated on the west side of the screen at All Saints' Church, Upper Sheringham, Norfolk.

It is interesting to note that at Sheringham, where the 15th-century rood screen and original rood beam still survive intact, a new nave altar sits to its *west* side, consistent with an ecclesiastical architectural practice now adopted in many larger churches and some cathedrals. Whilst this ostensibly defeats the original purpose of the screen – to symbolically separate the sacramental elements and protect the central mystery of the Eucharist – current thinking is that liturgical action should be more open and inclusive, and representative of God in our midst. This, however, evokes controversy from those who believe it epitomises secularisation of the Sacrament. Whether there should ever be a screen is a provocative question, as exemplified by the 'storm' occasioned by the removal of the screen at Hereford Cathedral in 1967.[439]

Pulpit

Revd Giles had already satisfied one of the most important ecclesiastical architectural requirements of the day by removing the three-decker pulpit (see p158). Revd Luxmoore clearly approved of the replacement, with its Jacobean panels, that had been made by George and Peter Milnes; he simply removed the associated clerk's desk and placed the pulpit on a new stone base, at a cost £7 10s 0d.[440]

Half a century later, in 1920, JB Firth notes that:

'The Jacobean pulpit is plentifully adorned with rusty nails driven into it in the name of church decoration at festival times. Wise vicars lay a

---

[438] *Rood Screen. Kathleen Kuiper (ed). Encyclopædia Britannica, 2008.*

[439] *To screen, or not to screen? Michael Tavinor. Church Times, November 17th 2017.*

[440] *John Stonhouse Luxmoore. Derbyshire Record Office, D7672/Lx.C-30.*

stern embargo on iron nails, however saintly the fingers which delicately ply the hammer.'[441]

In 1996 the sounding board, which had been stored in the vestry, was repaired and reinstated in memory of Thomas Nadauld Brushfield's grandson, the solicitor Thomas Nadauld Nugent Brushfield.

Heraldry

Two types of heraldic crest started to appear commonly in English churches in the 16th and 17th centuries: royal arms and funerary hatchments.

Memorial to Thomas Nadauld Nugent Brushfield (1916-1993), affixed in 1996 when the sounding board above the pulpit at Ashford Church was renovated.

The former reinforced visually the monarch's role as head of the Church of England. An example, dated 1724 from the reign of George I, survived Revd Luxmoore's renovation. It was restored in 1985 and rehung over the tower arch.[442]

The latter, a coat of arms memorialising a member of a prominent local family, would typically have first been suspended over the door of the deceased person's house for 6 to 12 months, before being moved inside the parish church.

It is recorded in 1829[443] that there was a hatchment in Ashford Church for 'the Chenys [sic] of Ashford Hall', inscribed with the motto *'mors janua vitae'* ('death is the gate to life'). Lysons,[444] Sleigh[445] and JS Luxmoore have all confirmed that members of the Cheney family lived in Ashford in the first

---

[441] *Highways and Byways in Derbyshire. JB Firth. Macmillan & Co Ltd, London, 1920, p 255.*

[442] *'The removal of the tower floor [during the installation of a new cast-iron bell frame: see footnote 408, p 169] enabled a large hatchment board dated 1724 to be brought down for cleaning and replacing. Obviously it had been placed in the tower in 1750, when the floor had been removed for the new bell [the third bell to be installed in the tower], and could not be brought down after that until 1953. The board seems to be one of the earliest forms of the royal arms, and is of some interest'. Report on the Fabric, Goods and Ornaments of the Church. Revd Thomas George. April 14th 1955. For a colour photograph, see: Holy Trinity Church, Ashford-in-the-Water, 1996, back cover.*

[443] *The History, Gazetteer, and Directory of the County of Derby. Part 2. Stephen Glover. Henry Mozley & Son, Derby, 1829, p 49.*

[444] *Magna Britannia, a concise topographical account of the several counties of Great Britain. Vol 5 (Derbyshire). Daniel & Samuel Lysons. T Cadell & W Davies, London. 1817, p cxxi.*

[445] *The Cheney Family. John Sleigh. The Reliquary, Vol 11, Llewellynn Jewitt (ed). Bemrose & Sons, Derby & London, 1870-1871, p 115 and plate XIII.*

half of the 18th century, and Cox cites that 'there is cut upon the altar rails (ca.1820) 'Thomas Cheney, Richard Whitby, Church-wardens, AD1715.''[446] The Cheney family hatchment is, therefore, most likely the 'coat of arms' that hung 'in the Chancel, on the south wall',[447] but it did not survive the 1870 building work.

The Cheney Arms: azure, six lions rampant, argent; a canton, ermine.

Windows

Prior to the 1870 restoration, Samuel Birley comments that 'the windows were all plain glass, the large east window and the window near the pulpit were square at the top.'[448] But 160 years earlier, in 1710, when the heraldic painter and antiquarian from Derby, Francis Bassano (1675-1746),[449] visited the church, he noted that the east window of the north aisle depicted the heraldry tinctures 'verry, argent and gules', indicating an alternating pattern of red and white panes. This heraldry was not unique to one family, but it has been suggested appropriate to attribute it to the Beauchamps, who were connected with the Nevilles.[450] That being the case, this window could at one time have been just one of several displaying heraldic tinctures.[451]

To bring his restoration vibrantly to life in the preferred Anglican ecclesiastical manner, Revd Luxmoore secured funding from local families for three significant new stained-glass windows that were installed in memory of their loved ones.

A four-light window with tracery in the west wall of the north aisle, reproducing existing designs of William Morris, Edward Burne-Jones and Philip Webb, was installed in 1880 in memory of John Gregory Cottingham

---

[446] *Notes on the Churches of Derbyshire, Vol II, The Hundreds of the High Peak and Wirksworth. J Charles Cox. Bemrose & Sons, Derby & London, 1877, p 577.*

This Richard Whitby (1660-1731) is likely the father of Margaret Nadauld, née Whitby (1689-1780), daughter-in-law of Henry Nadauld (see pp 99, 193).

[447] *Mr S Birley's Remarks on the Church Copied Verbatim, Jan 1900, Derbyshire Record Office, D7672/Lx.C-33.*

[448] *Ibid.*

[449] *The Bassano family. A-Z of Derby: Places-People-History. Maxwell Craven, 2018.*

[450] *Anne Beauchamp (1426-1492) was the mother of King Richard III's wife, who was a member of the House of Neville.*

[451] *Notes on the Churches of Derbyshire, Vol II, The Hundreds of the High Peak and Wirksworth. J Charles Cox. Bemrose & Sons, Derby & London, 1877, pp 49-50.*

(1813-1878). John was born at Hardwick Hall, where his father was employed as the house steward by the 5th Duke of Devonshire. He qualified as a solicitor, succeeded his father as steward of Hardwick Hall, and became Mayor of Chesterfield.[452] He was a cousin of Joseph Paxton's wife and, after the 6th Duke's death, he assumed Joseph's role as the land agent at Chatsworth.[453]

The 6th Duke appointed John's younger brother, Revd Henry Cottingham, to the living at St Michael and All Angels' Church, Hathersage. In 1852, during the term of this appointment, Revd Cottingham officiated at the marriage of his brother to Mary Anne Hallewell (1825-1882) in Cheltenham.[454] Mary was the second daughter of Edmund Gilling Hallewell (1796-1881), who was born in Boroughbridge. Edmund's father, Revd John Hallewell (also spelt Halliwell), had been appointed Curate of St James, Boroughbridge, in 1785. He was succeeded as the incumbent there, many years later, by William Cyril Luxmoore (see p141).[455] John Gregory and Mary Anne Cottingham are both buried in the churchyard of St Peter's Church, Edensor. Stained glass windows memorialising John's life are also installed in that church, as well as at St John the Baptist's Church,

The north aisle west window, depicting the Annunciation (top), St John the Evangelist and the poisoned chalice (bottom left), and Pope Gregory the Great (bottom right).

[452] *The Froggatts of Froggatt. Jennifer E Nicholas (née Froggatt), https://froggattsoffroggatt. wordpress.com/19th-century-secrets-and-revelations/*

[453] *Joseph Paxton (1803–1865). John Kenworthy-Browne. Oxford Dictionary of National Biography, Oxford University Press, 2004.*

[454] *Hereford Journal. August 11th 1852.*

[455] *St James Church, Boroughbridge: Transcription of incumbents. Jack Parry & Colin Hinson, https://www.genuki.org.uk/big/eng/YKS/WRY/Aldborough/BoroughbridgeStJamesIncumbents Transcription*

Ault Hucknall, where Revd Henry Cottingham had become the incumbent in 1859.[456]

The six-light window in the south wall of Ashford Church, adjacent to the pulpit, was installed in memory of Edmund Haworth (1797-1879), who lived in Churchdale Hall in the 1860s and 1870s. Haworth is also memorialised in a tablet on the south wall of the vestry, having bequeathed £500 to provide to the poor of Ashford 'useful articles of clothing or bedding'. The captions at the bottom of each window light reflect the practical Christian thinking that inspired his gift:

The window in the south wall of Ashford Church. Each light includes a Christian message about neighbourliness.

I was an hungred and ye gave me meat
I was naked and ye clothed me
I was thirsty and ye gave me drink
I was a stranger and ye took me in
I was sick and ye visited me
I was in prison and ye came to me

Edmund Haworth was second cousin to the two-times Prime Minister, Rt Hon Sir Robert Peel, MP. (His grandaunt, Elizabeth Peel (née Haworth), was the Prime Minister's grandmother.)[457]

The most prominent of the windows from this time is the east window, dedicated 'To the Glory of God and in Memory of Alfred Morewood, who died April 2 1872, aged 57'. The Morewood family has a pedigree that can be traced back to Bradfield in South Yorkshire at the advent of the Elizabethan era, but by the 17th and 18th century Alfred's ancestors are to be found in the Buxton area. His grandfather Andrew, a Manchester merchant, acquired Thornbridge Hall in Ashford from the Longsdon family of Little Longstone. He began to

---

[456] *The Cottingham Memorial Window. Derbyshire Times and Chesterfield Herald, November 1st 1879.*

History, Topography, and Directory of Derbyshire. T Bulmer et al. T Snape & Co, Preston, 1895, p 47.

[457] *The Haworths of Thurcroft, in the County of Lancaster [now Lancashire], and the Descent of the Right Hon Sir Robert Peel, Bart, MP, from the Haworths. William Haworth. Llewellynn Jewitt (ed). The Reliquary, Vol 18, Bemrose & Sons, Derby & London, 1877-1878, pp 29-32.*

rebuild it in the classical style, the work being continued by Alfred's uncle, John, and then his father, George.

The last of the Morewoods to live there were Alfred's sister Ann and her husband James McConnel: they were married at Holy Trinity in 1842, and sold the Hall back to the Longsdon family in 1859.[458] That same year, Revd James Burrow was the priest at the marriage of Alfred to one of the Longsdons, the widow Eliza Briggs.

Revd Luxmoore officiated at both Alfred's funeral, on April 6th 1872, and Eliza's funeral, on February 23rd 1898. They are buried together with Alfred's parents, George Morewood and

The east window at Ashford Church, depicting the crucifixion of Christ, is dedicated to Alfred Morewood (1815-1872).

Ellen Pierpoint Morewood (née Barrow), in a railed gritstone tomb in Holy Trinity's churchyard, on the south side of the old preaching cross.

The three stained-glass windows in the north wall were installed more recently, and are a gift of Alice Tinsley (died December 28th 1942); a memorial to Mary Hall Wall (died April 7th 1923); and a commemoration of William (1904-1992) and Kitty (1904-1998) Olivier.[459]

Maidens' garlands

Ashford Church is recognised for its maidens' garlands – once common but now very rare artefacts. They are a poignant reminder of an old English custom

---

[458] *Thornbridge Hall. Historic England, list entry number 1001275. The Hall was subsequently purchased from the Longsdons by John Sleigh, a Leek manufacturer; then it was acquired by Frederick Craven; and in 1896 by George Jobson Marples.*

[459] *William Herbert Olivier (1904-1992) was the cousin of the actor and director, Sir Laurence Olivier (1907-1989). William's and Laurence's fifth great-grandfather, Revd Jourdain Olivier (1643-1709), was a Huguenot refugee (see p 119). William lived in Ashford Hall with his wife, Kitty – Katherine Mary Olivier (née Jones). The window, designed in 2001 by the French artist Flore Sivell (née Vignet), reflects the Olivier family motto: 'Sicut oliva virens, laetor in aede Dei' – 'but I am like a green olive tree in the house of God; I trust in the mercy of God for ever and ever.' Psalm 52, v 8, King James translation.*

in which a garland was carried in a procession before the coffin of a young girl, and afterwards displayed in the church – a privilege given only to virgins. The custom and the garlands, the oldest of which dates from 1747, are described in detail elsewhere.[460] Originally seven in number, five were surviving by Revd Luxmoore's time:

Maidens' garlands at Ashford Church. Photograph by Revd JR Luxmoore, 1908.

'Fortunately, the five garlands at Ashford were scrupulously preserved at the time of the recent [1868-1870] restoration, and subsequently replaced in the same position that they had previously occupied.'[461]

One of the garlands fell to the ground in 1935 and could not be repaired; the four now remaining were expertly cleaned and conserved in 1987, before being resuspended inside protective transparent covers.

Bells

The oldest bell in Ashford Church is a small pre-Reformation sanctus bell, known as the 'ting-tang' bell after its characteristic sound, and also called the 'pancake bell' because it was traditionally rung on Shrove Tuesday.

The pre-Reformation sanctus bell in the belfry of Ashford Church.

---

[460] *Derbyshire Funeral Garlands. TN Brushfield. Journal of the British Archaeological Association, Vol VI, Bedford Press, London, 1900, pp 54-74.*

Holy Trinity Church, Ashford-in-the-Water, 1996, p 4.

[461] *Notes on the Churches of Derbyshire, Vol II, The Hundreds of the High Peak and Wirksworth. J Charles Cox. Bemrose & Sons, Derby & London, 1877, p 51.*

In 1864, Thomas Brushfield recounted this custom, which even then had been of at least 60 years' standing:

> '*SHROVE TUESDAY – Also called Goody's Tuesday – was held as a notable day in the village. At eleven o'clock in the morning of that day, a bell, called the 'pancake bell,' was rung in the church tower, and on the first sounding of that bell the children of the schools in the village were released from their studies, and had the rest of the day for holiday purposes – indeed it was a general holiday. The game of football was generally played during the after part of the day. These customs are still observed – the pancakes, the bell-tolling, and the football-playing – and there is no harm in them ...*

> '*I must, as a faithful recorder, mention another Shrove Tuesday custom, and one that is still, I believe, observed – it is for an unengaged youth to kiss the first young single female he meets on that day. This custom is called 'lousing,' and the salutation is considered to be a sure presage of a union for life of the parties concerned.*'

He goes on to say,

> '*But that such presage is not to be relied upon, I am a living evidence.*'[462]

However, JS Luxmoore tells of a more auspicious amorous encounter related to the ringing of this bell:

> '*Mrs George Furniss (née Sarah Green) said that the Pancake Bell was rung by women; and that a certain Elizabeth Twynham once rang so vigorously that she tore off a sleeve of her dress. Whilst ringing she saw a 'beau' (one Frederick Gale, a stranger) walking along by Gorse Furlong (i.e., near by where Rowland Holmes' house stood), and said she would like to marry a man like him. She married this identical man.*'[463]

Regarding the bell itself: 'from the appearance of its surface it plainly has been openly exposed to the weather for very many years'; ... it 'formerly hung in [an exterior] bell-cote above the chancel arch'[464] – a view confirmed at the time by an old villager, Joseph Smith.

James Medland Taylor's suggestions regarding this bell were not adopted during Revd Luxmoore's restoration. In 1899 the (by then retired) architect

[462] *A Second Notice of Customs, Notions, and Practices, at Ashford-in-the-Water, Sixty Years Ago.* Thomas Brushfield. *The Reliquary, Vol 5, Llewellynn Jewitt (ed). Bemrose & Sons, Derby & London, 1864-1865, p 153.*

[463] *John Stonhouse Luxmoore. Derbyshire Record Office, D7672/Lx.C-30.*

[464] *Ibid.*

comments, 'there was an old sanctus bell for which I designed a sanctus bell turret. But – as you know – I was not allowed to have this carried out.'[465]

The bell was therefore stored in the tower following the 1868-1870 renovation. It was rediscovered in 1893 and rehung in the tower, where it remains today; it is often chimed during the consecration of the Eucharist.

The sanctus bell is not hung for full-circle change ringing. However, in Revd Luxmoore's time three other bells were so mounted.[466] But because three

Bell-ringing instructions dated 1889, posted in the tower of Ashford Church.

bells provide only six possible orders of ringing (changes), there was little opportunity for the ringers to practise 'the Exercise' beyond a fairly rudimentary level. They could therefore not satisfactorily ring the methods that would be heard in neighbouring towers blessed with larger peals.

In 1889 it seems that the Ashford churchwardens wanted to restrict even further the ringers' freedom to practise their art, and instead adhere to a very specific set of ringing instructions. This is consistent with the efforts of the Established Church to maintain control in their belfries. It was during the 18th century that bell-ringers first acquired a reputation for inebriation and irreverent behaviour. Local tavern owners would have been very happy to relieve the ringers of the few shillings they had earned, and suggest that they should, in fact, ring for any and every occasion – not only for church services, but for all manner of essentially secular national or community events: to drive away evil; to calm storms; to bring plagues to an end; and to celebrate or commiserate successes or failures in wars.

---

[465] *Letter to Revd John Reddaway Luxmoore from James Medland Taylor, June 9th 1899, Derbyshire Record Office, D7672/Lx.C-29/16.*

[466] *These are now the fourth (originally cast ca. 1600-1612), fifth (1750), and tenor (1612) bells, all of which were recast in 1954. (See footnote 408, p 169.)*

By the early decades of the 19th century, some towers had become notorious as the bell-ringers engaged in heavy drinking and riotous behaviour, and some were even closed by their clergy. Therefore, within with the broader reform movement of the Established Church, an effort was made to reinstate the clergy's control of belfries and ringers. Many churches had the floor of the ringing chamber removed and the ropes lengthened, so that the ringers performed in full view of the congregation, as is now the case at Ashford.[467]

Although initial attempts to control bell-ringers met with resistance from bands who fought to maintain their independence, as the 20th century approached tower captains were appointed to help ensure proper behaviour and to improve ringers' skills. The number of bells was augmented in many towers, including, in 1954 and 1966, the addition of three new bells at Ashford (see footnote 408, p 169).

Prior to the renovations, the bell-ringers had to enter the tower by the exterior door on the south wall, the only means of access. Once the gallery and partition had been removed, they could enter from inside the nave. The Faculty Plan of 1868 indicates that new stairs were to be provided in the interior north-west corner of the tower, presumably to assist access to the clock and belfry. However, JS Luxmoore notes in about 1902 that, as is currently the case, 'there is no access to the bell chamber except by an ordinary ladder'.

The Churchyard

The recollections of Mr Birley and JS Luxmoore mention (among other interesting facts) some changes made in the churchyard at the time of Revd Luxmoore's restoration:

> 'In 1829 the burial ground was in a very neglected state. The children of the village used it as a playground, especially in the summer months, as there was no place, only the streets for them. The field where the manor house formerly stood was not then allowed them to play in from Shrove Tuesday until 5th of November, by the tenant who then occupied the land – George Hill of the Elms.

> 'At the entrance gate leading to the church was placed the stocks, for the punishment of the disorderly or unruly. I remember when a boy seeing a man in them.[468] Part of one of the stones is fixed in the stile leading from Ashford to Longstone.

---

[467] *History of Bell Ringing. Association of Ringing Teachers, 2019, http://www.bellringing.org*

[468] *John Norman states: 'The stocks which formerly stood near the entrance to the churchyard were removed ... on August 25th 1837.' Ashford-in-the-Water and its Church. John Norman. 1967 edition, p 11.*

James Medland & Henry Taylor's drawings of Ashford Church, as it was expected to appear following Revd Luxmoore's restoration.

'Just inside the yard, on the left hand leading to the church, stands a very old yew tree, which was probably planted there when the first church or chapel was built, and the burial ground first opened ... there was a very large ash tree at the west end, which was blown down a few years ago... ['The roots of the tree had encircled a memorial stone to the two children (Richard and Elizabeth) of Peter and Margaret Nadauld [née Whitby]. Some coffin plates, a cup, and coins were found when the remains of the tree were cleared away.'][469]

'At the time of the restoration, some waste ground was taken in, which increased the size of the burial ground a little, and a new wall was built all round, except at the west end.

'The new gate at the entrance to the church, the north gate, and the gate near the vestry were done away at this time, and gravel paths were made.'[470]

Reopening of Holy Trinity Church after Revd Luxmoore's restoration of 1868-1870

The church reopened for public worship on June 17th 1870, the Friday following Trinity Sunday. Bishop Selwyn presided, and the event was recorded in great detail in the local press.[471]

The bishop was 'assisted by a large number of his clergy' from Bakewell, Tideswell, Darley, South Darley, East Molesey[472], Youlgreave, Great Longstone, Chelmorton, Tideswell, Fairfield, Baslow, Millbrook, Taddington, and elsewhere.

There was a large congregation and the interior of the church had been decorated with 'garlands of flowers, and bannerets bearing suitable inscriptions and devices'.

---

[469] *John Stonhouse Luxmoore. Derbyshire Record Office, D7672/Lx.C-30.*

[470] *Mr S Birley's Remarks on the Church Copied Verbatim, Jan 1900, Derbyshire Record Office, D7672/Lx.C-33.*

[471] *The quotations following are from the Derby Mercury, June 22nd 1870.*

[472] *The incumbent of St Mary's Church in East Molesey, Surrey, was Revd William James Boys, who was Rector from 1869 to 1873. He had been a curate at All Saints' Church, Bakewell, from 1864 to 1866, which is when Revd Luxmoore would have met him. The Clergy List, Kelley & Co Ltd, London, 1897, p 118.*

A Topographical History of Surrey. Edward Wedlake Brayley, revised by Edward Walford. JS Virtue & Co Ltd, London, Vol 2, 1878, p 76.

Revd Boys' church was a few minutes' walk from Hampton Court Palace, where Henry Nadauld had worked 170 years earlier; a few miles from Friar's Stile Road, Richmond, where Revd Luxmoore's sister-in-law, Isabella Harriet Stonhouse, was about to live; and within about 25 miles of the two rectories at Frimley and Ash, Surrey, where Rosalie's uncles – Revd Charles Stonhouse and Revd Gilbert Heathcote – were the incumbents. There were therefore many reasons for Revd Luxmoore to keep in touch with Revd Boys after he had left Bakewell.

The service commenced with the hymn 'Christ is our Cornerstone', a 7th-century Latin text translated in 1837 by John Chandler. It was sung, quite probably, to Samuel Sebastian Wesley's tune, *Harewood*.

When the bishop entered the pulpit, he 'proceeded to address his hearers upon the various phases in the life of Christ represented by the ecclesiastical division of the calendar', leaving few of the major feasts and Holy Days unmentioned. He went on to promote the sacraments of baptism and the Eucharist, rebuking the 'thousands [who] have come to live among us who do not know the difference between Christian baptism and civil registration', and the 'men and women … in most congregations … who never received … the blessed sacrament of the Lord's Supper.'

Noting the bishop's criticism of those who 'abridged [their] prayers because they made the service a moment longer', and his suggestion to the congregation that 'if Christ had been stationed with us, he would have said, 'What, cannot ye watch with me one hour?'', we perhaps should not be surprised that 'the proceedings lasted upwards of two hours.'

Framed photomontage of Revd JR Luxmoore and the interior of his restored church.

The offertory, which amounted to £18 12s 6½d [£1,750], was undoubtedly a welcome addition to the church coffers.

A concluding observation is of interest:

'It had been announced that a confirmation would be held by the bishop, but that, from some cause, was departed from.'

Clearly, neither the reporter nor the congregation had received an explanation for this.

It will be recalled (see p140) that Revd Luxmoore and Rosalie's three-month-old son, Arthur Samuel Luxmoore, had been christened by the bishop on this day. As the infant died less than two months later, he might have already been in poor health. The christening would therefore have been a private and possibly emotional service, taking precedence over the scheduled confirmation ceremony.

Revd Luxmoore's further renovations (1890-1894)

Twenty years after its reopening, the church was closed again for a period of five weeks, when it had been found,

'that the work then done [in the 1868-1870 renovation] was not of a very permanent character. The roof was not perfectly waterproof and in addition the plaster upon the walls was of an inferior quality, causing the damp to strike through.

'A movement was set afoot by the vicar, the Revd JR Luxmoore, to remedy these defects, and a subscription list was shortly afterwards opened, to which several influential local gentlemen contributed very liberally, the Duke of Devonshire heading this list with a very handsome donation of £100.'[473]

On this occasion, the architect was a 'Mr Lord of Manchester',[474] the main building contractor was Mr T Allsopp of Bakewell, and,

'the work of plastering the interior, by a new process known as the 'adamant', has been very efficiently carried out by Messrs Hickson and Son of Manchester. The 'adamant plaster' when properly set closely resembles marble, and its inventors, a Birmingham firm, claim that among the most important of its qualities is its permanency.'[475]

---

[473] *Restoration of Ashford Church. Derbyshire Times & Chesterfield Herald, September 27th 1890.*

[474] *Likely Henry Lord (1843-1926). See: Henry Lord. A Biographical Dictionary of the Architects of Greater Manchester, 1800-1940. Manchester Group of the Victorian Society, https:// manchestervictorianarchitects.org.uk/architects/henry-lord*

[475] *Restoration of Ashford Church. Op. cit.*

The church was reopened by the Revd Balston, Vicar of Bakewell, before this latest round of renovations was completed, the stated reason being alleviation of the difficult challenge of conducting services in the Sunday School. However, the reality was that funds had been exhausted: of the total cost of £400, only £300 had been realised by that time, including the £100 donated by the Duke. Therefore, after his 'excellent sermon', an 'earnest appeal was made to the congregation on behalf of the restoration fund' by Revd Balston.

This insufficiency of funds was clearly frustrating for Revd Luxmoore. Even though the high Victorian gothic style was by this time in decline, he seems to have retained a love for polychromatic decoration, perhaps recalling the remains of frescos that had been found on the walls above the aisle arches during his earlier building work.[476] He needed to banish the bland appearance of the adamant plaster and make the walls as beautiful as the new stained-glass windows and the colourful tiles that had been laid in the chancel. He said to his faithful congregation,

'God could certainly be worshipped in a plain, whitewashed building as well as in one more pleasing to the eye, but it must be borne in mind that a church was a building set apart for the worship of God,'

and he was sure that his parishioners,

'would wish the walls of God's House to be different to a cottage bed-chamber.'

The chancel of Holy Trinity Church, Ashford-in-the-Water, showing the designs on the chancel walls added in 1894.

[476] *Ashford Church. TN Brushfield. Journal of the British Archaeological Association, Vol VI, Bedford Press, London, 1900, p 282.*

He returned to the fundraising theme at his evening sermon, saying he had 'never yet known any work for God left undone through lack of money.' The parishioners 'had helped in the work already done, and they would help in the work still to be done. It would be their blessed privilege to do so.'[477]

We cannot know whether Revd Luxmoore's concluding admonishment that 'a repaired congregation was even more important than the repaired fabric of the church' inspired them to dig deep into their pockets for the remaining £100. But we do know that the recolouring work was indeed eventually completed in 1894 by a Manchester artist, Mr Pearse, 'with hand-painted symbolical designs in which brown vines and angels figured prominently.'[478] A 1954 black-and-white photograph of the chancel can convey literally only a pale imitation of what must have been a strikingly vibrant scene.

John Norman reports in 1961 that these colourful designs 'were covered up some years ago in the process of redecoration.' Since he is not explicit about why or when such 'redecoration' occurred, it was probably before he became the vicar, and therefore between the date of the 1954 photograph and the year of his appointment (1957). This would have been during the incumbency of Revd Thomas George.

Once again, the walls of the church, in Revd Luxmoore's words, resembled 'a cottage bed-chamber'.

A reflection

The many hundreds of churches that were built or renovated in the 19th century did not result in the hoped-for rural religious renaissance. Indeed, one commentator has derided them as 'monuments to failure',[479] an ignominy shared with the twin towers of the unfinished Clifton Suspension Bridge (see p65). Certainly the Ecclesiological Society's claim in 1868 that 'we have the satisfaction of retiring from the field victors' rings hollow, to the extent that a tacit goal was to re-establish the pre-eminence of the Anglican Church. But Kenneth Clark's derogatory assessment that the gothic revival 'produced so little in which our eyes can rest without pain' with its 'unsightly wrecks stranded upon the mud flat of Victorian taste'[480] is not only extreme, but surely wrong.

---

[477] *Restoration of Ashford Church. Op. cit.*

[478] *Ashford-in-the-Water and its Church. John Norman. 1961.*
    Derbyshire Record Office, D747/A/PI/14/1.

[479] *A Little History of the English Country Church. Roy Strong. Vintage Books, London, 2007, p 223.*

[480] *Kenneth Clark. The Gothic Revival. Constable & Co, 1928. This statement was unchanged in his revised edition of 1950.*

Who amongst us today does not applaud the passion of Sir John Betjeman, who fought against the demolition of William Barlow's St Pancras Station and Gilbert Scott's accompanying Midland Grand Hotel? Now generally considered amongst the finest examples of Victorian architecture and engineering, these works represent 'a spectacularly-restored piece of history that will take your breath away.'[481]

Gilbert Scott had been restoring Tewkesbury Abbey for a period of 36 years when he became the target of a torrent of criticism inspired by William Morris' letter in *The Athenaeum* (see p154). He was offended by this, not least because he had himself advocated the principles of conservative restoration:

> *'It is therefore rather hard to bear that I should now be made the butt of an extreme party who wish to make me out to be the ringleader of destructiveness.'*[482]

In the context of the natural environment, Ruskin's sarcastic response to the supposed desecration of Monsal Dale (see p70) simply bewilders us: the area is now hailed as 'one of our most beautiful, tranquil and best-loved beauty spots',[483] and the Headstone Viaduct has been granted the status of a Listed Building by virtue of 'its national importance in terms of architectural or historic interest.'

The fact is that many churches would have fallen into disrepair (literally in some cases) had the Victorian restoration movement not saved them. Subsequent writers have sought more temperately to see the good amidst the bad, acknowledging that the definitive architectural history of the Victorian era may yet still have to be written.[484]

As we move into a future of declining congregations and limited funds, it seems desirable, as Isobel Combes advocates, to keep our churches alive with sensitive but imaginative modern renovations to make them more relevant to an increasingly secular society, so that they do not become museums to their own past.[485]

---

[481] *The Man in Seat 61. Mark Smith. 2020, https://www.seat61.com/stations/london-st-pancras.htm*

[482] *The Scott Dynasty, https://gilbertscott.org/tewkesbury-abbey/*

[483] *Derbyshire Life and Countryside, https://www.derbyshirelife.co.uk/out-about/places/wye-valley-1-5635976*

[484] *Gothic for the Steam Age: An illustrated Biography of George Gilbert Scott. Gavin Stamp. Aurum Press, 2015.*

High Victorian Gothic; or, The Dilemma of Style in Modern Architecture. James D Kornwolf. Journal of the Society of Architectural Historians, Vol 34, No. 1, 1975, pp 37-47.

[485] *Anglican Churches of Derbyshire. IAH Combes. Landmark Publishing Ltd, Ashbourne, 2004, p 11.*

Revd John Norman said of his predecessor's restoration, 'no doubt a number of interesting old features perished, but on the whole the resulting church is an example of the best Victorian restoration work.'[486] In its small-scale modesty it cannot, and does not, aspire to be hailed, like that magnificent bridge in Bristol (see p66), as 'the wonder of the age'. But to those who worship in it regularly, or rely upon it to be there to mark the biggest moments in their life's journey, it can most assuredly lay claim to be their personal 'ornament' of the village.

I suspect that John Reddaway Luxmoore would be gratified if he could peruse the positive comments in the Visitors' Book from some of the thousands of people every year who choose to spend a little time in Holy Trinity Church, Ashford-in-the-Water: they seem to me to attest to a potent and inspirational legacy.

---

[486] *Ashford-in-the-Water and its Church. John Norman, 1961.*

IV

THE VICARAGE

Citing the 1616 Ashford Court Rolls that itemise a 'vicar's house, yard and churchyard', John Stonhouse Luxmoore surmises that 'the Old Parsonage lies just across the Court Lane, and only a few yards from the church, near the east end'. He reports that 'it is claimed that the house [now Honeysuckle Cottage] was always occupied by the minister when there was a resident one.'[487] This is consistent with the recollection of a local resident that the vicarage was opposite the vestry and about 10 yards north of the Wesleyan chapel.[488]

As further evidence, JS Luxmoore notes the fact that, opposite this house, steps had been cut into the churchyard's north wall, 'whereby the minister could get into the yard, and proceed by a path leading from the steps round the east end of the church to the priest's door in the south side of the chancel.' He notes that during his father's restoration of the church, 'the steps were done away with when a new wall was built around the yard (except on the western side)', but that 'steps have recently been placed in the wall, practically in the same place as the former ones.'[489]

According to JS Luxmoore, the Old Parsonage was deemed 'not fit' for the residence of Revd William Galley Giles, who arrived in 1837, and he was therefore given permission by the 6th Duke of Devonshire to live at the much larger house, the Rookery, on Buxton Road.[490] Similarly, no suitable

---

[487] *John Stonhouse Luxmoore. Derbyshire Record Office, D7672/Lx.C-30.*

[488] *Notes about the Diaries of J James Middleton of Ashford (1812-1856). Derbyshire Record Office, D307/H/38/5, entry for June 22nd 1854.*

[489] *Repairs to the north wall, including the reinstatement of an entrance and steps at a cost of £40, were approved by the Parochial Church Council in October 1925.*

[490] *John Stonhouse Luxmoore. Derbyshire Record Office, D7672/Lx.C-30.*

History, Gazetteer and Directory of Derbyshire. Samuel Bagshaw. 1846, p 420.

Some 17 years earlier, the same Duke of Devonshire (1790-1858) – the 'Bachelor' Duke – had ensconced his mistress Eliza Warwick in the Rookery – one of a number of properties, known as 'birdcages', where the Duke had kept his lady friends. The Estate: A View from Chatsworth. The Duchess of Devonshire. Macmillan London Ltd, 1990, pp 123-124.

The Arrock hill, as viewed from the Old Vicarage.

parsonage was available in 1850 to his successor, Revd William Boyd.

It was during the incumbency of Revd James Burrow that the Bachelor Duke donated land in the village for a new vicarage, and it was built at a cost of £1,400, raised by public subscription. The house is situated on a hill on the north-west side of the village, its rear aspect facing south-west over the River Wye towards the Arrock, beneath which is one of the mines from where Ashford marble was quarried.

JS Luxmoore reports that the vicarage was designed by Sir Joseph Paxton. This would be three years after Paxton rose to fame as the designer of the Crystal Palace for the Great Exhibition of 1851, and four years before his retirement as the 6th Duke's Head Gardener.[491]

Although principally remembered as a designer of glasshouses and gardens,

> THE VICARAGE.
>   This was built during the time of the Revd. James Burrows (1852 to 1861)
>   The house was built on the side of the hill facing the north side of the Church, of limestone with gritstone quoins.
> It was designed by Sir Joseph Paxton, who seems to have wished to give an ecclesiastical appearance to the house, for the doorways, and the windows are gothic in character, in fact the front door might very well be a Church door.

John Stonhouse Luxmoore's comment on Sir Joseph Paxton's design of Ashford Vicarage.

---

[491] *John Stonhouse Luxmoore. Derbyshire Record Office, D7672/Lx.C-30.*

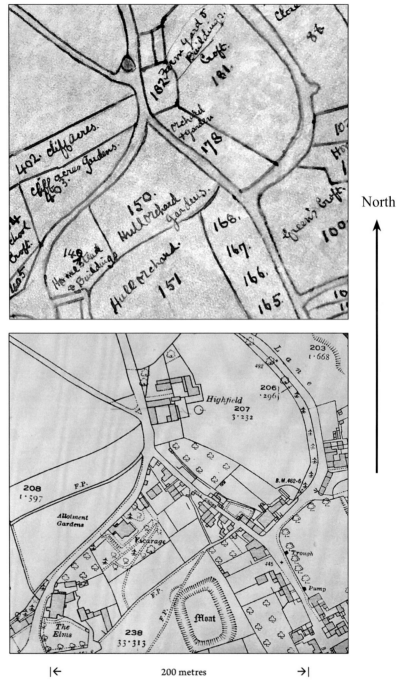

North

Sections of the Ashford allotment map, from the Ashford &
Sheldon enclosure plan of 1767 (top), and an Ordnance Survey
map of 1922 (bottom), depict the location of the vicarage, and
the development of adjoining lands in the intervening period.
The moat on Hall Orchard shows the site of the prior fortified
house of the Nevilles (see p19).

Paxton did design a number of buildings locally, including the station at Rowsley (now a shopping complex), the school in Pilsley, and the school and schoolmistress' house in Beeley. Some of these properties may have been designed in collaboration with the architect John Robertson of Baslow, who, it is believed, worked in Paxton's planning office at Chatsworth between 1840 and 1846. Indeed, Robertson drew the first plans of the Crystal Palace from Paxton's initial pen and ink sketch. Robertson also developed plans for the Ashford Marble Mine in 1840 and, in the same year, made some changes to Ashford's Churchdale Hall.[492] However, he had died before the vicarage was built.

The house was constructed by James Cox-Wilson (1813-1894), who operated his business in the village from a forge and sawmill at Watts Green. He staked out the plot on May 5th 1853, and the foundation stone was laid on June 9th 1853 by Louisa Cavendish of Ashford Hall.[493]

Within the curtilage of the vicarage a two-storey outbuilding was also constructed. The lower level accommodated a horse and one or two carriages, and the upper level provided general storage and dry space for keeping hay, which could have been let down directly to the lower-level stable through a chute.

A *Map of the allotments of the commons and common pastures of Ashford and Sheldon as the same were laid out and allotted in the year 1767* depicts a two-acre parcel of land (allotment 150 – the Hall Orchard Gardens), bounded on the north by what is now Vicarage Lane; on the south by Hall Orchard; on the east by Hill Cross; and on the west by a 'homestead and buildings'. A corresponding Ordnance Survey map of 1922 now shows the vicarage and carriage house, plus some additional properties on the easternmost ¾ acre of the two-acre parcel.

To the south of the vicarage, bordering Hall Orchard, a ½-acre rectangular plot of glebe land[494] was likely once used as an exercise area and pasture for the incumbent's horse. This notion is supported by the fact that there is a path marked on the Ordnance Survey map from the carriage house to this plot of land, and beyond into Hall Orchard. It would also have provided a direct route for the incumbent to Holy Trinity Church, which lies on the other side of Hall Orchard. However, the descent from the vicarage is steep, and in muddy or snowy conditions this route would have been unsafe for anything other than a sure-footed horse.

---

[492] *John Robertson of Baslow: Architect. Ann Hall. Baslow, Derbyshire, 2015.*

[493] *Transcripts of the Diaries of J James Middleton of Ashford (1812-1856). Derbyshire Record Office. Record No. D307/H/38/5, entries for May 5th 1853 and June 9th 1853.*

[494] *Land assigned to the incumbent of a parish as part of his benefice and the endowment of the church. The Local Historian's Glossary of Words and Terms. Joy Bristow. Countryside Books, Newbury, Berkshire, 2001.*

On March 27th 1930, Holy Trinity's Parochial Church Council adopted the following resolution:

'The Parochial Church Council has had under consideration the fact that the churchyard is practically full and does not admit of extension. The Parochial Church Council suggests that the Parish Council take steps with a view to the provision of a public burying ground, or cemetery.'

Having reviewed a number of potential sites over the ensuing three years, the Parish Council purchased a portion of this rectangular strip of glebe land on September 18th 1933, and it was duly consecrated by Bishop Edmund Pearce on Sunday, September 30th 1934.[495] Thirty years later, on June 5th 1964, the remainder of the ½ acre plot was sold to the Parish Council to extend the cemetery further.

The village's prior and current parish graveyards therefore comprise the ½ acre of land adjacent to Hall Orchard; Holy Trinity's churchyard; and the old Baptist burial ground on Ashford Lane.

Revd James Burrow (1820-1882), the first resident of the new vicarage, was born in Crosthwaite, Cumbria, and was previously a curate in Ramsgate. He arrived at Ashford in 1852, his wife Maria (née Skelton) joining him shortly thereafter with their seven-year-old daughter Mary Isabel Harriet and baby daughter Rose Diana Katherine. His first son, Charles James George, was born in Ashford in 1855, and the family moved in to the new vicarage in 1857, where his second son, Arthur Hughes Cornwallis, was born that same year, and his daughter Laura Henrietta Maria two years later. He left Ashford in 1861, ultimately becoming Vicar of St Mary's Church, Hampton, in west London.[496]

---

[495] *PCC Minutes, September 18th 1934. Derbyshire Record Office, D747/A/PC/1/2. The Rt Revd Edmund Courtenay Pearce was the inaugural Bishop of Derby from 1927 until his death in 1935.*

[496] *ASIDE: Revd Burrow was an aspiring entrepreneur. During the time he was resident at the vicarage he obtained provisional protection for three patents: 'improvements in coating wrought iron'; 'improvements in umbrellas and parasols'; and 'an improved floor scrubber and sweeper for carpets, floors, lawns, and other such like useful purposes.' As he remained a clergyman for the remainder of his life, it seems that these ideas did not achieve sufficient commercial success to allow him to take an early retirement! In fact, Revd Burrow had a propensity for becoming involved in matters beyond his ecclesiastical remit, which caused some controversy during his incumbency at St Mary's Church, Hampton: he came into conflict with members of the Vestry regarding the funding of the local grammar school; and dismissed a parishioner's complaint about the quality of the well water. (An expert scientist subsequently declared 'it is altogether a nasty water and in my opinion quite unfit for family use'.) Revd Burrow became paralysed in late 1881, and this – together with his becoming stuck in a snowbound train for several hours – were believed to be factors that contributed to his death the following year.*

The London Gazette, May 8th 1857; December 2nd 1859; and June 17th 1859.

St Mary's Vicars, Part 2. In: Hampton, Around and About. 'The Old Historian'. The Beveree, 2017, https://www.thebeveree.co.uk/threads/no-6-st-marys-vicars-part-2.18039/

James Burrow was succeeded very briefly by Charles Norman, but Samual Birley relates that 'this did not meet the wishes of the parishioners, consequently the exchange was set aside, and in the same year (1861) Revd John Reddaway Luxmoore was appointed to the living.'[497] The reason for the premature termination of Charles Norman's appointment is not known.

Prior to taking up residency in the vicarage, Revd Luxmoore and Rosalie had lived for a short while at the adjacent large house – the Elms – which is located at the corner of Vicarage Lane and Court Lane.[498] When the Luxmoores finally moved in to the vicarage, they were to stay there for over half a century.

In a cold winter, the three-storey stone building would have been difficult to heat to anything approaching a comfortable temperature, given its large rooms, high ceilings, draughty cast-iron window frames, and an exposed position on the hillside. And expensive, too, given that the house had nine fireplaces, plus an oven in the kitchen.

It would also have been gloomy in the vicarage when the sun went down, artificial light being available only from candles and oil lamps; many years were to elapse before gas lighting arrived in Ashford.

Gas street lighting was first demonstrated in 1807, on Pall Mall in London, by the German entrepreneur Frederick Winsor, who three years later founded the Gas Light & Coke Company. Shortly thereafter Winsor was ousted from the company, which went on to become, along with Thomas Brushfield's Commercial Gas Light & Coke Company, one of four London gas companies that eventually formed part of the North Thames Gas Board.[499]

In about 1850 gas street lighting arrived in Bakewell, and was gradually adopted by All Saints' Parish Church and some of the town's houses in the ensuing years. The Bakewell gasworks was located on Buxton Road, on a site adjacent to the Lumford Mill (now occupied by a supermarket).[500] Tideswell also had a gasworks by the 1860s,[501] but Alice Mary of Ashford states that

---

[497] *Mr S Birley's Remarks on the Church Copied Verbatim, Jan 1900, Derbyshire Record Office, D7672/Lx.C-33.*

[498] *The Old Orchard, built in the mid 20th century on land originally owned by the Elms, now stands between what are now known as the Old Vicarage and the Old Elms.*

[499] *Frederick Albert Winsor; Gas Light & Coke Company; and Commercial Gas Company. In: Grace's Guide to British Industrial History, https://www.gracesguide.co.uk*

FA Winsor and the Development of Gas Lighting. Survey of London. Volumes 29 & 30, St James Westminster, Part 1. FHW Sheppard (ed). London County Council, London, 1960, pp 352-354.

[500] *Bakewell: The Ancient Capital of the Peak. Trevor Brighton. Halsgrove, 2005, p 79.*

Conservation Area Appraisal, Bakewell. Peak District National Park Authority, 2013, p 16; Fig. 10.

[501] *Tideswell: Down Memory Lanes. Robert Dawson. 2004, p 19.*

her cottage had no gas, and neither did her grandmother Fanny Thorpe's house, even as late as the 1950s.[502]

The luxury of gas cooking was marketed to the public at the Great Exhibition of 1851, but the use of gas for anything other than lighting did not reach most homes until well into the 20th century; the widespread adoption of ovens occurred only after the invention of the oven thermostat in 1923. This slow growth was not helped by the fact that many gas companies prohibited the use of gas during the day.[503]

Unveiled in 2007, this plaque, at 100 Pall Mall in London, indicates the site of houses that were formerly occupied by Frederick Albert Winsor. It was on this road that Winsor was the first to demonstrate gas street lighting.

The vicarage would have been among the first houses in Ashford to boast a flushing indoor toilet. Although the concept of the flush toilet was invented as long ago as 1596 by a courtier of Queen Elizabeth I, Sir John Harington, it required technical improvements to prevent odours from entering the house, and the development of an infrastructure to deliver pressurised water and to remove and treat the waste. The Victorians came to the rescue with Joseph Bazalgette's municipal sewer system – built first for London between 1858 and 1865 – plus a rash of inventions from the 1850s to the 1880s, including Joseph Adamson's siphonic flush in 1853. Further impetus came with the passage of the Public Health Act of 1872, which made it a requirement for local authorities to provide water supplies to all.

Now technically feasible, and with investments being made in the required public fresh and waste water services, the new business of domestic sanitation gained traction. In the 1880s the pottery manufacturer Thomas Twyford

---

[502] *Even though electricity arrived in about 1930, it provided lighting downstairs only, paraffin lamps and candles still being used upstairs.*

My Ashford: A Century Past. Alice Mary Dawson. Robert Dawson (ed). Peak Advertiser, Bakewell, 2017, p 14.

Personal communication. Robert Dawson, 2020.

[503] *Cooking with Gas. National Gas Museum, Leicester, http://www.nationalgasmuseum.org.uk/cooking-with-gas/*

introduced single-piece ceramic flush toilets, the upper end of the range boasting painted designs that were 'pleasant to the eye'; and Thomas Crapper & Co achieved a Royal Warrant to supply 30 toilets with cedarwood seats for Sandringham House.

With no dedicated interior space provided when the vicarage was originally built, the water closet was added at a later time – rather inelegantly on the half-landing. The high-level cistern was refilled from a lead tank on the top floor. The location of the WC, adjacent to a large window extending almost to floor level, afforded its users the option of enjoying a front-seat view of the comings and goings on Vicarage Lane, but Victorian modesty no doubt required that a heavy curtain be pulled to block the view – in both directions!

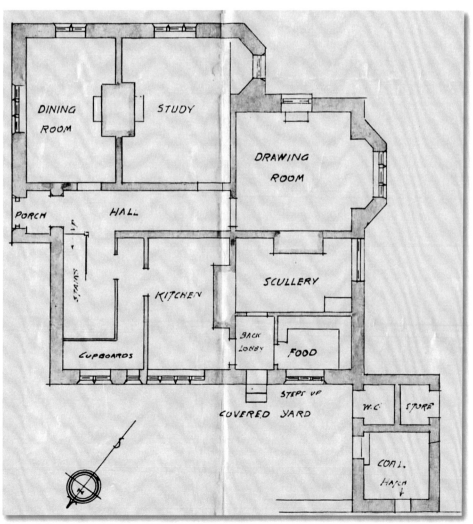

Ground-floor plan of Ashford Vicarage in July 1951.

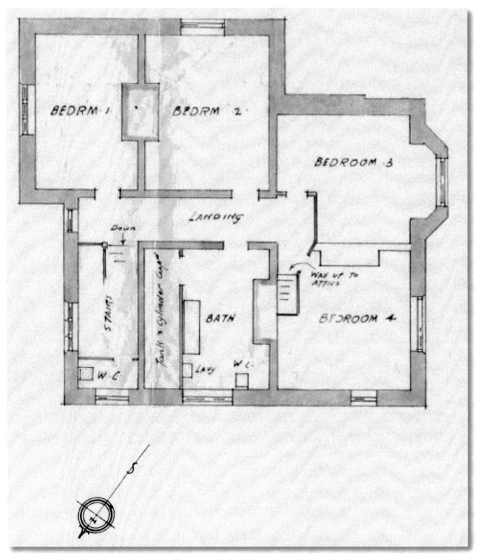

First-floor plan of Ashford Vicarage in July 1951 showing, in the northern corner, a water closet that had been added on the half-landing.

Summer surely brought blessed relief from the cold dark winter, with afternoon tea and sandwiches and croquet on the lawn, and a view over the village towards the Arrock from the warmth of the south-west-facing rear garden.

But less relief, no doubt, for the servants. Their working days would have typically run from 5.30 or 6.00am to 10.00pm. Even as late as the Edwardian era, they would be given only half a day off a week and a full day every month. So there was little time to enjoy the summer sun.

Revd or Mrs Luxmoore would rarely have set foot in the kitchen or scullery. Access to these working areas was kept separate from that of the main house:

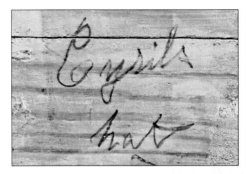
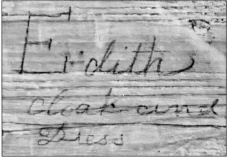
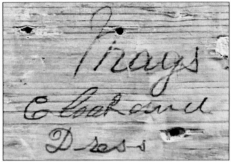

The names of the three youngest Luxmoore children were pencilled in the 1870s on boards in an under-stair cupboard in Ashford Vicarage. They indicate the locations for hanging articles of their clothing.

there was no communication with the main hallway other than via a swinging door hidden at the side of the stairway, to be used by the servants only when serving food in the dining room or otherwise attending to the needs of the vicar's family or their guests.[504] The servants would instead gain access to their food storage and preparation areas from a yard on the north-west side, that rarely caught much sun but at least would remain cool in the summer. They had their own toilet in a small space adjacent to the coalhouse. Coal and supplies would be delivered from the carts of vendors through the two hatch doors that open onto Vicarage Lane.

The live-in servants' quarters would have comprised the two rooms on the top floor. The bottom of their narrow stairs emerges adjacent to the door to the bedroom on the west corner of the house, which would most likely have been the nursery. This is supported by the fact that in this room there are boards in an under-stair cupboard, on which have been pencilled the names of the three youngest Luxmoore children, to indicate where various items of their

[504] *A key element in the design of parsonages was the separation of the family from the servants: 'What passes on either side of the boundary shall be both invisible and inaudible to the other.' Robert Kerr. The Gentleman's House, or How to Plan English Residences from the Parsonage to the Palace. Second edition, 1865. Quoted in: Kate Tiller. Parsonages. Shire Publications, Oxford, 2016, p 64.*

clothing were to be hung: Edith's, Mag's and Cyril's. The annotations would likely have been written by one of the servants in the mid 1870s, before these younger siblings were taking care of their own belongings. (William) Cyril would have been about 4; Margaret, 6; and Edith, 9.

During renovations in 2003 it was discovered that there had also been a second door into the nursery from the bedroom on the south corner, so that the parents could gain access to their children without having to walk onto the first-floor landing. This access has now been reinstated.

Whatever tranquility the Luxmoores enjoyed in their vicarage in rural Derbyshire was shattered when, on August 6th 1900, it suffered a lightning strike, sustaining very considerable damage to the roof. When JR Sterndale Bennett was corresponding with Revd Luxmoore the following December,

A DERBYSHIRE VICARAGE DAMAGED.

On Monday evening a terrific thunderstorm burst over Bakewell and district. The lightning was very vivid. The vicarage at Ashford-in-the-Water was struck, a chimney being thrown down, falling through the roof of the house into a bedroom. Much damage was done to the roof. The storm has done considerable damage elsewhere. The late hay crops, hundreds of acres of which are still ungathered, are nearly, if not quite spoiled. The corn, principally oats, is beaten down, and fruit, particularly apples and plums, has suffered severely.

Report of damage to Ashford Vicarage in 1900.

he wrote, 'please forgive my troubling you again – and trusting that yourself and Mrs Luxmoore have recovered from the shock of that dreadful accident to your house.'[505]

The gothic design of the vicarage, as remarked on by JS Luxmoore, lends itself to the invention (or reality?) of hauntings: 'Jennifer the Poltergeist' was said to have shared the vicarage with Revd Thomas George and his wife Margaret in the 1950s. Vicar from 1953 until 1957, Revd George said, 'it was something uncanny in the place and it was bad for the children.' Mrs George reported that 'all sorts

The key that was purportedly thrown by 'Jennifer the Poltergeist', who was named by the family of Revd Thomas George.

---

[505] *Letter from James Robert Sterndale Bennett to Revd John Reddaway Luxmoore, December 13th 1900. Derbyshire Record Office, D7672/Lx.C-47/6.*

of queer things used to happen', citing a 'big key to an outhouse' that 'flew in front of my husband.' They named it 'Jennifer' because 'it was mischievous, just like a woman'.[506]

This could be why the George family chose to remain in the vicarage for only four years. They may also have been overwhelmed with maintaining this large house. If so, Revd George was not the first clergyman to face such a challenge.

In 1868 Ven Archdeacon Balston, the Vicar of Bakewell, built a new gothic vicarage 'like a small bishop's palace' on what is now Yeld Road. His successors, not enjoying his level of private income, found it financially difficult to maintain.[507] Similarly, Revd George's successor at Ashford, Revd John Norman, agreed in April 1962 with the unanimous vote of the Parochial Church Council, 'that we consider selling the present vicarage in order to build a more suitable house on the land behind the church.' The vicar wrote to his parishioners:

> *'As long as the authorities continue to maintain a Victorian conception of the status and dignity of the parish priest, it is a problem which is likely to remain in this parish. One would have thought that the desire to foster vocations to the priesthood among grammar and secondary modern boys would have led to a modification of this attitude, in favour of houses in which such men might feel at home, but that time has not yet come!'[508]*

The initial idea to build a new house did not progress further, and most of the subsequent effort was instead directed towards the prospect of buying Barnfield on Mount Pleasant, once the home of Thomas Wheatley Cox-Wilson. Although the estate agent's assessment of the vicarage and associated land 'was not at all encouraging', the Parochial Church Council nevertheless secured approval from the diocese for its plans and 'was awaiting a firm offer for the vicarage' from a retiring naval officer.

That firm offer did not materialise, however. Moreover, the plan that had been put forward for converting Barnfield was 'too ambitious'. The only option left was to renovate the vicarage, including 'rewiring, central heating, and modernising the kitchen'; but it 'would then be a very expensive house in which to live, with a very large garden to keep up.' Ultimately, it was agreed that the cost of these improvements would be funded by a contribution of £250

---

[506] *"Is vicarage haunted?" ask village folk. Unidentified news clipping provided by Margaret Norman.*

[507] *Bakewell: The Ancient Capital of the Peak, Trevor Brighton. Halsgrove, 2005, p 62. Revd Balston had previously been headmaster of Eton College, and had secured the services of his former pupil, George Gilbert Scott, Jr, as architect for some restoration work at All Saints' Church, Bakewell.*

[508] *Vicar's annual report. Holy Trinity Church, Ashford-in-the-Water, 1962.*

from church funds, plus income from the sale of some glebe land.

After nearly two years of discussions, planning, negotiating and building work, Revd Norman was able to report to the PCC that the upgrades to the vicarage were almost complete, and that the sale of the glebe land was well underway.[509] This would have included the remainder

Induction of Revd John Norman, January 26th 1957. Left to right: Rt Revd George Sinker, Assistant Bishop of Derby; Revd J & Mrs M Norman; Revd RJ Stanford, Rural Dean.

of the ½-acre rectangular plot of glebe land to the south of the vicarage, that was to be sold to the Parish Council on June 5th 1964 to enlarge the parish cemetery. In what may have been a surprise to at least some PCC members, the vicar then 'spoke with regret of his impending departure.'

Twenty years later, on July 27th 1984, the vicarage was designated by English Heritage as a Grade II Listed building to mark its special architectural or historic interest.

Since the latter part of the 20th century, too few clergy have been available to serve the many parishes. In response, multi-parish benefices have been established in which several neighbouring churches and congregations are cared for by a team that may comprise one or more vicars, curates, licensed lay readers and other staff. In practice, the number of paid staff is often barely adequate for the number of parishes they must support, and the individual churches frequently need to rely on the *ad hoc* services of retired ministers, churchwardens and lay volunteers to sustain an effective ministry.

Whilst multi-parish benefices can certainly save money, they can place huge workloads on the diminishing number of clergy, especially in rural areas where the travel time between remote parishes can be long. And, as village parishes lose their 'own' dedicated priest, congregations can feel neglected. This trend is clear from the list of Parish Priests of Ashford-in-the-Water (see p 215), where the number of parishes for which the incumbent is responsible has increased from two in the time of Revd

[509] *PCC Minutes, January 31st 1964. Derbyshire Record Office, D747/A/PC/1/2.*

An aerial view of the Old Vicarage in 2020. The wide ground-level doors on the outbuilding at the top (north) of the photograph would have provided access to carriages, with the horse accommodated behind the stable door on the right. Behind the windows on the first floor of the vicarage were the nursery (left) and Revd and Mrs Luxmoore's bedroom (right), with the drawing room on the ground floor (right). The window on the lower left is shifted compared to that shown on the 1951 plan (see p 207); behind it was the scullery.

Luxmoore (Ashford and Sheldon) to five now.[510]

Fewer clergy means that there is a need for fewer parsonages. In 2000, anticipating the sale of Ashford's vicarage, emotions ran high in a way that would evidently have seemed irrational to Revd Norman and his Parochial Church Council a few decades earlier. As the new century approached, this was 'a move not welcomed by Ashford parishioners', who noted that 'in the last hundred years Ashford has lost its chapels, school, policeman, and its 'own' vicar, and seems likely to lose its vicarage.'[511]

This all said, a very positive parallel trend is the effort to establish and embed a much greater degree of collaboration, not only between Anglican churches of different churchmanship, but also between Anglican and other Christian denominations, and even those of different faiths. The spirit of this philosophy is captured in the declarations of the present Archbishop of Canterbury, Justin Welby:

'The Church when it is visibly united speaks more powerfully to the world – by the grace of the Spirit of God – than we can ever begin to imagine.

'Central to the Christian faith is the recognition that all human beings are made in the image of God. An important part of Archbishop Justin's ministry is to engage positively and lovingly with those of different beliefs, with the understanding that each person is a uniquely and wonderfully created child of God.' [512]

---

[510] *NOTE: The list of Parish Priests of Ashford-in-the-Water shown herein has been corrected and made consistent with the Clergy Database for the period 1732 to 1837, and extended to the present day. Clergy of the Church of England Database 1540-1835, https://theclergydatabase.org.uk*

The Ashford burial registers suggest that Revd Bache Thornhill (1785-1827) did not frequently officiate at Ashford; he was simultaneously Perpetual Curate not only at Ashford, but also at Winster and Great Longstone. During his curacy various other priests acted on his behalf, including, from about 1817, John Browne, who signs himself 'minister'. A decade later Revd Browne was formally appointed Perpetual Curate, when Revd Thornhill was tragically killed at the age of 42, as a result of an accidental discharge of a friend's gun. Nottingham Journal, January 5th 1828; On the Death of the Late Revd Bache Thornhill. The Ballads & Songs of Derbyshire, Llewellynn Frederick William Jewitt (ed). Bemrose & Sons, Derby & London, 1867.

Thomas Brushfield and J Charles Cox's suggestions that Revd Thomas Nadauld was the incumbent at Ashford commencing 1807 are based on Thomas Nadauld's name appearing in the Ashford Registers on November 13th 1807, but that entry is for his burial; his gravestone in Ashford churchyard clearly gives his date of death as November 9th 1807. It seems, therefore, that Revd Nadauld did not serve formally as an incumbent at Ashford. The Family of Nadauld. Thomas Brushfield. The Reliquary, Vol 10, Llewellynn Jewitt (ed). Bemrose & Sons, Derby & London, 1869-1870, p 118; Notes on the Churches of Derbyshire, Vol II, The Hundreds of the High Peak and Wirksworth. J Charles Cox. Bemrose & Sons, Derby & London, 1877, p 50.

[511] *A record of changes in Ashford during the 20th century. Compiled by John F Hollingworth. Ashford Time Capsule, 2000.*

[512] *Working With Other Faiths: Christian Unity. About the Archbishop, https://www.archbishopofcanterbury.org*

The vicarage was sold for the first time into private hands in 2002. Over the ensuing 18 years, I was privileged to join with prior and future residents as a custodian of a small part of our wonderful Victorian heritage.

Parish Priests of Ashford-in-the-Water

Assistant Curates at Bakewell Parish Church

1688	Samuel Mills
1707	Thomas Maddock
1724	Thomas Grove
1727	Richard Pughe
1727	William Deighton
1729	Samuel White
1729	Robert Lomas
1732	William Wingfield
1763	Peter Walthall
1812	Bache Thornhill
1828	John Browne
1837	William Galley Giles
1850	William Boyd
1852	James Burrow
1861	Charles Norman
1861	John Luxmoore

Vicars of Ashford with Sheldon

1872	John Luxmoore
1912	Henry Sherlock
1940	Reginald Absell
1950	Thomas Morris
1953	Thomas George
1957	John Norman
1964	John Legg
1967	Graham Foster

Priest in Charge of Ashford with Sheldon

1978	Gerald Phizackerley

Vicar of Ashford-in-the-Water with Sheldon and Longstone

1991	Clive Thrower

Vicar of Ashford-in-the-Water with Sheldon, Bakewell, Over Haddon & Rowsley

2007	Tony Kaunhoven

The list of parish priests that inspired the author to embark on his discovery of the life and times of Revd John Reddaway Luxmoore.

V

ASHFORD-IN-THE-WATER IN REVD LUXMOORE'S TIME

A stroll through the village of Ashford-in-the-Water on a typical Victorian weekday would have been less idyllic than it is today. The roads would have been dirty with the passage of horses, cattle and sheep, although the manure would have been welcome as fertilizer:

'Every time that a horse left some manure on the road, it was a race between neighbours' houses to get it for the gardens'.[513]

The stocking frames on Hill Cross would have been very noisy,[514] and the water-powered marble cutting and polishing machinery at the west corner of the village extremely dusty.

Hill Cross, Ashford-in-the-Water, ca. 1890s.

Ashford marble

The main industry of Ashford when Revd Luxmoore arrived was the marble trade, enabled by the marble works established in 1748 by Henry Watson,

---

[513] *My Ashford: A Century Past. Alice Mary Dawson. Robert Dawson (ed). Peak Advertiser, Bakewell, 2017, p 19.*

[514] *On Hill Cross, (then also known as the 'Rattle'), can be found one of the village's cottages which housed stocking frames. It has a long, horizontal row of small upper-floor windows, behind which the machines would have been placed. Villages of the Peak District. Denis Eardley. 2010.*

whose memorial can be seen in the church mounted on the south wall, adjacent to the south door.[515]

Many marble ornaments that were acquired at various times by the Dukes of Devonshire, on whose land the mines and the marble works were situated, can be viewed today by visitors to Chatsworth House.

When the 13-year-old Princess (Queen-to-be) Victoria visited Chatsworth in 1832, she wrote in her diary:

> *'We then went to the Rookery, a small cottage belonging to the Duke on the banks of the River Wye, very pretty and cool. From there we walked to the marble mills and saw how they sawed and polished the marble. There was a little cottage where they sold Derbyshire spar in different little shapes and forms, and some pieces of marble too.'[516]*

It was unusual for a rural village of that time to have so many livelihoods provided by such a substantial indigenous industry. Villagers were employed in all stages of the value chain, from mining and cutting, to turning, polishing and decorating. In 1846 there were four marble masons and statuaries and three marble turners in Ashford, all acting as principals in the marble trade. By 1850, there were more than 50 master craftsmen operating mosaic and inlay workshops in Ashford and surrounding communities.

Other employment

Agricultural employment in Derbyshire was affected less severely than it was in Devon by the agricultural depression of the last quarter of the 19th century. This was in part because, as a dairying county, Derbyshire was protected to some extent by the stability of milk demand from local urban markets.[517] It was also because the agricultural industry was a less dominant source of jobs, even before the onset of the depression. The 1851 census shows that only 2 per cent of farms in Derbyshire employed six or more adult males, versus 11 per cent in Devon; and farms in Derbyshire were

---

[515] *Samuel Watson, together with his son, also called Samuel, were stone-carvers who worked with Henry Nadauld at Chatsworth. It was Samuel's grandson (or possibly grandnephew), Henry, who inherited the stonemason's business around 1740, saw the possibilities afforded by water power, and created the Ashford marble works. Derbyshire Black Marble. John Michael Tomlinson. Peak District Mines Historical Society Special Publication No. 4, 1996, p 12.*

[516] *Ibid., p 34.*

'The Princes victori past (sic) through Ashford to Chatsworth.' Transcripts of the Diaries of J James Middleton of Ashford (1812-1856). Derbyshire Record Office, D307/H/38/5, entry for October, 1832.

[517] *Where was the 'Great Agricultural Depression'? A geography of agricultural bankruptcy in late Victorian England and Wales. PJ Perry. Agricultural History Review, Vol 20, 1972, p 45.*

smaller, with an average size of 67 acres, versus 109 acres in Devon.[518]

In Sheldon in 1891 there were 14 individuals who identified themselves as farmers. Indeed, there was only one person in commercial business who was not a farmer – the village shopkeeper, Miss Catherine Blamey. Even Maria Gyte, the innkeeper at the Devonshire Arms, also classed herself as a farmer. In Ashford, on the other hand, although the population was four times larger, there were only half as many farmers as there were in Sheldon.[519]

As was the case for all but the smallest rural villages in the 19th and early 20th centuries, Ashford was essentially self-sufficient, inasmuch as most of the trades, skills and labour could be found in the village itself, or in nearby villages, or in the town of Bakewell. Thus, villagers found work as domestic workers (mainly female), gardeners, grooms, shopkeepers and haulage contractors; and there was also a carpenter, wheelwright and blacksmith.

The power of the River Wye was harnessed for several village business undertakings, notably the Bobbin Mill, the Corn Mill, and the Cox-Wilson building business. The Cox-Wilson operation was a major employer for several generations, providing work for a variety of tradesmen, carters and general labourers. In addition to the vicarage, properties in the village built by the Cox-Wilsons include Bretnor House (once a post office, which had been erected on the site of an old thatched cottage); the terraced houses between Brushfield House and the village shop on Church Street, including Chandle House; the interwar houses on the west side of Greaves Lane, between a small bungalow (originally intended as a garage) and Arncliffe House at the foot of Hill Cross; and – on the south side of what is now the A6 trunk road, the Duke's Drive – Hillmorton, Underwood, Cornbrook, and Barnfield (the house championed in 1962 as a potential new vicarage by Revd John Norman, see p 211).[520] Further afield, in 1912 the Cox-Wilson family built Teapot Row on the Chatsworth estate, opposite Cavendish Hall, which 'got its name from the endless cups of tea drunk by the workmen. It is said that when the last house was completed their teapot was ceremoniously buried.'[521]

[518] *Family Farms and Capitalist Farms in Mid 19th-Century England. Leigh Shaw-Taylor. Agricultural History Review, Vol 53, No.2, 2005, pp 180 and 184.*

[519] *Kelly's Directory of the Counties of Derby, Notts, Leicester and Rutland. London, 1891, pp 30 and 298.*

The Gyte family had been innkeepers at the Devonshire Arms in Sheldon for over a century, and they continued to run it until it closed in the 1960s. The Diaries of Maria Gyte of Sheldon, Derbyshire, 1913-1920. Gerald Phizackerley (ed). Scarthin Books, 1999, p xv.

[520] *A record of changes in Ashford during the 20th century. Compiled by John F Hollingworth. Ashford Time Capsule, 2000.*

[521] *Round About Chatsworth, Dowager Duchess of Devonshire. 2005, pp 30-31.*

Members of the Cox-Wilson family lived at various times in Greatbatch, a large house on Church Street dating from the 17th century [Francis James Cox-Wilson (1863-1939), James Cox-Wilson's elder son]; and in some of the houses they had built themselves, including Chandle House on Church Street [Clifton Evans Cox-Wilson (1898-1967), son of Francis James Cox-Wilson]; and on Mount Pleasant [James Cox-Wilson, and his younger son Thomas Wheatley Cox-Wilson (1869-1940), who lived in Barnfield].

Further downstream towards Bakewell, employment could be found spinning cotton at Richard Arkwright's five-storey mill at Lumford. Built in 1777, the mill employed around 300 people at its peak, and in 1829 was supplying cotton to 80 frames in Ashford cottages for the manufacture of stockings. There were difficulties in recruiting for the cotton mill locally, so girls were brought in from Manchester. However, the mill was destroyed by fire in 1868 and many lost their jobs. Although operations were resumed in 1875, it was on a much smaller scale. In 1898 the Dujardin-Plante Company opened a factory there, initially to manufacture the batteries required for the electrification of large English houses.[522]

Ashford people were also employed outside the village at Cressbrook Mill, the quarries in Buxton, the new railway, and in Bakewell retail businesses, including the grocers Messrs Orme & Co.[523]

Financial hardship

Most village residents had little money. In the early years of the 20th century, the rent for each of the small cottages in the village would have consumed 2s 6d each week, and some would struggle to provide the basic necessities for their families. One might expect that this would have been known to the Parish Council; however, in 1895 some members were clearly turning a blind eye to the problem of poverty:

'Despite the fact that certain members of the Ashford Parish Council

---

[522] *Conservation Area Appraisal, Bakewell. Peak District National Park Authority, 2013, pp 12, 17, 27, 30, 37, 70.*

Bakewell: The Ancient Capital of the Peak. Trevor Brighton. Halsgrove, 2005, pp 72-73 and 144.

DP Battery Co. In: Grace's Guide to British Industrial History, https://www.gracesguide.co.uk

Following various changes in ownership and product lines, the Dujardin-Plante battery operations closed in 1970. Multiple businesses now operate on the premises, but in 2017 planning permission was given for the development of a 72-bedroom hotel, and other office and factory space. It is planned that subsequently the Mill Race Building and Retort House will be refurbished. Derbyshire Times, June 7th 2019.

[523] *A record of changes in Ashford during the 20th Century. Compiled by John F Hollingworth. Ashford Time Capsule, 2000.*

are of the opinion that no distress exists in that parish, a house-to-house canvass by one of its members has proved otherwise. Subscriptions towards a fund for providing soup for the poor have kindly been collected by Messrs George Lowe and Samuel Ashton, and on Saturday over 70 persons were given a supply of excellent soup. The thanks of the recipients are due to the Misses Frost, of the Devonshire Hotel, who generously made the soup and distributed it.'[524]

Transport

With no public transport available, villagers who were not employed in the village itself had no option but to walk to and from their place of work.[525] Very few would be able to afford a horse, unless it could be supported financially by their farming or haulage business. Revd Luxmoore's possession of his own horse and carriage would therefore have placed him in a small elite, along with the major local landowners. Early versions of the motor car were available to an even narrower social class; there were only about 14 or 15 cars on Britain's roads by the end of 1895.[526]

In the diaries of William Hodkin, a Victorian farmer and agricultural trader in Beeley, it is noted that, 'reading the diary, it is remarkable for us now to realise the distances which had to be walked.' Although 'the coming of the railways had made travel and the movement of goods very much easier,' William 'does have to rely on the stagecoach to reach certain areas, or walk.'[527]

Even well into the 1920s, our Ashford chronicler Alice recalls,

'Ordinary people had no private transport and there was little public transport. From Ashford you usually had to walk to Bakewell to see a doctor and then walk back. On one particular occasion, I remember mum having to walk both ways despite being really ill.' … 'A group of us set off from Ashford at about 5.00am to walk to the mill [at Cressbrook]. Similar groups walked from Wardlow, Great and Little Longstone, and other villages.'[528]

---

[524] *Derbyshire Times & Chesterfield Herald, February 23rd 1895. The Misses Frost (Bertha and Emily) were the daughters of Mrs Fanny Frost who, two years earlier, had provided the 'capital spread' for the Men's Friendly Society. (See p 96.)*

[525] *The first public motorbus came through Ashford in about 1920. My Ashford: A Century Past. Alice Mary Dawson. Robert Dawson (ed). Peak Advertiser, Bakewell, 2017, p 29.*

[526] *National Motor Museum Trust, https://nationalmotormuseum.org.uk*

[527] *A Victorian Farmer's Diary, William Hodkin's Diary 1864-66: Life in and around Beeley on the Chatsworth Estate. TA Burdekin (ed). 2003, pp 9, 18.*

[528] *My Ashford: A Century Past. Alice Mary Dawson. Robert Dawson (ed). Peak Advertiser, Bakewell, 2017, pp 37, 42.*

Those who were in a position to be able to travel using horse power would need to be aware of the peculiar accompanying dangers. We have already heard of the fatal riding tragedy that befell John Nicholl Luxmoore at a young age (see p 32).

In 1870 Revd Luxmoore will have been reminded of this event when he learned of another death from

Inscription on the Mill Bridge, Ashford-in-the-Water, where tradition suggests a Mr M Hyde was thrown from his horse in 1664 and drowned in the River Wye below.

a riding accident: his uncle, Squire James Reddaway, then living at Burdon House, was thrown from his horse when returning from the Hon Mark Rolle's Hunt. The 'high-spirited animal' shied whilst descending a steep hill, and one of the stirrups broke. At the subsequent inquest, a verdict of accidental death was returned; James was 62 years of age.[529]

Locally, tradition suggests that the inscription 'M HYDE 1664' on Ashford's Mill Bridge, downstream from the mediaeval Sheepwash Bridge, memorialises another tragic accident when this man, returning from a mill near Taddington, seated on a bag of meal flung over the horse's back, was blown by a sudden gust of wind into the River Wye and was drowned.[530]

Less serious accidents were commonplace: Alice recalls that she sometimes managed to catch a ride with her brother Fred, one of Cox-Wilson's workers, in the firm's dray, which was drawn by two horses. On one occasion,

'the horses shied at a car on the way back and Fred and I were thrown off as the dray overturned ... Mr Cox-Wilson took us back to Ashford in his car but gave Fred the sack instantly.'

---

[529] *Western Morning News, March 16th 1870.*

[530] *The Reliquary, Vol 7, Llewellynn Jewitt (ed). Bemrose & Sons, Derby & London, 1867-1868, p 255.*

This story is conjectural, as is another version suggesting that the drowned man was Revd Hyde, Vicar of Bakewell Church. The parish priest at Bakewell from 1661-1668 was, in fact, Revd John Beardmore, as per the list of parish priests mounted on a board on the west wall of the church, and also in: Vicars of Bakewell. Revd Charles T Abraham. Sheffield Independent, July 30th 1901.

The diaries and letters of Fred Brocklehurst of Sheldon reveal that:

'The milk was taken by horse and float to Longstone Station every morning to catch the 8.40 train, a 35-minute journey. Some of the journeys could be very bad in winter, with two horses being required to pull the milk float through the snow drifts up the 1-in-6 hill between Ashford and Sheldon. Fred recalls that on one occasion the road had been so icy that going down the hill he could not stop the float sliding down the hill sideways and the horse finishing up facing up hill'.[531]

In 1915 Maria Gyte tells us (no doubt appreciating a funny side to the incident):

'Mr Sherlock [Vicar of Ashford & Sheldon 1912-1940] paid us a visit, on horseback. Having fastened his horse to the ring at our end of house, he came and had a cup of tea. Some lads kicked a football into the horse and it (the horse) bolted and ran into the Bland Croft. [We] were helping Mr Sherlock to mend the bridle which was broken in two parts.'[532]

The new safety bicycle was being produced in the late 1880s to a design essentially the same as today's basic bicycle, and John Dunlop's pneumatic tyre, invented in 1888, made the ride much more comfortable. Writing in 1899, George Lacy Hillier, a prominent cycling journalist, proclaimed:

'What a wonderful thing is the modern cycle! In years to come, when the historian writes of the Victorian age, he will, without doubt, feel himself constrained by the force of circumstance to write at length of the genesis and development of 'the bicycle' – that curious vehicle which in the 19th century added new and altogether unequalled powers of locomotion to those already possessed by man, powers which were dependent on man's muscles alone, and which enabled him to travel farther and faster than he has before been able to progress by their use.'[533]

In the 1880s and 1890s cycling was largely enjoyed only by the middle classes but, by the turn of the century, a second-hand safety bicycle could be bought for as little as £2 and, by the time Alice was 14 (in 1926), a quarter of that. She was then employed at Cressbrook Mill, being paid on a

---

[531] *FW Goes to War: from the diaries and letters of FW Brocklehurst of Sheldon, Derbyshire.* Brian Greasley. *Country Books, Little Longstone, Derbyshire, 2016, p 20.*

[532] *The Diaries of Maria Gyte of Sheldon, Derbyshire, 1913-1920.* Gerald Phizackerley (ed). *Scarthin Books, 1999, entry for September 15th 1915, p 62.*

[533] *All Round Cycling.* George Lacy Hillier. 1899. *Quoted in: Revolution – How the Bicycle Reinvented Modern Britain.* William Manners. *Duckworth, 2019, p xxix.*

piecework basis. In order to increase her pay she took the risk of side-stepping the mandated method for knotting snapped cotton threads, which, although slower, provided neater results. Unfortunately the gamble did not pay off, and for this transgression she lost her job. But, almost as if to celebrate, she bought a bicycle:

> 'That same day, I bought a second-hand bike from another worker for 12s 6d from my savings, and went home on it. My mum was angry and told me to take the bike back when she found out about the lost job. However, I kept it and used it a lot.'[534]

A few years later, motor vehicles were starting to offer even greater freedom, and we find Alice with her beau on faster wheels:

> 'Occasionally we took a trip to Castleton on his motorbike for tea and cake ... we really enjoyed dancing, and with the motorbike went as far afield as Tideswell and Bradwell.'[535]

Sanitation and health

For most people, sanitary arrangements were very basic. Cold piped water may have been available but, when this failed, water would have had to be collected from one of the village wells. Exterior dry-earth toilets were the norm, and Alice's grandmother Fanny Thorpe's dry toilet was shared between two houses.

The scourge of life-threatening infectious disease was ever-present. In 1887 smallpox had been 'imported from Sheffield, where the disease was epidemic', resulting in two deaths in Ashford and others in Hathersage. There was concern that it could become 'a very serious thing if it got amongst the young people at the cotton mill on Ashford Road'.[536] The following year, ten cases of typhoid fever were diagnosed in the village, two of which proved fatal.[537]

Alice herself had pleurisy twice, and her elder sister, Margaret, died of pneumonia, aged just seven. Alice writes poignantly,

> 'Illness spread quickly under those cramped, unhealthy conditions [of her small, end-of-terrace cottage].'[538]

---

[534] *My Ashford: A Century Past. Alice Mary Dawson. Robert Dawson (ed). Peak Advertiser, Bakewell, 2017, p 39.*

[535] *Ibid., p 45.*

[536] *Derbyshire Advertiser & Journal, November 4th 1887.*

[537] *Derbyshire Advertiser & Journal, March 18th 1898.*

[538] *My Ashford: A Century Past. Alice Mary Dawson. Robert Dawson (ed). Peak Advertiser, Bakewell, 2017, p 16.*

This was more than 30 years after the medical examiner had reported in 1883 that there was 'overcrowding in some of the houses in Ashford-in-the-Water'.[539]

However, for those who were lucky enough not to succumb to one of the childhood infectious diseases or tuberculosis in young adulthood – which together accounted for a third of all deaths[540] – a life that was long even by today's standards was not uncommon: Revd Luxmoore's mother, maternal grandparents and paternal grandparents lived into their 70s, 80s and even 90s; Revd Luxmoore and Rosalie themselves lived to well into their 80s. And Alice Mary Dawson lived to be 93; her mother Jane, 79; and her grandmother Fanny Thorpe, 89.

The NHS did not arrive for another half a century, in 1948. Until that time, doctors' advice was expensive and not available to most people. In 1930, when she was working as a maid for a doctor, Alice Mary wondered why he had so many grandfather clocks and oak chests in the rooms and corridors: apparently, he would take these in lieu of cash when patients were unable to pay their bills.[541]

Fanny Thorpe, although unqualified and scarcely able to read and write, worked in Ashford as a midwife, providing birth services for people who could afford to pay only a little. She also assisted the undertaker (JW & J Mettam of Bakewell) by providing a quick response when someone died. Fanny 'was very religious' and would have been well known to the Luxmoores, as she was 20 years old when they arrived in the village and worked well into her mid 70s, by which time Revd Luxmoore was retired.[542]

Those who had been able to afford regular subscriptions to the village's Men's and Women's Friendly Societies may have received some help with meeting their medical bills. A few may have been able to afford ready-made proprietary medicines, such as chlorodyne for coughs and colds, and camphorated tincture of opium ('paregoric'), used when first discovered to treat asthma and, in the 19th century, to control diarrhoea. Opium was also available in pill form, coated in varnish for the working class, silver for the rich, and gold for the very rich.[543] In a letter to 'Brushfield' from James Green,

---

[539] *Derbyshire Advertiser & Journal, June 22nd 1883.*

[540] *F Condrau and M Worboys. Epidemics and Infections in 19th-Century Britain. Social History of Medicine, Vol 22(1), 2009, pp 165-171.*

[541] *My Ashford: A Century Past. Alice Mary Dawson. Robert Dawson (ed). Peak Advertiser, Bakewell, 2017, p 41.*

[542] *Ibid., pp 8-10.*

[543] *Drugs in Victorian Britain. Wellcome Collection, https://wellcomecollection.org/articles/ W87wthIAACQizfap*

the writer notes that Revd Luxmoore 'is still suffering from violent face and head neuralgic pain and is moving south for a month as soon as he can find someone to take his duty.'[544] He may have resorted to laudanum: a pain-killing (and highly addictive) cocktail of morphine, codeine and alcohol.[545]

However, most families relied on home remedies, such as those found in *Mrs Beeton's Book of Household Management*. The first edition was published in 1861 – the same year the Luxmoores arrived in Ashford – when author Isabella Beeton was just 25 years old. Typical remedies included bread yeast, camphor bags, vinegar cloths, mustard, and brimstone and treacle. Bicarbonate of soda or soot were often used as toothpastes.

Unfortunately, no remedies of the time could save Isabella herself, who died three years later of puerperal fever after giving birth to her fourth child. Her legacy is her collection of articles that has remained constantly in print in various versions over the subsequent 160 years.

Demographic perspectives

It is instructive to compare the demographics of the parishes of Ashford and Sheldon during Revd Luxmoore's time with the statistics that characterise these villages today.[546]

The population has decreased substantially and continually since June 1841, when the number of residents in Ashford alone totalled 950, comprising 460 males and 490 females.[547] By 1891, midway through Revd Luxmoore's incumbency, the parishes of Ashford and Sheldon together had a combined population of 844.[548] By 2011, this had reduced to 559. The average number of members in each household is now around one third of what it was in 1846 (2.2 versus 6.2 people per household, respectively).

At the present time, about 84 per cent of the area of the Peak District National

---

[544] *The address of the letter is 'Seaforth'. Derbyshire Record Office, D7672/Lx.C-47/39. In the Ashford burial registers for December 22nd 1874, it is noted that Ann Walker Green, who died aged 47, was from Twembrook House, Crosby Road, Seaforth. Her husband James, also noted to be from Seaforth, was buried on April 23rd 1904, aged 78 years. Revd Luxmoore officiated at both burials.*

[545] *Victorian Era Medicine: Laudanum. VL McBeath, 2020, https://valmcbeath.com*

[546] *Modern demographic statistics have been drawn from: Draft Assessment of the parishes of Ashford-in-the-Water and Sheldon, Peak District National Park; Derbyshire Life and Countryside, Archant Community Media, Ltd, July 19th 2017; ZoomLocal (CliqTo Ltd), Shrewsbury; Nomis Official Labour Market Statistics for GSS code E04002718, sourced from the 2011 Census.*

[547] *Transcripts of the Diaries of J James Middleton of Ashford (1812-1856). Derbyshire Record Office, D307/H/38/5, entry for June 7th 1841.*

[548] *Kelly's Directory of the Counties of Derby, Notts, Leicester and Rutland. London, 1891, pp 30, 298.*

Park is farmed land. However, the majority of the combined population of Ashford and Sheldon comprises skilled tradespeople and those employed in professional and management capacities, whilst across the Peak District as a whole, tourism provides employment for 25 per cent of the residents. About 35 per cent of people in the Ashford postcode areas are in the highest social grade (AB), compared to a national average of 27 per cent.

These changes reflect the increase in the general standard of living across the whole country, but they are also undoubtedly due in part to the protections – and corresponding enhancements in prestige – that were conferred in 1951 when the Peak District was designated the country's first National Park and, in 1981 and 1995 respectively, when Ashford and Sheldon were designated Conservation Areas. The Park's beautiful views, created by contrasting landscapes and dramatic geology, are perceived to be its most special qualities, attracting 12 million visitors every year.[549]

The Peak District National Park faces a number of challenges that result directly from its popularity. One such challenge is the upward pressure on house prices, due in part to the fact that about 20 per cent of its properties are second homes or holiday lets: over the first nine months of 2021, the average house price in the Derbyshire Dales was £296,996 – 16 per cent above the UK national average.[550] A direct consequence is a lack of affordable housing. Other challenges include traffic congestion and the effect that large numbers of visitors can have on fragile landscapes.[551]

Although these problems have a real impact on the Peak District in general and the residents of Ashford and Sheldon in particular, they are easier to bear than the daily struggles and life-and-death anxieties that were endured by many of the villagers of Revd Luxmoore's time.

---

[549] *National Park Management Plan 2018-2023. Peak District National Park, Bakewell.*

[550] *UK House Price Index. January to September, 2021, http://www.gov.uk*

[551] *National Park Management Plan. Op. cit.*

VI

CONCLUDING REMARKS

My glimpse behind the curtain of history has revealed an imperfectly focussed portrait of a country vicar that has, nevertheless, become clearer with every new light shone upon it. However, I am aware that I may be found guilty of having interpreted facts through a lens that has accentuated my own biases.

On my journey of discovery, I have enjoyed the constant company of my now familiar Victorian friends – Thomas Brushfield, JP, Thomas Nadauld Brushfield, MD, FSA, Revd John Stonhouse Luxmoore, and Samuel Birley. Their enthusiasm for recording their local history has been both infectious and inspirational.

The facts tell us that the lands inherited by Revd John Reddaway Luxmoore enabled his elevation to a social position above that of most of his agricultural forebears. Although the income that these properties could generate was relatively modest, especially during the agricultural depression, it provided for him and his family a life that was more comfortable than the livings at Ashford-in-the-Water and Sheldon could offer by themselves.

We have seen in Charles Bennett (Rosalie's uncle), and in Ashford-born Thomas Brushfield, examples of entrepreneurially-driven Victorian risk-takers, who sought and won their fortunes in environments that would initially have been both intimidating and exciting: the untamed wilderness of the New World, and poverty-stricken East London. But Revd Luxmoore did not have that kind of ambition. He sought, and was happy to find, long-term security and respect as an Anglican vicar, in a rural community that was essentially similar to the villages of west Devon in which he had been born and raised.

He was a follower of the social mores of the time. He willingly participated in all the activities that were expected of a Victorian village clergyman – from village fêtes, fundraising events and horticultural pastimes, to revelries with the landed gentry. His beliefs and values were rooted in an obedient Victorian understanding of what was right and what was wrong, and he struggled when these came into conflict with theological Dissent and an increasingly secular society. The few examples we have of his preaching suggest that it was conventional, founded firmly on traditional Christian precepts and late 19th-century moral values.

His children were inculcated to respect the Established Church (John Stonhouse Luxmoore and William Cyril Luxmoore were both to become Anglican clergymen) and to adhere to the strict moral principles by which their father lived. Their social lives were limited to pastimes that were socially acceptable for those of their class – village sports for the boys; singing for the girls – and to the support of charitable causes and church functions in their own and neighbouring communities. None of his three daughters married, most likely because their financial future was secure, but perhaps also because they were given little rein to mingle with eligible bachelors in the local area.

But Revd Luxmoore was also distinctive, not least by virtue of his 52-year tenure at Holy Trinity Church, Ashford. As his bishop had noted on the occasion of his 50th Jubilee in 1911, 'there was no one in the deanery who could come within twenty years of Mr Luxmoore.'

And he was quite unlike some wealthy pluralists in the 'other' Luxmoore branch of his family tree: his income, although high compared to most people in the village, provided no possibility that he might fall prey to the sin of avarice; and his simultaneous service to two rural parishes was a calling, not an opportunity for enrichment. If his network of influential churchmen expanded upon his marriage, he did not exploit it: the greatest benefit that derived from his union with the Stonhouse family – apart, of course, from 56 years of loyal love and support from Rosalie – was the financial independence of his unmarried daughters, secured through the generosity of Charles Bennett.

There was a growing acceptance – even approbation – of the non-graduate training that was being increasingly provided by 'second-tier' theological colleges such as St Bees. But the mere fact that such institutions were established for ordinands who could not afford an Oxbridge education would have carried an unwelcome stigma. This would have been a strong reason why he chose to invest in Oxford educations for his two sons.

Perhaps as a result of his modest roots in rural working communities, Revd Luxmoore did not stand aloof or separate from his flock. He, his wife and his family all shared and participated fully in village life. He worked diligently to improve the lot of his parishioners – for example, via his provision of opportunities for the education of older children and adults in Ashford; his industrious and tenacious completion of the restoration of Holy Trinity Church; and his conscientious grassroots work to establish and help manage the school at Sheldon. He opened the school with a prayer in 1878; remained constantly involved with its day-to-day activities; and visited for a final time shortly after his retirement in 1912.

He had witnessed and endured tragedy, loss and grief in his own family: the sudden and dramatic confinement in the Exminster Asylum of his uncle, Charles; the mental illnesses of his wife's sister Alice and brother Edward; and the death of his infant son, Arthur. These painful experiences allowed his humanity to escape the emotional straitjacket of Victorian stoicism.

The fact that he remained in post for 52 years was therefore not simply a consequence of a lack of ambition, nor a lethargy induced by an ample and secure lifestyle. It was because he had a true empathy with his parishioners' often difficult lives, providing 'practical sympathy and kindly help in times of sickness and need'. He 'endeared himself to everyone in the parish' because of his abiding sense of loyalty – just as he travelled at a particularly busy time to support Alice Stonhouse in her hour of need, notwithstanding her inevitable condemnation by Victorian society.

His clear and never-changing signature on 52 years' worth of church registers is a metaphor for the constancy of purpose of his ministry, and his steadfast devotion to the members of his two parishes.

The signature of Revd John Reddaway Luxmoore.

It is facile to say, 'behind every good man there stands a good woman.' Rosalie is certainly a constant presence, supporting her husband as would be expected of a good Victorian vicar's wife. But she is also reported to have been equally empathetic and self-denying. I do not apologise for repeating what can be no greater testament than the quiet firsthand reflection, that:

'There is a warm corner in many hearts, especially amongst the older folk who were her contemporaries in Ashford and Sheldon, for Mrs Luxmoore.'[552]

---

[552] *Vide supra, p 146.*

Wikipedia, a gateway to some of my historical research, states,

'Today the term 'antiquarian' is often used in a pejorative sense, to refer to an excessively narrow focus on factual historical trivia, to the exclusion of a sense of historical context or process. Very few people today would self-describe themselves as an 'antiquary".[553]

I have no such shame. I choose to concur with Rosemary Sweet that,

'Interest in the customs, habits and dress of 'ordinary' people [is] one of the foundation stones of social history.'[554]

I have thoroughly enjoyed uncovering a wealth of information about Ashford and Sheldon, and the people who lived here some 150 years ago. Their stories have better informed my appreciation of these villages today.

I hope that my readers may have an equally enjoyable experience.

---

[553] *Antiquarian, https://en.wikipedia.org/wiki/Antiquarian*

ASIDE: Wikipedia is aware that it is often derided for its assumed low quality, inaccurate, or biased articles. Examples supporting this assertion can indeed be found by anyone who uses it enough. However, armies of contributors and users essentially 'auto-correct' content, to the extent that many entries achieve impressive levels of accuracy. The prestigious journal 'Nature' reported that 'Wikipedia comes close to Britannica in terms of the accuracy of its science entries.' Encyclopædia Britannica naturally disagreed, and promptly published a vigorous rebuttal, following which Nature issued its defence. The debate rolls on (see, e.g., 'the more, the wikier' below); the truth is that 'truth' is elusive. Certainly, the internet can very effectively bestow unwarranted authority to errors via their uncontrolled proliferation. From a practical perspective, I have found Wikipedia to be an invaluable starting point; it has more often than not pointed me to original source documents, or otherwise provided a basis on which to dig deeper. Because it has not been possible to verify every 'fact' independently, I have extensively referenced my sources. I apologise to the extent that I may have perpetuated any errors, or neglected to cite a source, and I would be happy to make appropriate corrections in any subsequent edition.

https://en.wikipedia.org/wiki/Wikipedia:Not_ready_for_primetime

Internet encyclopædias go head to head. Jim Giles. Nature, vol 438, 2005, pp 900-901.

http://corporate.britannica.com/britannica_nature_response.pdf

Britannica attacks. Nature, vol 440, 2006, p 582.

The more, the wikier: The secret to the quality of Wikipedia entries is lots of edits by lots of people. Philip Ball. Nature, News, February 27th 2007.

[554] *Antiquarianism and history. Rosemary Sweet. Making History. Institute of Historical Research. School of Advanced Study, University of London, https://archives.history.ac.uk/makinghistory/ resources/articles/antiquarianism.html*

Appendix

The History of the Dissenting Chapels in Ashford

by David Windle

The Baptist Chapel on Ashford Lane

A small copse of trees alongside the B 6465 road between Ashford and Monsal Head probably draws little attention from most passing travellers, but those who do investigate are often puzzled to find it is a small cemetery with no apparent reason for its existence. Local opinion has often referred to it as a Quaker cemetery, but in fact the ivy-covered gravestones mark the last resting place of members of a Society of Baptists, who, as Dissenters, had broken away from the Established Church. The Act of Uniformity of 1662, following the restoration of the monarchy, required ministers to pledge allegiance to the Established Church, and those who 'Dissented' were ejected from the ministry.

Baptist cemetery in Ashford Lane.

Ivy-covered gravestones in the Baptist Cemetery.

Perhaps the most famous of them in our area was William Bagshawe, popularly known as the 'Apostle of the Peak.'[555] Although strongly identified with Ashford, he was not associated with the Chapel on Ashford Lane, but more of him later.

It appears that the area around the Mother Church of Bakewell had a high concentration of Dissenters (and Papists, notably the Eyres of Hassop), and a report made for the archdeaconry of Derby in 1677[556] recorded 65 Papists and 200 Dissenters, more than anywhere else in the county, and it is likely that the Established Church would not permit the burial of such non-conformers in their churchyards (see p 116).

The area centred on the cemetery at Ashford included the Longstones and Wardlow and as far north as Abney and Bradwell, and possibly Monyash to the south, and can be seen as a stronghold of the Baptists. This in itself is unusual, since the Baptists had little presence in the rest of the county at that time.[557] It is possible that the cemetery in Ashford Lane predates the Act of Uniformity and was established during the Cromwellian period.[558] In the absence of a chapel, members would have met in various private houses, with travelling ministers visiting from time to time.

---

[555] *Transactions of the Congregational Historical Society, Vol.VI, 1913-1915.*

[556] *Victoria County History: Derbyshire, Vol II, 1907.*

[557] *Transactions of the Baptist Historical Society, Vol I, 1908-1909.*

[558] *The History of the English General Baptists, Vol 2. Adam Taylor. London, 1818, pp 261-269.*

It is not known how many interments may have been made, our only record being the legible inscriptions on the surviving 17 gravestones (see Additional Note 1, p 246).

A fundamental belief of the Baptists is in adult baptism by total immersion, replicating the work of St John the Baptist, who baptised his followers in the River Jordan in readiness for the coming of the Messiah. It is not clear how the congregation at Ashford carried out this ceremony, but tradition has it that a pond, not now accessible, in an adjoining field, with steps leading into it, was used.

There is a record of a Baptist ceremony taking place in the River Wye at the Sheepwash Bridge in 1898,[559] long after the Ashford Lane Chapel had ceased to exist, and a transcript is given in Additional Note 2 (see p 251). It is also possible that the sheepwash in Monsal Dale might have been similarly used. Local tradition also has it that after the minister's house was built, a large trough may have been installed, but there is nothing to corroborate that.[560]

At the end of the 17th century the Society appears to have been flourishing, and was served by two preachers, a Mr Mason and Mr Samuel White, both church members. Samuel White was particularly zealous and effective in spreading the Baptist message, and was noted for his constant travelling on horseback all around the Peak, in all weathers, often delivering his sermons from the saddle. Samuel White died in 1727, aged just 47, and he is buried in the cemetery in Ashford Lane. It is reputed that his preaching saddle was preserved in the former Bull's Head public house in Wardlow.[561]

Following the death of Samuel White, and later that of Mr Mason, the local Society went into decline and almost extinction, with no regular minister to attend the members. Eventually a former native of the district, who was a Baptist pastor in Lincolnshire, Mr Israel Cotton, visited and preached on occasion at a house in Monsal Dale. He persuaded a friend of his, Mr Jeffery of Gamston in Nottingham, to take on the venture, which he did with a missionary zeal. He asked a colleague, Mr Dossey, to join him, and between them they visited the congregation regularly once a month, alternating with each other, and at their own expense.

Eventually they decided that meeting in various private houses was not

---

[559] *Derbyshire Courier, August 13th 1898.*

[560] *Following the procession on June 11th 2017 to bless the Ashford village wells, the Bishop of Repton, Jan McFarlane, invited anyone who had not been baptised to take the opportunity to do so in the River Wye, with the exhortation 'Wye not?' A teenager accepted the offer, and the unscheduled baptism duly took place at Sheepwash Bridge, immediately following the parade.*

[561] *Personal recollection of the late Leonard French Blackwell, one-time Landlord of the Bull's Head at Wardlow.*

Baptist minister's house, now part of Red House, about 200 yards south of the Baptist Cemetery on Ashford Lane.

satisfactory and they set about building a meeting house, or chapel. They acquired a piece of land adjacent to the burial ground, and with local help, and almost entirely at their own expense, proceeded with the construction. Mr Jeffery funded the enterprise to the tune of £30, while Mr Dossey contributed £40. The pulpit and pews were made in Gamston and carted to the site by themselves; the building was finished and opened in 1761.

Not satisfied with this, they then purchased a further three acres of land close to the meeting house, and proceeded to build a dwelling house for a regular minister. Again, all the materials were transported to the site from Gamston by their own efforts. These materials included bricks, which were the standard building material in that area of Nottingham, and the resulting edifice presented a striking contrast to the typical limestone cottage of our own landscape, so much so that it became known as the 'Red House'.

The house was completed by 1762 and the first occupant and resident preacher was Mr Benjamin Fox, also from Gamston. He was succeeded in 1766 by Mr William Kelsey, but he moved on in 1778 and the Society was again left with intermittent visits. In 1782 the Society joined the New Connexion of the General Baptists, by which time the members had declined to just ten, recovering to 15 by 1783. In 1789 the Society was joined by Mr

William Pickering as its resident minister and he increased membership dramatically. He held meetings at Wardlow and Bradwell, as well as at the Chapel on Ashford Lane, and even gave evening lectures at a room licensed in Ashford village, possibly the Boys' Schoolroom. He was instrumental in having a meeting house built at Bradwell, to better serve the members there, which was completed in 1790.

William was acting in a lay capacity at this time, but was eventually ordained at Ashford Lane on August 14th 1794. By 1796 he had baptised another 18 members, who now numbered 43, but this was probably the pinnacle of his success, and by 1800 membership had declined to 23. The decline was accelerated when Mr Pickering left Ashford on August 14th 1800 to take up a position in Nottingham. (See the flyer on p24 advertising his return as a visiting preacher.)

Again the Society was left with no regular minister and, despite the efforts of local preachers – firstly Mr Robert Bradbury and then Mr Bramwell – the decline continued. In 1811 the Society split,[562] with one group of nine forming the church at Bradwell, including Abney, while Ashford, with Wardlow and now Longstone, continued alone with 20 members. There was a transient revival at Ashford, but by 1816 the numbers had decreased to 16. By 1832 regular attendance was down to five or six,[563] and by 1844 the Society was considered extinct,[564] its death occurring in 1839 when the membership was officially recorded as eight.

When the Congregational Chapel in Little Longstone was opened in 1844,[565] it was reported that the Revd Joseph Spencer of Bakewell and Revd J Sargent of Tideswell, who had preached from time to time in the Ashford Lane Chapel, would jointly occupy the pulpit there.

So today the cemetery remains as a reminder of a former age, overgrown and in need of care and attention. The chapel building itself was swept away long ago, possibly as a result of roadway realignment. Yet, a small fragment remains, as the crumbling roadside wall is believed to be part of the building itself, and the author remembers the entrance as a complete stone door frame. As for the minister's dwelling house, that still survives. It remained in occupation into the 20th century and, when the modern farmhouse was built close by, it was sympathetically constructed of brick and the new building assumed the name of the 'Red House'. The old building later saw service as an outbuilding

---

[562] *The History of the English General Baptists, Vol 2, London, 1818, pp 368-369.*

[563] *Minutes of an Association of the New Connexion of General Baptists, 1832.*

[564] *J Taylor. Statistics of the New Connexion of General Baptists, 1844.*

[565] *Sheffield and Rotherham Independent, December 28th 1844.*

to the farm, but in recent years it has been restored and modernised as living accommodation again.

The Presbyterian Chapel on Buxton Road

The road we know today as Buxton Road was formerly known as Cliff End Lane, and the chapel under consideration here took its name from that of the Lane. The old lane gave access to the Rookery and the fields beyond, and, after the middle of the 18th century, to one of the marble works in the village. It was not until the early 19th century that the route was turnpiked through to Buxton and the name changed to Buxton Road.

The chapel retained the name 'Cliff End Chapel' and occupies a particularly important place in the history of our village, because it owes its existence to William Bagshawe,[566] otherwise known to posterity as the 'Apostle of the Peak'. The life of William Bagshawe has been well documented, but a brief history is worth repeating here.

The Bagshawes were an old-established and eminent Derbyshire family, and William was born in 1628 at Litton, near Tideswell, where his family were well-to-do local squires. His early education was in two local grammar schools, and it is possible that one of these may have been at Ashford and the other at Tideswell. The grammar school at Ashford had been founded in 1630,[567] and it and Tideswell were closest to Litton. At this time there were probably less than 10 such schools in the whole of the county.

William appears to have been an able scholar and was sent to Corpus Christi College, Cambridge, where he graduated by the time he was 18. He had decided to go into the ministry, much against the wishes of his family, and to a large extent he was cut off from the family fortunes. He preached for a short time at Wormhill (another Bagshawe estate), and in a Sheffield parish. In 1650 he was ordained at Chesterfield, and soon after became the minister at Glossop, where he remained for 11 years, and where his children were born.

That would probably have been the end of the story for William, but, following the Restoration of the Monarchy in 1660, an Act of Uniformity was passed which required all ministers to accept the Articles of Faith of the Established Church. Along with many others, William felt he was unable to do this and, on St Bartholomew's Day 1662, he was forced to relinquish his living at Glossop.

He retired to Ford Hall, near Chapel-en-le-Frith, the only part of the Bagshawe estates left to him, from where he embarked on an Evangelical

---

[566] *J Tilley. Old Halls, Manors and Families of Derbyshire, Vol 1, High Peak Hundred, 1899.*

[567] *Charity Foundation Board in Holy Trinity Church, see pp 165-166.*

mission, preaching from there and in private houses at a number of locations around the Peak. This put him at some risk of arrest, but it seems that those sent to arrest him never carried out their warrant, presumably out of respect for him. While a relaxation in the law in 1689 made it possible for William to sign a modified Act of Uniformity, he maintained his Presbyterian principles and continued with his adopted mission.

Although William visited places as scattered as Tideswell, Chinley, Chelmorton and Hucklow, his most frequent visits were to Malcoff (near his home at Ford Hall) and Ashford, where he preached on alternate Sundays. He clearly had a particular affection for Ashford, which may stem from his possible early education in the village, and also from the fact that his mother was a member of the Oldfield family, which had a long-established connection with Ashford, as well as other places in the Peak. It is also evident that his Ashford congregation had a strong affection for him, culminating in the building of the Cliff End Chapel for his use; it opened in 1701. Surviving photographs show the chapel as a simple single-storey gritstone building under a stone roof, with a door and windows in the gothic revival style.

Cliff End Chapel, ca. 1920.

Unfortunately, William was unable to make much use of his new chapel, as on April 1st 1702 he passed away, aged 74, and was laid to rest at Chapel-en-le-Frith, alongside his wife. He had remained a Presbyterian to the end, and had continued to preach until a few days before his death.

Grave of Revd John Ashe in the churchyard of Holy Trinity Church, Ashford.

During his later years, William was assisted by his nephew, Revd John Ashe,[568] whose mother was Susannah, William's sister. John had been ordained as a Presbyterian minister in 1696 and had helped his uncle by preaching at Ashford on two Sundays in the month, and one Sunday each at Chelmorton and Hucklow.

John Ashe now assumed full responsibility for the Chapel at Ashford, and in addition preached in neighbouring parishes such as Tideswell, Bradwell, Hucklow and Litton on Feast Days and Wakes Days. He had a number of assistants at various times,[569] including George Lowe of Norton (Norton being part of Derbyshire at that time); Mr Clark of Hucklow; Thomas Bott, who became rector of a parish in Norfolk; and Joseph Hankinson of Altrincham, who became pastor at Wirksworth in 1727. By 1730 John was in poor health and not up to travelling; he relinquished charge of Hucklow and Bradwell to the Revd Robert Kelsall, also of Altrincham, who served Hucklow for 41years, up to his death in 1772.

John Ashe remained in charge at Ashford until his sudden death on October 2nd 1735. Like his uncle before him, Revd Ashe had earned himself much respect and devotion in Ashford. He was interred on October 4th 1735 in the

---

[568] *Transactions of the Congregational Historical Society, Vol.VI, 1913-1915, p 345.*

[569] *Ibid., p 346.*

churchyard of Holy Trinity Church, although the incumbent at the time made quite sure that the entry in the Parish Register identified John as 'a Dissenting minister'.[570] The table tomb of John Ashe stands in the churchyard to the west of the tower, but weathering has removed all traces of the inscription. Fortunately, his epitaph was recorded long ago,[571] and a transcript is given in Additional Note 4 (see p 253).

However, William Bagshawe and John Ashe were not the only persons of note to be associated with this old chapel. Towards the end of the 17th century in Catholic France, the Protestant Huguenot minority, although tolerated, were frequently persecuted, and following the revocation of the Edict of Nantes, which had guaranteed their rights, they were actively discriminated against. As a result many Huguenots were forced to flee their country, including Henri (Henry) Nadauld who made it to London with his wife and family in about 1697 or 1698.[572] Many of these refugees were skilled craftsmen and artisans, and Henry was a stone carver or sculptor. Along with some of his countrymen, he came to the attention of the Duke of Devonshire, who at the time was rebuilding his home at Chatsworth into the mansion that we see today. Henry was brought to Chatsworth and spent most of his working life there, and at some other Cavendish properties, also doing occasional jobs at Castle Howard in Yorkshire. He worked mainly with Samuel Watson, whose son Henry is credited with founding the black marble industry in Ashford in 1748. One of the best examples of Henry's work can be seen today on the Temple at the head of the Great Cascade in the gardens of Chatsworth House (see p 100).

Henry had settled in Ashford, anglicising his name from Henri to Henry, and after retirement he lived out the rest of his life there, becoming a respected member of the community. He was also a loyal member of the Cliff End Chapel, where he enjoyed the religious freedom denied him in his homeland. When he died in 1723, aged 70, he was accorded the honour of being buried within the chapel, no doubt with the full approval of his friend, John Ashe. An original poem celebrating Henry Nadauld is transcribed in Additional Note 5 (see p 253).

John Ashe was followed at Ashford by the Revd Samuel Evatt,[573] who ministered there and at Stoney Middleton for many years. During his time

---

[570] *Ashford Parish Registers, transcripts copyright Val Neal.*

[571] *The History, Gazetteer, and Directory of the County of Derby. Part 2. Stephen Glover. Henry Mozley & Son, Derby, 1829, p 49. See also p 99 et seq.*

[572] *Chatsworth: A Short History. Francis Thompson. 1951. See also p 99 et seq.*

[573] *Transactions of the Congregational Historical Society, Vol VI, 1913-1915, p 347.*

at Ashford, he helped to establish in 1761 the Thomas Roose (or Goodwin) charity,[574] which was entrusted to pay 40 shillings (£2) to the Dissenting minister, and 20 shillings (£1) to the master of the grammar school. It was also during Samuel's ministry, in 1741, that repairs were made to the building, which was apparently in a state of decay. A plaque was added, recording 'Presbyterian Chapel, erected 1701, repaired 1741'. Eventually, Samuel conformed and was accepted back into the Established Church, and consequently resigned his ministry at Cliff End. By now the congregation at Ashford had so reduced that it almost ceased to exist. It was supplied by occasional preachers, mostly drawn from the Great Hucklow Chapel, which had a thriving congregation.

The state of the Chapel at Ashford was improved during the 1770s when the then minister at Great Hucklow, a Mr Evans, who had also added the pastorates of Bradwell and Stoney Middleton to his care, took on the ministry at Ashford. The four congregations remained united under one minister until 1798, firstly Revd Evans, and then the Revd Allard. It was during Revd Evans' ministry that the chapel underwent substantial rebuilding work, funded by two benefactors – Samuel Shore of Meersbrook and Robert Newton of Norton – who had also invested heavily for the benefit of the minister.[575] By this time the group had become Unitarian and the congregation at Ashford was small but regular. (See also: Attorney-General v Samuel Shore; The Shore family scandals, pp 125, 128.)

In 1870 the Chapel was acquired by the Congregational Church at Bakewell, and from that time it appears to have been little used for its intended purpose, although it occasionally served as a venue for church and other public meetings,[576] as well as for public entertainment.[577] A singular reference to its use by the Plymouth Brethren and the Baptists is transcribed in Additional Note 2 (see p 251). By the 1900s the building was being rented by the Young Men's Christian Association, when the initials of the organisation were displayed on each of four panes of the central window. It was subsequently used as a club for the young men of Ashford into the 1930s.

This historic old building came to a sudden and ignominious end in 1937 when the roof collapsed, an event that was recorded in newspapers far and wide.[578] The structure of the chapel seems to have always been problematical and

---

[574] *Charity Foundation Board in Holy Trinity Church. See pp 165-166.*

[575] *Transactions of the Congregational Historical Society, Vol VI, 1913-1915, pp 349-350.*

[576] *Tea Meeting. Derbyshire Times & Chesterfield Herald, January 10th 1883.*

[577] *Fundraising Event. Derbyshire Times & Chesterfield Herald, May 10th 1890.*

[578] *Gloucester Echo, August 5th 1937; Hull Daily Mail, August 5th 1937.*
    See also p 120.

had clearly deteriorated towards the end, but its final demise was attributed to vibration caused by traffic passing by on the Buxton Road. Although the Duke's Drive bypass (now the A6) had been constructed four years earlier, it had done little to alleviate the traffic to and from Sheffield, and the steelworks of that city had a voracious appetite for the high-grade limestone from the quarries around Buxton. Consequently, a steady stream of lorries passed by, day and night – a situation that continued for another four decades, until a second bypass (A6020 diversion) was opened in 1979.

After the bulk of the rubble had been cleared away and the 'Frenchman' had been reinterred in the churchyard,[579] the site remained as a playground for children like myself. Although a modern dwelling now stands on the site, the gable end of the chapel and a small remnant of masonry can still be seen against the end of the row of cottages on Buxton Road. (See also: The burial and reinterment of Henry Nadauld, p 119.)

The Wesleyan Methodist Chapel on Court Lane

The Methodist Chapel in Ashford[580, 581] is sandwiched between old cottages in a quiet corner of Court Lane overlooking Holy Trinity Church. Over the entrance porch the date of 1899 appears to indicate the date of its establishment, but in fact it was founded 70 years earlier.

Methodism began as a movement within the Established Anglican Church pursuing the doctrines of John Wesley and others, including his brother Charles. Although Wesley remained within the Established Church, he pursued his Evangelical mission, travelling the country and preaching his message, particularly to the working classes and to the poor. After John's death in 1791, his fellow leaders broke away and set up the Methodist Church as a separate denomination. By the beginning of the 19th century, Methodism had become a growing force.

So it was that a group of local men, enthused by the Methodist message, were keen to establish a chapel in the area and they set up a trust to further their cause. They were able to advance their aims when, at a manorial court at Ashford on October 29th 1829, the trustees gained possession of a building in Court Lane, on payment of a fine of £25. The building had been used as a stable, but was at the time a blacksmith's workshop in the occupation of Richard Dunn of Ashford; the trustees now set about adapting the building to its new use. The property was held subject to payment of copyhold rent of two

---

[579] *Personal recollections of the late George Thomas Millward Lowe Doxey.*

[580] *The bulk of this history is based on private papers donated by Mrs D Daybell.*

[581] *High Peak News, April 26th 1930.*

pence (2d) per year, which continued to be paid up to 1930.

The trust deed, dated December 30th 1831, refers to the building having been converted into a Methodist Chapel, and it is interesting to note that only one of the named trustees was actually an Ashford resident. That was George Oldfield, described as a mason, the same George Oldfield who was about to take over the Ashford Marble Works at the foot of Kirkdale. We have come across the Oldfield family before in connection with the family of William Bagshawe and the Cliff End Chapel. Interestingly, George lived on Cliff End Lane, close to the chapel, and may even have been a member of the congregation there at one time.

The other trustees were: Stephen Holmes, John Gibbons and George Ludlam, all farmers of Rowsley; Charles Harrison of Sheldon and Lawrence Furniss of Pilsley, also farmers; and William Willis, a currier of Grindleford Bridge, who appeared to be the leader.

It is not known what this early chapel looked like, but given its previous uses, it would presumably have been just a single-storey building of humble construction, quite unlike the building we see today. Typically for the period, heating would have been by coal fire and lighting by candles, later replaced by oil lamps. An account for 1862 shows the cost of lighting amounted to ten shillings (50p). In 1874 the cost of candles was 10d (4p) per pound. The cost of coal in 1874 was 1s 3d per cwt (approximately 6p per 50kg), but by the early 1930s it had increased to 2s 6d (12p per 50kg); annual consumption was about two tons.

The chapel apparently prospered, and apart from religious service, much secular work was done. One of the keystones of Methodist doctrine was the promotion of education, and the Sunday School was particularly well supported, presumably in competition with the Anglican Sunday School. Despite this success, the chapel clearly left something to be desired, and various repairs and improvements needed to be made over the years. For example, the interior was painted in 1868 at a cost of £2, and in 1871 Matthew Thorp, a mason and builder working there, charged 4s 6d (23p) per day. In 1874 a more ambitious scheme to rebuild the interior was carried out. One of the contributors to the fund for this work was Lord George Cavendish, brother of the 7th Duke of Devonshire. Lord George, who lived at Ashford Hall, had been the Liberal MP for North Derbyshire and was a noted benefactor to the village. After he died in 1880, his widow, Lady Louisa, had shelters built over the two main village pumps, which still stand to his memory today.

As the Society grew in strength, a scheme was put forward to expand the chapel and renovate the old structure, and fundraising started in earnest. One of the main members driving the project forward was Mr William Daybell, who was a particularly zealous Methodist. William was a Nottinghamshire man who had come originally to Bakewell as a signalman on the railway. He and his family moved to Ashford in the 1870s, and in the 1881 census he is described as a coal agent and carter. He was very active in the movement, becoming a senior local preacher on the Methodist Circuit, occasionally known to some as 'Bishop' Daybell.

Eventually it was possible to proceed with the plans, and Messrs Alfred & Hedley Hill of Tideswell were appointed contractors for the work at a cost of £400. Earlier attempts to find more land to accommodate the new chapel had failed, so building commenced on the existing plot, with the result that the premises effectively filled the site. The development involved building a separate school room, which could also be used for hosting social gatherings, alongside the existing room. The Wesleyan school here attracted pupils from the established village school, as noted in the Ashford School logbooks.[582] The original chapel was to be completely renovated, with a new roof, doors and windows, and an entrance porch, the whole being in the gothic style. The two rooms were separated by a folding screen. The opportunity was taken to fit gas lighting in place of the oil lamps, which had previously replaced the candle lighting. Electric lighting was not installed in the premises until 1930.[583]

At 3.00pm on Thursday July 27th 1899, a ceremony to lay the memorial stones of the new building was held, with much celebration, prayers, hymn singing and speeches. On an improvised platform were the Revd J Rogers (Superintendent Minister of Bakewell); Messrs T Clarke (of Leeds) and W Robinson (Evangelist); Mr J Norcross (of Middleton, Lancashire); and William Daybell. The Sunday School stone was laid by Mr G Thorpe, and Mr and Mrs Daybell each laid a stone either side of the new doorway. Stones were also laid by Mrs Norcross, Miss Bridge and Mrs M Percival. William Daybell noted in his speech that two stones remained that needed to be attributed but, although they were laid, they remain blank to this day.

Later in the day a public tea, attended by 125 people, was held at the Cliff End Chapel on Buxton Road, which was being used by the Methodists while their new chapel was being built. In the evening a public meeting was held at the same place, and collections during the day amounted to £50.

---

[582] *Ashford-in-the-Water School, 1631-1988. Unpublished history by the late Miss Sheila Hurst.*

[583] *During its centenary celebrations the building was redecorated at a cost of £70, and the electric lights were added by a Miss Norcross in memory of her parents. Derby Daily Telegraph, May 2nd 1930.*

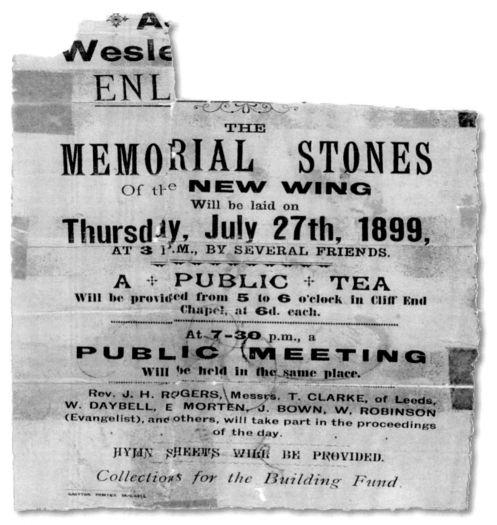

Notice of the laying of memorial stones for the Wesleyan Chapel.

By the end of 1899 the chapel was completed, and on Thursday December 21st a reopening and dedicatory service was held and sermons were preached by Revd HT Smart of Sheffield. A public tea was held later at the Cliff End Chapel, and in the evening Revd Smart gave a lecture entitled 'Nineteenth Century Miracles'. The photograph opposite shows William Daybell sitting on the wall outside the recently completed chapel. The wall at the time was unadorned, but later a wrought iron gate and railings were added, which survive to this day.

On September 12th 1900 the chapel was registered to perform marriages, meaning that it was now able to provide all the spiritual needs the community might have, from baptism, through marriage, and eventually to the end of

William Daybell outside the newly-enlarged Wesleyan Methodist chapel, ca. 1900.

life, and continued to do so for nearly a century more.

Eventually, falling numbers of members and smaller congregations made the chapel less viable. An entry in the Ashford School Logbook records that pupils had returned from the Wesleyan school by 1932. Like many similar institutions in recent years, the chapel finally closed its doors in 1994. Although the building was sold and converted to a private dwelling, the outward appearance remains just as it was in 1899.

Additional Note 1: Transcription of gravestones in the Baptist cemetery

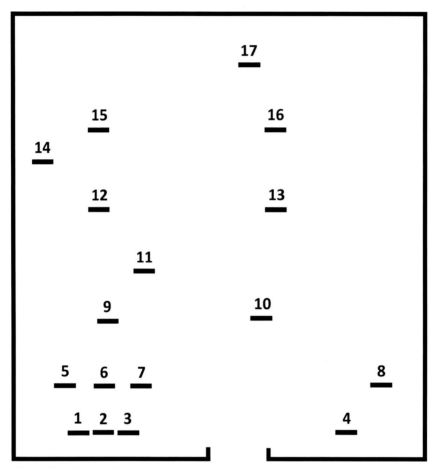

Plan of the Baptist Cemetery.

1.   (Gr.H.)[584]   Here lyeth the body
                                   of SAMUEL WHITE who
                                   departed this life
                                   October ye 17. 1727
                                   aged 47 years

(Samuel White was a member of the Society of Baptists at Ashford. He was particularly zealous and travelled across the Peak on horseback, preaching from the saddle.)

---

[584] *See key on p 251.*

2. (Gr.H.)

M.W.
Dyid Octr
ye 28. 1713
aged 22
years

3. (Gr.H.)

RALPH WHITE
Dyid Nov. 7. 1709
aged 68
Here let his bones
rest in the dust
Until the resurrect-
ion of the just

4. (Lm.H.)

HERE
LIE THE REMAINS
OF
GEORGE BRUSHFIELD
WHO DIED FEBY 25TH 1825
AGED 52 YEARS
MORTAL – WAIT NOT FOR MONUMENTAL STONE
TO TELL THE VIRTUES ONCE BY THEE POSSESS'D
FOR ALL AROUND THEE MAKE THY GOODNESS KNOWN
E'RE THOU ART CALL'D TO EARTHS LAST BED OF REST
AND THOUGH MANS ENVY MAY THY WORTH DISOWN
STILL CONSCIOUS UPRIGHTNESS SHALL FILL THY BREAST
REWARD THY LIFE WITH PEACE AND MAKE THY MEM'RY BLEST

5. (Sa.H.)

IN MEMORY OF JOSHUA
BIRLEY of BRADWELL who
departed this life May 3.....aged.....9 years
Also of his wife
who departed this life
Feb.....9th 1767 aged .....years
Also
PHILIP who departed this life.....
1791 aged 6 years

6.   (Sa.H.)   SACRED
                          TO THE MEMORY
                               OF
                          JOHN BIRLEY
                             late of
                      BRADWELL, who depar
                      ted this life Decr 2nd 1831
                         aged 81 years

(George Birley of Ashford, a member of this family, was a noted missionary preacher. He was ordained in 1786. He had settled in St Ives, Huntingdonshire, in 1777, and was buried there in 1824.)

7.   (Sa.H.)   IN MEMORY OF
                      JOSIAH BIRLEY (late of
                      WARDLOW) who departed
                      this life August 24 AD 1842
                         aged 82 years
                      Also of HANNAH the wife of
                      the said JOSIAH BIRLEY
                      who died November 23rd
                      AD 1800 in the 38th year
                         of her age

(Monumental mason – W CHAPMAN, WINDMILL)

8.   (Lm.H.)   HERE
                            LIE THE
                      REMAINS OF JOSEPH
                           the son of
                      JOHN and ANN BIRCH
                          of OAKS
                      He departed this life
                      July the 18th 1803 aged 18 years

9.   (Gr.H.)   Here Lyeth the
                                body of ANN ye
                                wife of HUGH
                                HANDEFILD who
                                died March the
                                31. 1723 aged
                                46 years

10. (Gr.H.)   T.H.
                                 died Oct.
                                 22. 1707

11. (Gr.H.)   Here lieth the
                                body of SAMUEL
                                SKIDMORE who
                                departed this
                                life May the 25
                                in the 34 year
                                of his age
                                1739

12. (Lm.H.)   IN MEMORY OF
                            WILLIAM BRAMWELL
                                OF ASHFORD
                            who died June 4th 1845
                               aged 57 years
                      And of FRANCES BRUSHFIELD his wife
                            who died May 18th 1843
                               aged 53 years
                          Also of RICHARD, their son
                      who died Novr 18th 1821 aged 6 years
                        and of ELIZABETH, their daughter
                      who died March 14th 1834 aged 8 years
                          Also of WILLIAM, their son
                      who died Decr 5th 1836 aged 16 years
                        and of BENJAMIN, who died
                             in his infancy

13.   (Sa.H.)   IN
                     AFFECTIONATE REMEMBRANCE OF
                              GRACE
                          youngest daughter of
                     WILLIAM & FRANCES BRAMWELL
                       Born the 13th January 1830
                       Died the 11th November 1878
                       Also of ROBERT BRAMWELL
                          their youngest son
                       who died March 1st 1904
                            aged 74 years

(Monumental mason – J TWIGG, ASHFORD)

14.   (Gr.H.)   H.S.
                               1705

15.   (Gr.H.)   SAMUEL SHAW dyed
                        January ye 18th 1728

16.   (Gr.H.)   HERE LIETH THE
                         BODY OF WILLIAM
                         THORP who de-
                         parted this life
                         in the year.....

(Stone deeply set in ground)

17.   (Lm.H.&Ft.)   IN MEMORY OF
                              SAMUEL
                         BIRLEY of ASHFORD
                  who died October 19th 1870 aged 75 years
                     Also of ANN his beloved wife
                  who died March 29th 1870 aged 76 years

and to MARY ANN their daughter
who died 1831 aged 17 years
and to MARY their daughter
who died 1849 aged 12 years

Key: Gr.H. = gritstone headstone
Sa.H. = sandstone headstone
Lm.H. = limestone headstone
Ft.   = footstone
.....   = illegible

Additional Note 2: Record of a Baptist baptism

The following is a transcription of an article that appeared in the *Derbyshire Courier* on Saturday August 13th 1898:

> *'The village of Ashford-in-the-Water was the scene of a somewhat novel religious ceremony on Sunday [August 7th]. A congregation of Baptists at Buxton, a few months ago, acquired the old Plymouth Brethren's Chapel on the Buxton Road, Ashford, in which to hold services. On Sunday, their first convert was publicly baptised by immersion, in accordance with the tenets of their faith. As there was no accommodation for such a rite at the chapel, the sheepwash at Bridge End, Ashford, off the River Wye was utilised. The pastor, Mr James Underwood, of Litton, accompanied by a young man named McFadden, clad simply in shirt and trousers, walked into the water up to the waist, and there the latter was totally immersed in the water. A short religious service was also held at the riverside. The novel scene was witnessed by a large and curious crowd.'*

This clearly refers to the Cliff End Chapel which, at the time of this event, had long been in the possession of the Congregational Church at Bakewell. If this unique reference to the Plymouth Brethren is correct, the Congregational Church must have let it to that sect and, subsequently, to the Baptist group from Buxton. Neither group could have held it for long, as by the early 1900s it was being used by the YMCA.

It is possible that the river at Ashford was often used for this ceremony when the Ashford Lane Chapel was active, and it is thought that the sheepwash in Monsal Dale was similarly used on occasion. The Monsal Dale sheepwash adjoined the footbridge over the river, but little trace of it remains today.

Additional Note 3: Chapel near Monsal Dale (transcript from *The Reliquary*)[585]

'In the graveyard of a chapel (now a ruin) near Monsal Dale, lie the remains of several who were once persons of note in Ashford; among them lie, at his particular wish, my father, George Brushfield. At the request of my mother, I wrote at the time an epitaph for his headstone, and as the stone is now broken, I send a copy of the lines which were on it should you think them worth preserving.

Mortal wait not for monumental stone
To tell the virtues once by thee possessed;
But make thy goodness all around thee known
Ere thou art called to earth's last bed of rest.
And though man's envy may thy worth disown,
Conscious integrity will fill thy breast,
Reward thy life with peace, and make
The memory bless'd.

'On the evening of my father's funeral, the guests who had followed his remains were assembled around the table and about to take tea, when I heard some whispering going on in the adjoining room, and found the gravedigger apparently terror stricken; on enquiry, he stated that he had heard noises in the grave which he was filling up, and fancied he heard raps on the coffin lid. I with two others immediately went with him, had the earth thrown out of the grave and the coffin lid opened, but, alas! my dear father slept in his last sleep, and the noises the gravedigger had heard were caused by the plate on the coffin. We went back and informed the company of the acts, and relieved all from a most painful anxiety.'

This macabre, yet somewhat amusing, anecdote was recounted by George Brushfield's son, Thomas, for whom some biographical notes are given on p 103 et seq. It is not known how or why the original headstone came to be broken; perhaps an act of vandalism. Whatever the reason, the stone visible in the cemetery today is clearly a replacement, and the engraving on that stone differs very slightly from the epitaph quoted above.

---

[585] *Chapel near Monsal Dale. Thomas Brushfield. The Reliquary, Vol 11, Llewellynn Jewitt (ed). Bemrose & Sons, Derby & London, 1870-1871, p 254 (see p 117).*

Additional Note 4: Epitaph of Revd John Ashe[586]

In Memory of
JOHN ASHE
A minister of the Gospel
whose mind was enriched with that learning and piety,
that candour and humility
that simplicity and godly sincerity
that greatly adorned his inoffensive and useful life,
which suddenly and happily
ended with his labours
in his 64th year
October 2nd 1735

Additional Note 5: Original poetry: Henry Nadauld's grave

The following poem, relevant to Cliff End Chapel (see p 239), is transcribed from *The Derbyshire Times & Chesterfield Herald*, September 11th 1880:

'On the revocation of the Edict of Nantes, one Henry Nadauld fled from France, and settled in Ashford, Derbyshire; there he died and was buried in the chapel.

This should be hallowed ground, and these poor walls
And ruder roof esteemed a noble shrine,
Fair as a work of gems and carven capitals,
In thy dear land of beauty and the vine.
An exile's dust should rest where splendour falls
On a brave record, or where flowers entwine,
Commingling beauties, the union is so rare
Of a right noble nature and a spirit fair.

Thy heart oft yearn'd for thine own sunny clime,
As here reposing 'neath a colder sky,
The feeble daylight died at eventime,
And mirrored in the pale mists rising high,
Thy friends and kindred with endearing mime
Beckoned thee back; thy choice was here to die,

---

[586] *The History, Gazetteer, and Directory of the County of Derby. Part 2. Stephen Glover. Henry Mozley & Son, Derby, 1829, p 49.*

France thrust thee forth, with truth the loss was hers,
Thou wert not of France only, but the universe.

The cold green hills that cluster round thy dust
Remember thee, their children tell of thee,
As one on whose firm heart reposed a sacred trust,
The grave that gave thee welcome still is free,
For freedom ever dwelleth with the just,
Men gather round thy grave still with humility,
But the poor place doth open to the sky
When the true word is spoken, and thy friend is nigh.'

Ashford, August 31st 1880.   *MNH*[587]

---

[587] *The identity of MNH is not known but is possibly a descendent of Henry Nadauld.*

ACKNOWLEDGEMENTS

Nobody can create a local history book without leaning heavily on the work of others, and I have been fortunate that many details of the histories of the small villages of Derbyshire have been recorded by those passionate Victorian chroniclers that I introduced in the Preface.

I am no less indebted to modern-day chroniclers: I mentioned earlier the importance to Revd Luxmoore's story of David Windle's history of the Dissenting chapels in Ashford, and I appreciate this most valuable contribution. Local historians of today and tomorrow will delight in his archive of hitherto unpublished facts and photographs.

Robert Dawson has carefully documented the affecting reminiscences of his mother, Alice Mary Dawson; his kind permission for me to quote directly from his book has helped in painting a touching, but inspirational, picture of the frequently challenging lives of early 20th-century Ashford villagers.

It has been a real privilege to hear anecdotes and first-hand recollections of Revd JR Luxmoore's children from Robin S Luxmoore and Paul J Luxmoore, his grandson and great-grandson respectively, and to reproduce some photographs from their family albums. Robin's memories, photographs and documents relating to a trip he made to Devon in May 1989 to research his forebears and namesakes have been most interesting and informative. I am also extremely grateful for the permission granted to me by the Luxmoore family to use writings from the *Luxmoore of Ashford* archive at the Derbyshire Record Office. The enthusiasm and practical assistance that has been provided by Bruce, James, Judith, Melissa, Paul, Robin, Rory and Sarah have made this book possible.

Graham and William Yeo generously hosted me at Lewtrenchard, shared the histories of the Yeo family and Orchard Barton, and directed me to Ron Wawman's transcription of the diaries of Sabine Baring-Gould. Erma Luxmoore kindly gave me permission to use photographs of the Luxmoore-Yeo family from the genealogy collection of her late husband, Charles Emerson Luxmoore.

The clergy, officers and members of the congregation of Holy Trinity Church, Ashford, have all been highly supportive of this project. I am pleased to have received practical assistance from Revd Canon Tony Kaunhoven (Vicar of Ashford-in-the-Water with Sheldon, Bakewell, Over Haddon & Rowsley); John Foster and John Winkworth-Smith (Churchwardens); John Gibson (Secretary of the Parochial Church Council); Linda Foster (Church Administrator); Linda Pelc (Tower Captain) and John Thorpe; and prior incumbents Revd Clive Thrower and Ven Gerald Phizackerley.

Along with many other researchers and genealogists worldwide, I have referred many times to the online searchable databases of the monuments and inscriptions in the churchyards of Ashford, Sheldon and other local parishes that have been meticulously prepared by Revd Clive Thrower.[588] We are indebted to him for the huge amount of time he has invested in creating and making available this most valuable resource.

Ian Cox, David Windle and Laurence Knighton provided their marvellous photographs of various Ashford village scenes and celebrations. Lillias Bendell directed me to the *Diaries of J James Middleton of Ashford*, and proffered the framed photomontage of Ashford Church and Revd JR Luxmoore that was so treasured by her grandaunt Mary Bolsover. The late Margaret Norman gave freely of her time and allowed me access to her written and photographic archives relating to her husband John's incumbency at Ashford and Sheldon from 1957 to 1964. The photograph of Bishop Luxmoore's memorial tablet in St Asaph's Cathedral would be of little value without the translation of its inscription by the learned Michael Hannon. I am also grateful to Roger Allum, Paul Brittain, Edward Caudwell, Maurice Daniel, Pearse Fee, the Hooper Kindon family, and the other individuals and organisations named below for permission to reproduce their photographs.

My thanks also are due to Brian Greasley of the Sheldon Local History Group, for bringing to my attention Revd Luxmoore's involvement in the establishment and operation of Sheldon School; and to Ann Hall of the Longstone Local History Group, for supplying valuable information regarding Joseph Paxton's design of local buildings and the recent archaeological dig at Fin Cop (for which Ann was Project Manager).

Shane Wadman contributed additional helpful insights into Sabine Baring-Gould and the Luxmoore family in Devon, and Barry Sterndale Bennett

---

[588] *Monuments: Ashford-in-the-Water, Holy Trinity; Sheldon, St Michael and All Angels. Clive Thrower. See Bibliography, p 265.*

allowed me to quote extracts from his great-grandfather's correspondence with Revd JR Luxmoore.

I have spent many happy hours sharing with Richard Crosby our love of local history, and I am indebted to him for loaning me several of the books that I have listed in the Bibliography, and which have aided my research.

I am thankful for the expertise and patience of staff at the Derbyshire Record Office, including especially Paul Beattie, Anne Lawley, Karen Millhouse and Becky Sheldon; Ruth Barber of the Derbyshire Family History Society; and the Devon Archives and Local Studies Service of the South West Heritage Trust.

To help provide an idea of the value of 19th-century financial transactions in today's money, I have used the relevant online calculators provided by the MeasuringWorth Foundation.[589]

In order to improve the readability and accessiblity of historical materials, I have on occasion taken the liberty of making some minor revisions to quotations and transcriptions, whilst endeavouring to preserve both the meaning and essential flavour of the source documents. I apologise to those who, after researching the original texts, believe that I have strayed too far from academic exactitude.

I am delighted to have found in Roger Allum someone with an equal passion for the past, who also shares with me a scientist's love of accuracy, but who has a far more discriminating and scholarly appreciation of literary style. I am immensely grateful for his enthusiastic support of the project, for his editing and proofreading, for his guidance regarding illustrations, and for his suggestions for layout and typography. To the extent that there remain any non sequiturs, grammatical faux pas, out-of-place hyphens, stray apostrophes, or an excess or insufficiency of commas, the reader may be assured that I will have introduced, or refused to rectify, such horrors, against his better advice. Jonathan Taylor of Spiral Publishing, indexer Anna Lord, and image restoration expert Ian Wright, have patiently provided their guidance and applied their professional skills in converting our drafts into a book of which I hope they can be proud.

Notwithstanding the encouragement and assistance from so many enthusiastic collaborators and supporters, I take full responsibility for the final product.

---

[589] *Measuring Worth. MeasuringWorth Foundation. 2019, https://www.measuringworth.com*

See also: Cost of Living Over Two Hundred Years. Joy Bristow. The Local Historian's Glossary of Words and Terms. Countryside Books. 2001, pp 223-225.

Copyright credits and references for illustrations, photographs, and quoted extracts

I am indebted to the many organisations, families and individuals named below for their kind permission to use their copyright material. Every effort has been made to trace copyright holders: I apologise in advance for any unintentional errors or omissions, which I would be pleased to correct in any subsequent editions. Where relevant and available, literature citations, archive catalogue numbers, and the creation dates of all illustrations and photographs are provided below.

DRO: Derbyshire Record Office. www.derbyshire.gov.uk/recordoffice.

BNA: British Newspaper Archive. www.britishnewspaperarchive.co.uk. BNA newspaper images are copyright the British Library Board. All rights reserved. Reproduced by permission of the British Newspaper Archive.

TK: Permission and confirmatory authorisation to reproduce a number of Ashford and Sheldon church illustrations and documents in the DRO archives have been provided by Revd Canon Tony Kaunhoven, Vicar of Ashford-in-the-Water with Sheldon, Bakewell, Over Haddon & Rowsley.

DRO, D7672: The *Luxmoore of Ashford* family archive at the Derbyshire Record Office. Works of John Reddaway Luxmoore and John Stonhouse Luxmoore in this family archive are published by permission of the Luxmoore family. The collection was given in 1940 by Miss Edith Rosalie Luxmoore, daughter of Revd John Reddaway Luxmoore.

Front cover: Left: Revd JR Luxmoore, 1911. Reproduced by permission of Revd Canon Tony Kaunhoven. Right: Proposed post-restoration exterior south elevation of Holy Trinity Church, Ashford. James Medland & Henry Taylor, 1868. TK. DRO, D7672/Lx.C-67.

Page 18: Domesday Book for Ashford, folio 272 verso, 1086. Open Domesday Project. John Palmer, George Slater and Anna Powell-Smith. opendomesday.org. **Page 19**: Hall Orchard, Ashford, ca.1920. Reproduced by permission of Laurence Knighton. **Page 20**: Neville Old Hall, Ashford, ca.1930s. Reproduced by permission of Peak in the Past. Ref. Ashf003. **Page 21**: Norman tympanum, Holy Trinity Church, Ashford. Drawing by George S Ramsey. In: On Norman Tympana, with especial reference to those of Derbyshire. TN Brushfield. Journal of the British Archaeological Association, Vol VI, Bedford Press, London, facing p 241. Description of carving from:

Notes on the Churches of Derbyshire, Vol II, The Hundreds of the High Peak and Wirksworth. J Charles Cox. Bemrose & Sons, Derby & London, 1877, p 45.

Page 21: Norman corbel, Holy Trinity Church, Ashford. Ecclesiastical Antiquities, Derbyshire. Thomas Nadauld Brushfield. The Anastatic Drawing Society, Vol 20. 1882, plate XXVII, no. 3. **Page 22**: Norman lintel, Holy Trinity Church, Ashford. Ecclesiastical Antiquities, Derbyshire. Thomas Nadauld Brushfield. The Anastatic Drawing Society, Vol 20. 1882, plate XXVII, no.1. **Page 24**: Flyer re. Ashford Baptist Chapel event, 1805. TK. DRO, D7672/Lx.C-61. **Page 28**: Map of west Devon locations superimposed on 1848 background map by Samuel Lewis, 2020. Ian Pykett. **Page 29**: Cholera victim illustration, 1832. Science Photo Library, Ref. N506/0017. **Page 30**: John and Alice Yeo, ca.1870s, and (inset) Alice Yeo, ca.1860s. Reproduced by permission of Erma Luxmoore. **Page 31**: Samuel Luxmoore Yeo, ca.1870s. Reproduced by permission of Erma Luxmoore.

Page 33: Memorial to Bishop John Luxmoore, St Asaph Cathedral, 2020. Ian Pykett. The translation of the Latin inscription is by, and reproduced by permission of, Michael Hannon. **Page 35**: Robin Stonhouse Luxmoore with the bronze bust of Henry Elford Noble Luxmoore, 1989. Reproduced by permission of Robin Stonhouse Luxmoore. **Page 36**: Reddaway Farm, 2018. Reproduced by permission of Stags, Tiverton, Devon. **Page 37**: Okehampton Castle, Devon. In: Devonshire Illustrated in a Series of Views of Cities, Towns, Public Buildings, Streets, Docks, Churches, Antiques, Abbeys, Picturesque Scenery, Castles, Seats of the Nobility. Engraved by W Taylor from an original drawing by Thomas Allom. Fisher, Son & Co, London, 1829.

Page 39: Bridge Street, Hatherleigh, Devon, ca.1890. Reproduced by permission of the Hooper Kindon family. **Page 45**: Overlake Cottage, Eworthy, Germansweek, Devon, 1989. Reproduced by permission of Robin Stonhouse Luxmoore. **Page 46**: Headstone of James and Susanna Luxmoore, St Peter's Church, Lewtrenchard, Devon, 1989. Reproduced by permission of Robin Stonhouse Luxmoore. **Page 48**: West Week Barton, Lifton, Devon, 1989. Reproduced by permission of Robin Stonhouse Luxmoore. **Page 50**: Farm at East Risdon, Jacobstowe, Devon, 1989. Reproduced by permission of Robin Stonhouse Luxmoore. **Page 51**: Headstones of Samuel & Patience Luxmoore, St James' Church, Jacobstowe, Devon, 2020. Ian Pykett. **Page 58**: Report of presentation to Revd JR Luxmoore at Smalley, Derbyshire. Derby Mercury, October 26th 1859. BNA. **Page 65**: Avon Gorge and the 'monuments of failure', ca.1861. Reproduced by permission of the Bristol Museum & Art Gallery. Object number Mb3694. Copyright Bristol Culture.

Page 66: Guide to P&A Campbell's Paddle Steamer Cruises on the Bristol Channel, 1936. **Page 71**: Headstone Viaduct, Monsal Dale, Derbyshire, ca.1914. Reproduced by permission. Copyright the Francis Frith Collection. **Page 75**: Memorial to Sir William Sterndale Bennett and his father, Sheffield Cathedral, 2015. Reproduced by permission of Andrew R Abbott. Creative Commons CC BY-SA 4.0. **Page 79**: St Michael and All Angels' Church, Sheldon, ca.1870. TK. DRO, D7672/Lx.C-64. **Page 85**: Parish Notice, Ashford, 1867. TK. DRO, D7672/Lx.C-62. **Page 86**: Flyer re. Diamond Jubilee, Ashford, 1897. TK. DRO, D7672/Lx.C-69. **Page 87**: Diamond Jubilee celebrations, Ashford, 1897. Reproduced by permission of Ian Cox. **Page 88**: Village parade, Ashford, ca.1900. Reproduced by permission of David Windle.

Page 90: 'Peace Memorial Seat' plaque under Top Pump, Ashford, 2020. Ian Pykett. **Page 91**: Band of Hope medallion. Reproduced by permission of Pearse Fee. **Page 93**: Menu, County Ball, Chatsworth House. Derbyshire Times & Chesterfield Herald, January 14th 1899. BNA. **Page 93**: Band music list, County Ball, Chatsworth House. Derbyshire Times & Chesterfield Herald, January 14th 1899. BNA. **Page 95**: Samuel Birley's Ashford marble table, designed by James Randall. Copyright Victoria & Albert Museum, London. (To view high-resolution colour photographs online, go to Victoria & Albert Museum, Item O18958, at http://collections.vam.ac.uk.) **Page 96**: The Devonshire Arms in Ashford, ca.1910. Reproduced by permission of the DRO. **Page 98**: Headstone of the Birley family, Holy Trinity Church, Ashford, 2020. Ian Pykett.

Page 100: The Cascade House, Chatsworth, 2016. Creative Commons Universal CC0 1.0. **Page 101**: Headstone of Ann Brushfield, née Nadauld, Holy Trinity Church, Ashford, 2019. Ian Pykett. Inscription reference from Thomas Brushfield: A Memory. Llewellynn Jewitt. The Reliquary, Vol 16. Llewellynn Jewitt (ed). Bemrose & Sons, Derby & London, 1875-1876, p 210. **Page 109**: Organ at Christ Church, Spitalfields. Angelo Hornak/Alamy Stock Photo. **Page 111**: Christ Church Spitalfields. Anonymous, 1815. Heritage Image Partnership Ltd/Alamy Stock Photo. **Page 120**: Report of collapse of Cliff End Chapel. Nottingham Journal, August 5th 1937. BNA. **Page 124**: Memorial to Richard Nadauld Brushfield, Holy Trinity Church, Ashford, 2019. Ian Pykett.

Page 133: TN Brushfield as 'The Ruling Spirit'. Illustrated London News, January 22nd 1881. Reproduced by permission of the Illustrated London News/ Mary Evans Picture Library. **Page 134**: Memorial plaque to TN Brushfield,

Budleigh Salterton, Devon, 2018. Reproduced by permission of Maurice Daniel. **Page 137**: Revd JR & Mrs Luxmoore, 1911. Reproduced by permission of Revd Canon Tony Kaunhoven. **Page 138**: Report of Coronation celebrations, Ashford. Derbyshire Advertiser & Journal, June 23rd 1911. BNA. **Page 139**: Coronation Day, Church Street, Ashford, 1911. Reproduced by permission of David Windle. **Page 140**: Revd JS Luxmoore, ca.1900. Reproduced by permission of Paul Jeremy Luxmoore. **Page 140**: Edith Rosalie Luxmoore, ca.1933. Reproduced by permission of Paul Jeremy Luxmoore.

Page 141: William Cyril & Constance Evelyn Luxmoore, 1921. Reproduced by permission of Robin Stonhouse Luxmoore. **Page 142**: Christopher Charles & Robin Stonhouse Luxmoore at Boroughbridge Vicarage, ca.1934. Reproduced by permission of Robin Stonhouse Luxmoore. **Page 144**: Servants' bell box in the Old Vicarage, Ashford, 2020. Ian Pykett. **Page 144**: Report of Revd JR Luxmoore's retirement, Derbyshire Courier, October 5th 1912. BNA. **Page 145**: Report of Revd JR Luxmoore's funeral. Sheffield Daily Telegraph. May 16th 1917. Reproduced by permission of Sheffield Newspapers. **Page 146**: Revd JR Luxmoore's burial register entry, Holy Trinity Church, Ashford, May 15th 1917. DRO, D747/A/PI/5/2. **Page 150**: Memorial to Revd & Mrs JR Luxmoore, 2013. Ian Pykett.

Page 152: Dukinfield Old Chapel, Greater Manchester, 2017. Reproduced by permission of Gerald England. Creative Commons CC BY-SA 2.0. **Page 155**: Chancel, Tewkesbury Abbey, 2019. Ian Pykett. **Page 157**: Three-decker pulpit illustration in: Antiquities and Curiosities of the Church. William Andrews (ed). William Andrews & Co. 1897, p 127. **Page 160**: Pre-restoration photograph of south elevation of Holy Trinity Church, Ashford, ca.1868. TK. DRO, D7672/Lx.C-66. **Page 161**: Pre-restoration drawing of north elevation of Holy Trinity Church, Ashford, 1898. TK. DRO, D7672/Lx.C-68. **Page 162**: South entrance of Holy Trinity Church, Ashford, showing location of tympanum, ca.1868. TK. DRO, D7672/Lx.C-66. **Page 164**: Norman tympanum and voussoir stones, Holy Trinity Church, Ashford, 2020. Ian Pykett. **Page 165**: Charity board in Holy Trinity Church, Ashford, 2020. Reproduced by permission of Roger Allum. **Page 167**: Church Choirs – the Old Style, 1891. Sydney Prior Hall. Bridgeman Images UK.

Page 170: Romesse stove, St Michael and All Angels' Church, Edmondthorpe, Leicestershire, 2016. Terence Wright/Alamy Stock Photo. **Page 171**: Gurney stove, Tewkesbury Abbey, 2019. Ian Pykett. **Page 176**: Pre-restoration plan of Holy Trinity Church, Ashford, 1867. TK. DRO, D7672/Lx.C-68. Annotations,

2020. Ian Pykett. **Page 177**: Proposed post-restoration plan of Holy Trinity Church, Ashford, 1868. TK. DRO, D747/A/PI/8/1. Annotations, 2020. Ian Pykett. **Page 180**: Rood loft and screen, All Saints' Church, Upper Sheringham, Norfolk. Printed by M&N Hanhart. In: Illustrations of Monumental Brasses, Cambridge Camden Society, 1846, facing page 6. **Page 182**: Nave altar and screen, All Saints' Church, Upper Sheringham, 2014. Reproduced by permission of Paul Brittain.

Page 183: Memorial to TNN Brushfield at Holy Trinity Church, Ashford, 2019. Ian Pykett. **Page 184**: Cheney Arms. The Cheney Family. John Sleigh. The Reliquary, Vol 11, Llewellynn Jewitt (ed). Bemrose & Sons, Derby & London, 1870-1871, plate XIII. **Page 185**: The Cottingham west window at Holy Trinity Church, Ashford, 2021. Ian Pykett. **Page 186**: The Haworth south window at Holy Trinity Church, Ashford, 2021. Ian Pykett. **Page 187**: The Morewood east window at Holy Trinity Church, Ashford, 2021. Ian Pykett. **Page 188**: Maidens' garlands, Holy Trinity Church, Ashford. Revd JR Luxmoore. Nooks and Corners of Old England. Allan Fea. New York. Charles Scribner's Sons. 1908, p 221. **Page 188**: Sanctus bell, Holy Trinity Church, Ashford, 2006. Ian Pykett. **Page 190**: Bell-ringing instructions of 1889, Holy Trinity Church, Ashford, 2020. Ian Pykett. **Page 192**: Proposed post-restoration exterior aspects of Holy Trinity Church, Ashford. James Medland & Henry Taylor, 1868. TK. DRO, D7672/Lx.C-67.

Page 194: Photomontage, Holy Trinity Church, Ashford & Revd JR Luxmoore. Reproduced by permission of Lillias Bendell. **Page 196**: Chancel of Holy Trinity Church, Ashford, 1954. Reproduced by permission of Revd Canon Tony Kaunhoven. **Page 201**: The Arrock, Ashford, 2019. Ian Pykett. **Page 201**: Facsimile extract: The Vicarage. In: Notes on the Church of Holy Trinity, Ashford. JS Luxmoore, ca.1900. DRO, D7672/Lx.C-30. **Page 202**: Top: Ashford allotment map, 1767. DRO, D747/A/PI/12/1. Bottom: Ashford Ordnance Survey map, Derbyshire Sheet XXIII, 1922. Reproduced by permission of Ordnance Survey, OS Crown copyright 1922, CS-150432-V8W1B8. DRO, D747/A/PI/17/1. **Page 206**: Memorial plaque to Frederick Albert Winsor, 2009. Reproduced by permission of Simon Harriyott. Creative Commons CC BY 2.0.

Page 207: Ground-floor plan of the Vicarage, Ashford, 1951. Edited, 2020. Ian Pykett. Reproduced by permission of Revd Canon Tony Kaunhoven. **Page 208**: First-floor plan of the Vicarage, Ashford, 1951. Edited, 2020. Ian Pykett. Reproduced by permission of Revd Canon Tony Kaunhoven.

Page 209: Locations for hanging articles of Luxmoore children's clothing, 2020. Ian Pykett. **Page 210**: Report of damage to the Ashford Vicarage. Nottinghamshire Guardian, August 11th 1900. BNA. **Page 210**: Key of 'Jennifer the Poltergeist', 2019. Ian Pykett. **Page 212**: Induction of Revd John Norman, 1957. Reproduced by permission of the late Margaret Norman. **Page 213**: Aerial view of the Old Vicarage, Ashford, 2020. Reproduced by permission of Edward Caudwell. **Page 215**: Parish priests of Holy Trinity Church, Ashford, 2020. Ian Pykett.

Page 216: Hill Cross, Ashford, ca.1890s. Picture the Past, Derbyshire County Council. Image Ref: DCHQ006529. **Page 221**: Inscription on the Mill Bridge, Ashford, 2013. Reproduced by permission of Tony Bacon. Creative Commons CC BY-SA 2.0. **Page 229**: Signature of Revd John Reddaway Luxmoore. In: Parish registers, Holy Trinity Church, Ashford. DRO. Edited, 2019. Ian Pykett. **Page 231**: Baptist cemetery in Ashford Lane. David Windle. **Page 232**: Ivy-covered gravestones in the Baptist cemetery. David Windle. **Page 234**: Baptist minister's house. Reproduced by permission of Mr G Webster. **Page 237**: Cliff End Chapel, ca.1920. David Windle. **Page 238**: Grave of Revd John Ashe. David Windle. **Page 244**: Notice of the laying of memorial stones for the Wesleyan Chapel. David Windle. **Page 245**: William Daybell outside the newly-enlarged Wesleyan Methodist chapel, ca.1900. David Windle. **Page 246**: Plan of the Baptist Cemetery, David Windle.

BIBLIOGRAPHY

Adrian Andrews & Michael Pascoe. *Clifton Suspension Bridge*. Broadcast Books, Bristol, 2008.

Roger Bowen. *Lunacy to Croquet: The Life and Times of Dr Thomas Nadauld Brushfield*. CreateSpace Independent Publishing Platform, 2013.

Trevor Brighton. *Bakewell: The Ancient Capital of the Peak*. Halsgrove, 2005.

Jonathan Brown. *The Edwardian Farm*. Shire Publications, 2010.

Julie Bunting. *Bygone Industries of the Peak*. Wildtrack Publishing, Sheffield, 2006.

Kathryn Burtinshaw & John Burt. *Lunatics, Imbeciles and Idiots: A History of Insanity in 19th-Century Britain and Ireland*. Pen & Sword History, 2017.

IAH Combes. *Anglican Churches of Derbyshire*. Landmark Publishing Ltd, Ashbourne, Derbyshire, 2004.

John Charles Cox. *Notes on the Churches of Derbyshire, Vol II, The Hundreds of the High Peak and Wirksworth*. Bemrose & Sons, Derby & London, 1877.

Robert Dawson (ed). *My Ashford: A Century Past. Alice Mary Dawson*. Peak Advertiser, Bakewell, 2017.

Edward Goodricke Draper. *The Great Sheffield Flood, 1864. A Collection of Lantern Slides and Accompanying Text*. Hillsborough Community Development Trust, 1995.

Simon Goodenough. *The Country Parson*. David & Charles Ltd, Newton Abbott, Devon, 1983.

Brian Greasley. *This Remote Little School*. Country Books, Little Longstone, Derbyshire, 2013.

Brian Greasley. *FW Goes to War: from the diaries and letters of FW Brocklehurst of Sheldon, Derbyshire*. Country Books, Little Longstone, Derbyshire, 2016.

Michael Hall. *What do Victorian Churches Mean? Symbolism and Sacramentalism in Anglican Church Architecture, 1850-1870*. Journal of the Society of Architectural Historians, Vol 59, No. 1, 2000, pp 78-95.

John Hibbs. *The Country Chapel*. David & Charles, London, 1988.

Charles Frederick Coryndon Luxmoore. *The Family of Luxmoore*. William Pollard & Co Ltd, Exeter & London, 1909.

Trevor May. *The Victorian Clergyman*. Shire Publications, 2006.

GE Mingay. *Rural Life in Victorian England*. Book Club Associates, 1976.

Sally Mitchell (ed). *Victorian Britain – An Encyclopædia*. First published by Garland Publishing, New York & London, 1988. Republished by Routledge Revivals, Abingdon, Oxfordshire, 2011.

John Norman. *Ashford-in-the-Water and its Church*, 1961. Extended 1962; revised and enlarged by Graham Foster incorporating notes by the late George Pace, 1979; revised, reprinted and retitled *Holy Trinity Church, Ashford-in-the-Water*, 1996.

David Parker. *Early Victorian Devon 1830-1860*. Halsgrove, 2017.

Gerald Phizackerley (ed). *The Diaries of Maria Gyte of Sheldon, Derbyshire, 1913-1920*. Scarthin Books, 1999.

John Martin Robinson. *Antiquarian Revival*. In: *Treasures of the English Churches*. Sinclair-Stevenson, 1995, pp 155-178.

Roy Strong. *A Little History of the English Country Church*. Vintage Books, London, 2007.

Clive Thrower. *Monuments: Ashford-in-the-Water, Holy Trinity; Sheldon, St Michael and All Angels*, http://www.thrower.org.uk/ashford/monuash.htm & http://www.thrower.org.uk/sheldon/monuments.htm

Kate Tiller. *Parsonages*. Shire Publications, Oxford, 2016.

John Michael Tomlinson. *Derbyshire Black Marble*. Peak District Mines Historical Society Special Publication No. 4, 1996.

Margery Tranter (ed), in collaboration with David A Barton & Paul S Ell. *The Derbyshire Returns to the 1851 Religious Census*. Derbyshire Record Society, 1995.

Andrea Yount. *William Morris and the Society for the Protection of Ancient Buildings: 19th and 20th-Century Historic Preservation in Europe*. Western Michigan University, 2005.

INDEX